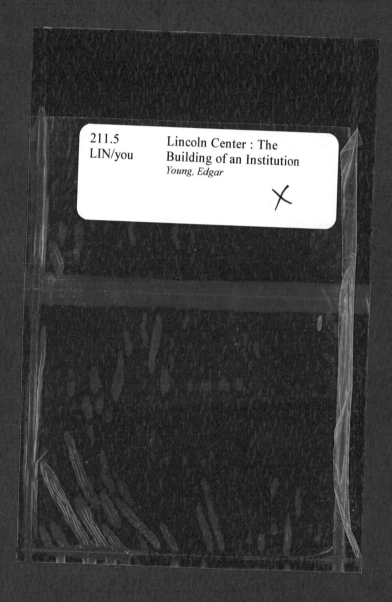

LINCOLN CENTER

THE BUILDING OF
AN INSTITUTION

Edgar B. Young

LINCOLN CENTER
THE BUILDING OF
AN INSTITUTION

EDGAR B. YOUNG

With a Foreword by
FRANK STANTON

New York and London
New York University Press

Library of Congress Cataloging in Publication Data

Young, Edgar B   1908-
  Lincoln Center, the building of an institution.

  Includes bibliographical references and index.
  1. Lincoln Center for the Performing Arts, New
York. I. Title.
PN1588.N5Y68   790.2'09747'1   80-17725
ISBN 0-8147-9656-7

Manufactured in the United States of America

My appreciation goes to the following for permission to reprint material in this book:

To Hoyt Ammidon, Sir Rudolf Bing, Robert Moses, William Schuman for quotations from their correspondence.
To the Private Archives of the Messrs. Rockefeller for quotations from John D. Rockefeller 3rd.

To the Metropolitan Opera Association for quotations from its Guide book to the Metropolitan Opera House.

To Prentice-Hall, Inc., Englewood Cliffs, New Jersey 07632, Publisher and The Sterling Lord Agency, Inc., New York, for an excerpt from *Lincoln Center for the Performing Arts* by Ralph Martin, Copyright (c) 1971 by Ralph G. Martin.

To *The New Yorker* and to Winthrop Sargeant for permission to use an excerpt from "Housewarming" by Winthrop Sargeant from their May 9, 1964 issue.

To the *New York Post* for two excerpts reprinted by permission of the New York Post, from December 27, 1964 and September 22, 1965 issues. (c) 1964 and (c) 1965 by the New York Post Corporation.

To The Twentieth Century Fund for an excerpt from William J. Baumol and William G. Bowen, *Performing Arts: The Economic Dilemma*, Copyright (c) 1966 by the Twentieth Century Fund, Inc. Reprinted by permission.

To the *Daily News* for two excerpts from their September 24, 1962 and October 22, 1965 issues, Copyright 1962 and 1965 New York News Inc. Reprinted by permission.

To the *Architectural Record* for an excerpt from an article on the Juilliard School, *Architectural Record*, January 1970, (c) 1970 by McGraw-Hill, Inc. with all rights reserved.

To *High Fidelity/Musical America* for permission to reprint an excerpt from the May 1964 issue of *Musical America*, all rights reserved.

To *The New York Times* for permission to reprint numerous excerpts from issues 1959-1979, (c) 1959/62/63/64/65/66/69/79 by The New York Times Company. Reprinted by permission.

To the *Saturday Review* for permission to reprint a quotation from Irving Kolodin's column "Music to My Ears" in the May 9, 1964 issue, Copyright (c) 1964 by Saturday Review. Reprinted by permission.

Dedicated to
the memory of

John D. Rockefeller 3rd
1906-1978

Contents

Foreword

Edgar B. Young's history of Lincoln Center for the Performing Arts is the traditional American saga. It records the adventures of a small band of sturdy pioneers, men of vision, who undertook to carve out of the wilderness a "path toward the stars," in Robert Sherwood's words. It records their tribulations and their ultimate triumph.

That the pioneers were men of our own century, that the wilderness they attacked was not the forest of Daniel Boone but the blighted west side of New York City, that their vision was artistic, not material, that their tools were not the axe and the scythe but management and money, and still more money, does not invalidate the comparison. They had a dream, as surely as did Lewis and Clark, and they had their courage and determination too.

Dwight Eisenhower, who was President and present when the ground was broken in a field adjacent to Lincoln Square or, as it was known a century earlier, Bloomingdale Road, on May 14, 1959, said to the leader of this band of latter-day pioneers, John D. Rockefeller 3rd, ". . . once again is demonstrated that one of the great strengths of America lies in our willingness, even desire, to share the good things of life with all our citizens."

President Eisenhower accurately assessed the motivations of Mr.

Rockefeller and his associates in this enterprise. They were united by their desire to give, not to get, to improve the quality of life of their fellow citizens, to accept their responsibility in a democracy to provide a home for the arts of performance, a place for education and refreshment of the spirit. And in our free enterprise system, they were determined that government patronage would take second place to private initiative. It is a source of deep satisfaction to me that I was allowed to be one of that band.

Again and again during the 15 years which Edgar Young records so candidly and with such meticulous care, the task seemed insurmountable. There were no muddy rivers to cross, no mountain passes to conquer, no parched plains to traverse, no Indians, no hurricanes. But there was bureaucratic red tape to unwind, there were strikes in the building trades to sit out, there were rising costs of steel and stone, there were prickly prides of institutions and individuals to be assuaged; and always there was the spectre of running out of money before the job was done.

The history recorded in this book is only partially that of building a great and complex center: an orchestra hall, an opera house, theatres for dance and drama and chamber music, a conservatory for training the specifically gifted and talented, a library of the performing arts. It is also a history that documents the way the hundreds of artists, their patrons, leaders and support staffs struggled to develop a familial modus vivendi.

Never was the underlying purpose of all this effort lost sight of. Finally when the fund-raisers came to the end of the line and Lincoln Center could announce the completion of its funding, the heretofore unheard-of sum of $185 million, John Rockefeller reminded us all that "what counts is how the Center will be used for the advancement of the arts and for the benefit of the people who come to attend its performances."

If this story has a hero, it must certainly be John D. Rockefeller 3rd. He was not, it is true, there at the start. Robert Moses and Mayor Wagner, architect Wallace Harrison, lawyer Charles M. Spofford were there before him and all of them (especially Spofford) must share in the glory. But this volume makes it quite clear that it was John's qualities of leadership, his perseverance, his vision, his tact, his modesty, and his generosity, which make him the center of the great panorama laid out in these pages.

I feel it necessary and agreeably appropriate to speak a few words concerning the historian himself. Edgar Young emerges from these pages as a second hero. In spite of himself. The careful reader will easily recognize the importance of his contribution to the enterprise, despite a degree of self-effacement equal to his good friend and mentor. At all times, but especially in moments of crisis, Ed's skill, dedication and tact kept the venture from foundering. He was at various stages in its history Secretary of the Corporation, Executive Vice President, Acting President, Chairman of the Building Committee. All those successive roles he performed with diligence and care. Now he has made this authoritative record of an extraordinary undertaking, as one uniquely qualified for the task. I salute his notable accomplishment with admiration.

Frank Stanton

Chronology of Lincoln Center

1955		City designates Lincoln Square area for urban renewal
	April	Metropolitan Opera Association decides to build new opera house at Lincoln Square
	April	New York Philharmonic-Symphony Society decides to build new concert hall at Lincoln Square
	Sept.	John D. Rockefeller, 3rd invited to join representatives from Opera and Philharmonic to explore music center possibilities
	Oct. 25	First meeting of Exploratory Committee for a Musical Arts Center
1956	June 22	Incorporation of Lincoln Center for the Performing Arts; initial constituents: Metropolitan Opera Association and New York Philharmonic-Symphony Society; Rockefeller elected president
1957	Feb. 1	The Juilliard School becomes a constituent
	Sept. 23	Start of Lincoln Center Capital Campaign; Chairman: Clarence Francis; goal: $75 million

	Nov. 26	Final approval by city of Lincoln Square Urban Renewal Project
1958	Feb. 28	Lincoln Center site purchased from city
	Oct. 1	Juilliard site purchased from city
1959	May 14	Ground Breaking by President Eisenhower
1960	Feb. 15	Repertory Theater Association becomes a constituent
	May 23	Campaign goal increased to $102 million
	June 20	Lincoln Center Student Program started
1961	Jan. 1	Gen. Maxwell D. Taylor becomes Lincoln Center president; Rockefeller becomes chairman
	Feb. 13	New York Public Library becomes a constituent
	March 21	Agreement with New York World's Fair for performing arts portion of fair to be at Lincoln Center
	March 24	N.Y. State Legislature authorizes $15 million for New York State Theater
	June 30	Gen. Taylor resigns to become Military Adviser to President Kennedy; Edgar B. Young becomes Acting President of Lincoln Center
	Nov. 28	City authorizes $7.587 million for Library & Museum of Performing Arts
1962	Jan. 1	William Schuman becomes President of Lincoln Center; Young becomes Executive Vice President
	Aug. 30	City authorizes $4.383 million for New York State Theater
	Sept. 23	Philharmonic Hall opened
1963	Feb.	Music Theater of Lincoln Center becomes a constituent
	Apr. 15	Campaign goal increased to $120.6 million
1964	Apr. 23	New York State Theater opened
1965	Jan. 11	City Center of Music and Drama becomes a constituent
	Oct. 14	Vivian Beaumont Theater opened
	Nov. 30	Library & Museum of Performing Arts opened
1966	Jan. 31	Capital Campaign goal reached and surpassed; additional capital needs recognized
	Sept. 16	Metropolitan Opera House opened
1967	June 12	Festival '67 - international summer festival
1968	Dec. 31	William Schuman resigns; Amyas Ames becomes Chairman of Executive Committee; John Mazzola appointed Executive Vice President and General Manager

1969	Feb. 17	The Chamber Music Society of Lincoln Center becomes a constituent
	May	Film Society of Lincoln Center becomes a constituent
	June 30	Capital Fund Raising completed; project total (including government funds): $185.4 million
	Sept. 11	Alice Tully Hall opened
	Oct. 26	The Juilliard School opened
1970	May 11	Amyas Ames becomes Chairman; Rockefeller elected Honorary Chairman
1971	April	Music Theater terminates operation
1973	March	New York Shakespeare Theater becomes a constituent, succeeding Repertory Theater
1974	Aug.	First "Lincoln Center Out-of-Doors"
		Lincoln Center Institute is established
1976	Jan. 30	First "Live from Lincoln Center" telecast
	Oct. 19	Avery Fisher Hall opened after acoustical rebuilding
1977	May 16	John W. Mazzola becomes President of Lincoln Center
	August	New York Shakespeare Theater withdraws from participation in Lincoln Center
1979	May	20th Anniversary of Ground Breaking is celebrated
1980		Vivian Beaumont Theater, Inc. becomes a constituent

Author's Note

This history of the creation of Lincoln Center for the Performing Arts is an insider's account. It was a self-imposed task and a sequel to my personal involvement in the enterprise from its earliest planning to the present day. In spite of my effort to be objective and factually accurate in all respects, this account cannot help but be biased; from the start of the project, I have endorsed the goals of Lincoln Center and have had confidence in its value to the arts, to artists, to the community, and to the nation.

In preparing this recollection of the evolution of the center, the facts and events have been told as they were perceived by those engaged in them at the time. The text itself indicates in most instances the documentary source of information. Conversations with many colleagues have refreshed memory; all official minutes of meetings and other records have been available to me. Peter Johnson and Curtis Clow were especially helpful in locating material in The Private Archives of the Messrs. Rockefeller. John O'Keefe and his staff at Lincoln Center located or verified a number of the press references, and Susanne Stevens was especially helpful in selecting the illustrations.

Lincoln Center was a group effort that benefited from the time and talents of a very large number of people. In telling its history, if I were to mention all who were involved, the story would have a cast of hundreds. To those not named, I offer my apology and my recognition that without the infusion of their many and varied contributions, Lincoln Center could never have been accomplished.

I am grateful to Carlos Moseley and Howard Taubman for their insistent urging that I write this history and for their counsel in the early stages of its preparation; to Florence Thompson, who was my secretary throughout the years recorded here and who helped me research the facts and prepare the first draft; to Dr. Jerrold Ross, whose judgment and encouragement helped me turn a draft into a text for publication; to Dorothea O'Hair and Robert Stone for their patiently careful manuscript typing; to Robert Bull at New York University Press for his editorial assistance. My deepest gratitude is to Jane, my partner of fifty years, who shared in the experience of the Lincoln Center years and has been my most helpful, penetrating critic during the writing of this book.

E. B. Y.

LINCOLN CENTER

THE BUILDING OF
AN INSTITUTION

Prologue

Lincoln Center for the Performing Arts is a nonprofit institution dedicated to fostering the arts of music, dance, and drama and to encouraging the widest possible public enjoyment of those arts. It was established and built through the sustained, voluntary public service of a group of New York citizens during the years from 1955 to 1970. It endures as a vital force in the artistic and community life of New York and of the nation.

The history told here recounts the facts of the origin and evolution of Lincoln Center as a place and as an organization. It is a record of urban renewal and of collaboration between private, nonprofit organizations and agencies of city, state, and federal governments. It is a story of architecture and construction and of capital finance on a scale never before attempted in the realm of the performing arts. It is the account of the growth of artistic and educational institutions, some old and some new, into a composite whole. It is the human story of the way a group of devoted people, led by John D. Rockefeller 3rd, met a succession of sometimes frustrating, always challenging problems and brought the project through from conception to fruition. It is a case study of how the "Third Sector," the voluntary, nonprofit sector, functions in American life.

3

A place for work.

A place for study and training.

LINCOLN CENTER: What meanings do this place and this concept conjure in the minds of the millions of people whose lives are touched by it? There are scores of answers, as many as there are points of view about this artistic and educational conglomerate.

At ground breaking in 1959, President Eisenhower saw the Center as a "mighty influence for peace." To the people who make up the nightly audiences of over ten thousand for an annual attendance of nearly five million, Lincoln Center is a place to enjoy great music, dance, and drama. To millions of devoted Saturday and Sunday afternoon radio listeners, it is the home of the Metropolitan Opera and of the Philharmonic. To millions more it is the source of "Live from Lincoln Center" and other telecasts which bring the home viewers into the halls and theaters of the center.

To many of the world's great performing artists, conductors, and directors, the stages of Lincoln Center offer opportunities to present their art. For more than 6800 musicians, dancers and actors, stagehands, ushers and ticket takers, costume makers and set builders, engineers, porters and guards, teachers and librarians, and permanent office personnel, Lincoln Center is the source of their livelihood. Lincoln Center and its constituent institutions have become a $92 million annual enterprise providing payrolls of over $62 million.

To aspiring and talented young artists in training, the Juilliard School is the place where their dreams become career possibilities. To many a playwright, composer, choreographer, or set designer, the Library & Museum of the Performing Arts is a storehouse of creativity and inspiration. Each year the Lincoln Center Student Program exposes over a half million high school young people to music, dance, and drama of quality, in live performance.

Those who are concerned for the vitality of the city recognize that Lincoln Center inspired a renewal of the West Side of Manhattan. They see its presence at Lincoln Square as the economic reason for a surge of new apartment building, for numerous new restaurants, music stores, and other service facilities. And they also see Lincoln Center as the stimulus for many more millions spent for travel, hotels, meals, clothing, taxi fares, and parking fees. Each year, to hundreds of thousands of visitors to New York City, Lincoln Center is a tourist attraction second only to the United Nations headquarters.

Not everyone perceives Lincoln Center in such glowing terms. To some artists and critics it is a concentration of money and power and an excessive application of millions of dollars to steel and stone that they feel might more usefully have gone into the support and training of creative and performing artists. To some urban planners, Lincoln Center is a concentration of too many of the city's great institutions in one geographic location to the detriment of other parts of the city. To some former residents of the area and to some urbanologists, the renewal project is perceived as the destroyer of homes and of a neighborhood.

People who follow the trends of private giving see the success of Lincoln Center's capital fund drive as a philanthropic breakthrough. It broke new ground, in the recognition of artistic needs, in levels of giving, and in the participation of business in cultural enterprises. Some, whose loyalty is centered on important but less conspicuous artistic endeavors, see Lincoln Center as the giant that cornered more than its fair share of available philanthropic money.

Photo: Victoria Beller-Smith

Most members of the immense public that come to Lincoln Center find in its buildings, parks, and plazas a bright and safe oasis in the City. But some architectural critics see the center and its buildings as a lost opportunity, if not a disaster.

However Lincoln Center is seen, the inescapable fact about the center is that it is there. It exists and it works. Today, Lincoln Center is recognized throughout America and in remote corners of the globe. The center is alive and throbbing with human activity. The place itself and the arts presented there touch and influence the lives of millions of people.

PART I

Origin

CHAPTER 1

Needs and Opportunity

It is often assumed that Lincoln Center was one person's dream. Actually, it evolved out of a combination of very real needs and opportunities that existed in New York City in the mid-fifties. In its evolution it brought together the knowledge and judgment, the inspiration and generosity of voluntary civic-minded citizens. Late in 1954 and early in 1955, before there was any thought of Lincoln Center for the Performing Arts, three separate and significant decisions were made that led to the center.

The first decision was governmental, made in the framework of the city's urban renewal program. It was reached by the Committee on Slum Clearance under the chairmanship of Robert Moses and by Mayor Robert Wagner. The committee determined that a 17 block area on the west side of Manhattan (between 62nd and 70th Streets) should be redeveloped. This resulted in the Lincoln Square Urban Renewal Project, taking the name of the double triangle formed by the intersection of Broadway and Columbus Avenue.[1] Moses at first visualized commercial and cooperative real estate development, middle-income housing, a university center, a small public park, stores and commercial property along Broadway, and several new theaters. Significantly for the origin of Lincoln Center, his vision included an opera house.

Moses turned to an old friend, architect Wallace K. Harrison, for consideration of his idea for a new opera house. Harrison had, for more than a quarter of a century, worked with leaders of the Metropolitan Opera on opera house designs and had also been in the center of planning for such projects as Rockefeller Center and the United Nations headquarters. Harrison recalls that Moses telephoned one Sunday evening and asked if he might come over. After customary pleasantries, Moses described his hopes for the Lincoln Square project. "What would you think," he asked, "of a site for an opera house west of Broadway between 63rd and 64th Streets?" Harrison was enthusiastic; the Lincoln Square proposal offered real possibilities for a solution to the long-standing need of the Metropolitan for a new home. Harrison agreed to bring the proposal to the attention of Charles M. Spofford, then chairman of the Metropolitan's Executive Committee.

Spofford became a key figure not only in the opera's response, but in all the subsequent evolution and building of Lincoln Center. Spofford brought to any subject a broad perspective gained from a career that ranged from a distinguished place in the legal profession through military service with the rank of Brigadier General to participation in the formation of NATO. In business he was a director of several corporations; in philanthropy, a trustee of the Carnegie Corporation, Union Theological Seminary, and the New York Chapter of the Red Cross. In addition to his position on the opera board, he was also a Director of the Juilliard School and a trustee of its related Juilliard Musical Foundation. A personal love of music undergirded all his involvement with Lincoln Center. An impressive man in voice and bearing, as well as in intellect, he was influential in any group. His sense of fairness and his objectivity were judicial; his analytical mind could break down complex problems into soluble parts.

Spofford moved promptly to bring Moses' offer of an opera house site to the Metropolitan's New House Committee and to its full board. On April 14, 1955, the directors of the Metropolitan Opera Association made the second of the three decisions. They formally and unanimously

RESOLVED, that it is the opinion of this Board that a new Opera House is essential to the continued advantageous existence of the Metropolitan Opera; and further

RESOLVED, that the New Opera House Committee be instructed to advise the City authorities and the Honorable Robert Moses, Chairman of the Committee on Slum Clearance, of its continued interest, and the Committee is directed to vigorously continue its efforts to acquire a site for a new Opera House and to develop a practical plan to finance the project.

This "new house decision" was the culmination of years of dissatisfaction with the old house and years of unsuccessful searching for a new home. Later, Rudolf Bing described the old opera house:

The auditorium was of course one of the glories of the world—that deep Diamond Horseshoe that gave the box holders, who had once owned the house, an opportunity to look at each other unrivaled in any other opera house anywhere. But the depth of the Horseshoe meant an immense number of side seats that had limited views of the stage, and the public areas were seriously inadequate . . . .

Behind the proscenium and its golden curtain, however, the theater had nothing at all to recommend it. Everything backstage was cramped and dirty and poor. There were neither side stages nor a rear stage; every change of scene had to be done from scratch on the main stage itself, which meant that if an act had two scenes, the audience had just to sit and wait, wondering what the banging noises behind the curtain might mean. The lighting grid was decades behind European standards, and there was no revolving stage . . . .

Dressing rooms were inadequate—and had to be used during the day for coaching sessions, because of the lack of rehearsal space. (The chorus rehearsed in the public bar!)[2]

Storage facilities, so necessary for any repertory operation, were almost nonexistent as witnessed by the sets stacked daily on Seventh Avenue at the stage doors waiting to be hauled to the warehouse. The backstage area was a dangerous firetrap. Even the auditorium, the part of the old house that was so loved by the public, had serious deficiencies. Its highly regarded acoustical properties were overrated; sound distribution was uneven; reverberation time was shorter than optimum for opera. Singers had difficulty in projecting their voices from certain points on stage.

The Metropolitan had made repeated attempts to relocate or to rebuild for nearly 50 years. Their most highly developed plan for a new house fell victim to the stock market crash of October 1929 and to the depression of the 1930s. The Opera board, acting under the pressures of financial crisis, withdrew from participation in the Rockefeller Center project. In 1951, after negotiations with Moses, a plan for an opera house at Columbus Circle in conjunction with the Coliseum was abandoned. Later there was talk of building on opera house in a corner of Central Park, but without success.

The third decision was made by the board of the New York Philharmonic-Symphony Society in 1955. The Philharmonic required a new home but for very different reasons. The Philharmonic had been a tenant in Carnegie Hall since it was built in 1891. But Carnegie Hall was privately owned, and its owners felt the return on their investment was inadequate. Early in 1955, they decided to replace the concert hall with an office building and notified the Philharmonic the Carnegie Hall lease would not be renewed after its expiration in 1959. The Philharmonic was forced to relocate, despite its general satisfaction with Carnegie Hall and the public affection for it. The Philharmonic board decided that they must seek a new site and build a new home. Arthur A. Houghton, Jr., an influential director and soon to become board chairman, also turned to Harrison for advice and for preliminary architectural work.[3] Harrison was the catalyst who brought together the three separate decisions and the decision makers.

A few days after the Metropolitan's decision, four representatives of the New House Committee met with Moses, who indicated that a site of 120,000 square feet (approximately three acres) was available at a price of $8.00 per square foot under the "write-down procedures" of urban renewal. His offer was conditioned on the Met acting promptly (his deadline was July 1, 1955) and on assurances that they were serious about wanting a new site and could obtain funds for it. He thought the Opera might need to raise $1.5 million to cover not only land costs, but also preliminary planning, relocation of tenants, and clearance of the site.

In this first discussion with Moses, the Metropolitan representatives raised the idea of a music center which might include additional space for the Philharmonic. Moses registered strong opposition, urging that if the Met "wanted to go ahead with this project they should not attempt to associate with any other group, or try to build a temple of music in which other organizations could participate, or any other joint venture."

Three days later, after talking again with Harrison, Moses changed his mind and wrote that the Committee on Slum Clearance could make additional space in the site available not only for the Opera but for other related purposes such as the Philharmonic.[4] Moses tentatively reserved a four-acre plot, but pointed out that this would raise the Met's financial need to $1.75 million instead of the $1.5 million earlier discussed.

Within another three days the Met's New House Committee reported to Moses that,

> Everyone present was of the opinion that we should go ahead vigorously with endeavoring to raise the money so as to give you a prompt answer that the Opera Association wants to avail itself of the opportunity to obtain the site.

They proposed that the Opera should first raise the $1.5 million needed for the Opera alone; after that,

> We don't believe anyone would have any objection to then considering entering into a joint venture for related purposes. . . .[5]

The money-raising effort was undertaken immediately and within a month $400,000 had been pledged, half from the Juilliard Foundation and half from the Avalon Foundation. C. D. Jackson, another Met director and member of its New House Committee, then appealed to Mr. John D. Rockefeller, Jr. for a contribution of $500,000 or more toward the site fund.[6] He stressed the unity and enthusiasm of the Met board for this project. He praised the location, saying it "is excellent from the standpoint of mass subway transportation and is no less convenient for the Cadillac trade." Jackson then extolled the music center idea and reported that "the Philharmonic, out of funds available, has appropriated the sum necessary to acquire its section of land." Mr. Rockefeller, Jr. responded with a pledge for $500,000, and in due course the Met succeeded in raising the $1.5 million required.

The die had been cast. The Metropolitan and the Philharmonic had determined to build new homes and to locate them at Lincoln Square in the new urban renewal project. During the late summer of 1955 the new house momentum was increasing among the leadership of both the Metropolitan and the Philharmonic with Harrison continuing to serve as the catalytic agent between them and with Moses. Several of their board members, especially Houghton, Jackson, and Spofford, were thinking in even broader terms. They were asking themselves whether some form of an art center at Lincoln Square might make

Photo © Katrina Thomas

Wallace K. Harrison

sense. There were no clearly formulated plans, but there was a willingness to pause long enough to explore possibilities.

The Met was then anticipating a $15 million building, and the Philharmonic's early estimates called for one costing $5 million. Both groups recognized that they would have to approach many of the same major sources for contributions and that there were risks in competitive appeals. There was tentative talk of some kind of a joint campaign and agreement that in whatever way their plans might evolve, they needed the judgment, interest, and support of civic leaders outside their immediate groups. They hoped one of the Rockefeller brothers could be brought in. Harrison suggested they consider John D. Rockefeller 3rd, the eldest of the five brothers and, at that time, the board chairman of the Rockefeller Foundation. Spofford discussed the matter with Dean Rusk, president of the Rockefeller Foundation, who also advised consideration of John 3rd. The focus on John Rockefeller became clear.

Meanwhile, Rockefeller had some knowledge of what was under consideration at Lincoln Square, for Harrison had briefed him and his associate, Edgar Young, on the status of the project with hints of an art center possibility. Rockefeller and Young subsequently discussed the pros and cons of a possible center with Rockefeller Foundation officers, and with such people as William Schuman, president, and Mark Schubart, dean of the Juilliard School, Lincoln Kirstein, managing director of the New York City Ballet, and Henry Heald, president of New York University.

John D. Rockefeller 3rd

Charles M. Spofford

Arthur A. Houghton Jr.

Devereaux C. Josephs

During the weekend of September 8 and 9, 1955, Spofford seized an opportunity to talk with Rockefeller while they were both attending a week-end conference of the Council on Foreign Relations in the Poconos. Spofford described the "three coincidences," the Metropolitan decision to move, the Philharmonic's need for a new home, and the availability of land.

Later, Rockefeller wrote:

For me new horizons began to open. Since the war my work had been concentrated in the international area. I had begun to think more seriously of my responsibilities as a citizen of New York . . . Therefore I accepted with enthusiasm Spofford's invitation to join his committee and to help enlist others.[7]

Spofford had presented the situation as he believed it to be, an opportunity for public service and not primarily a financial problem. Rockefeller admired the willingness of the Metropolitan and Philharmonic leaders to sit down together to examine whether their plans for new institutional homes created an opportunity for something of even greater importance to the community. It was this potential that challenged Rockefeller then and throughout the evolution of the project.

The world Rockefeller knew best was that of voluntary, nonprofit citizen participation. He had experience and judgment in the management of such enterprises; he knew how money was raised. Rockefeller made no pretense of professional knowledge or expertise in any of the arts. He was not an opera buff, a symphony fan, or a balletomane. But he believed that opportunities to experience the arts should be available to everyone; he recognized that the arts could play a significant role in the lives of large numbers of people.

CHAPTER 2

The Exploratory Committee
1955-1956

On October 25, 1955, six men concerned about the future of the performing arts in New York City came together at luncheon to explore the possibilities for a cultural project. The Metropolitan Opera Association was represented by Charles M. Spofford, chairman of its Executive Committee, and Anthony A. Bliss, its president. Representatives of the New York Philharmonic-Symphony Society were Floyd Blair and Arthur A. Houghton, Jr., its chairman and president. Architect Wallace K. Harrison and John D. Rockefeller 3rd completed the group.

This was the first of a long succession of working luncheons that has continued to the present. They met at the Century Association—an old and distinguished New York club on West 43rd Street, housed in its landmark building designed by McKim, Mead, and White.

The six men had a common understanding of the situation that had brought them together. The Metropolitan was committed to building a new opera house; the Philharmonic to a new concert hall. Both had accepted Lincoln Square as a suitable location. The group launched immediately into discussion of the fundamental question that had brought them together: Would anything more than an opera house and a concert hall be desirable and feasible at Lincoln Square? To determine desirability they needed to ask: What might foster the arts of serious music? What might bring those arts to a wider public? Are facilities needed for other arts? What would be constructive and important in the life of New York City and of the nation? Feasibility depended on answers to practical questions: What could be financed? What could be accommodated in the space available? Were there problems of easy access, traffic congestion, parking?

In approaching these questions, this group of men recognized the complexity and interrelationship of the issues they would be considering. Rockefeller felt strongly, and the others agreed, that their small group should be enlarged to bring in other leaders with a variety of experience and judgment. Accordingly, Devereux C. Josephs, Robert E. Blum, and Lincoln Kirstein were invited to join the group, and each agreed to do so.

Josephs was chairman of the New York Life Insurance Company, an Overseer of Harvard University, and a trustee of the New York Public Library and the Metropolitan Museum of Art. He was knowledgeable in philanthropic circles. He was formerly president of the Carnegie Corporation and currently a trustee of the Rockefeller Foundation. Most important for the new project, he was a practical, down-to-earth person with experience in facing tough questions and cutting through to the heart of a problem.

Blum, from a distinguished Brooklyn family, was a vice president of Abraham & Straus department store and president of the Brooklyn Institute of Arts and Sciences. He was familiar with the intricacies of dealing with city officials and the city bureaucracy, and his long, close friendship and working relationship with Robert Moses were certain to be helpful. Kirstein was utterly devoted to the art of the dance and, in particular, to the New York City Ballet. He was an idealist and a perfectionist. He also had personal knowledge about the arts and could render opinions that the business and legal members of the group could not supply.

A need was recognized for a small management consulting staff to coordinate the committee's work, to conduct research, to estimate space needs and costs, and to draft reports.

When the Committee members assembled for a second meeting on November 8, they chose John Rockefeller as Chairman. At their third meeting they approved his recommendation to retain the Philadelphia firm of Day & Zimmermen, which assigned to the project its vice president, A. L. Fowler, and a senior staff member, Henry D. Johnson, Jr.

A change in the leadership of the Philharmonic soon brought a change in their representation on the Exploratory Committee. On the Philharmonic board, Houghton succeeded Blair as chairman, and David M. Keiser became president, replacing Blair on the committee. Keiser brought to the committee a combination of business acumen and artistic sensitivity, for, in addition to his business success in the sugar industry, he was a concert pianist. He had studied at the Juilliard School and was a trustee of that institution.

The Metropolitan Opera Association kept Spofford as chairman of its executive committee and their chief spokesman on the exploratory group. The Met also added to the committee two of its directors, Irving S. Olds and C. D. Jackson. Olds, the retired chairman of U. S. Steel, was a respected elder statesman in the Met family. Known for his keen legal mind and for his sense of fairness, Olds became the group's most influential member in working out the organizational relationships among the several participating institutions. Jackson, the publisher of *Fortune* magazine, had been an ardent and articulate member of the Met's New House Committee. He brought unfailing optimism to the group, a quality needed in the face of frequent unforeseen obstacles. Along with creative ideas of substance and strategy, he brought wit and humor to the committee's discussions.

When the enlarged committee met on December 13 they chose as their official name "The Exploratory Committee for a Musical Arts Center." A budget was prepared totaling $50,000 to cover anticipated expenses for five months. Discussions of these needs were held with staff of the Rockefeller Foundation, and a formal request for a $50,000 grant was sent on December 29. In that letter Spofford summarized the thinking of the committee up to that time concerning its self-imposed mission:

> to determine the feasibility of a musical arts center in the City not only for the opera and symphony but also for such activities as chamber music, ballet, light opera, and spoken drama, and possible educational programs related thereto. Other questions to be considered by the Committee, should it reach an affirmative decision regarding the Center, will touch upon the proper organizational relationships of the various participating groups, the facilities that would be required, and the best methods of financing such a project.

The Rockefeller Foundation made the grant requested, and the expenses of the Exploratory Committee beyond the five-month initial period were further underwritten by a grant of $25,000 from the New

York Foundation and by smaller grants from the New York Community Trust. Thus a principle of diversified support was established at the beginning.

The amount of work faced by the Exploratory Committee called for frequent meetings and the pattern of regular luncheon meetings every other Monday was adopted. Though the committee members were full-time business or professional men, they were interested, serious, and committed to their task. Seldom were any of them absent or even late. While discussions in the committee were informal, often spirited, the members had no difficulty in coming to a consensus or a formal decision when it was needed. The nature of these meetings was described by several committee members:

"We didn't wait for food; business started right away," said Blum. "The Chairman never could eat much lunch, but the others did."

"People are always asking what goes on at meetings like this," Josephs remarked. "They think it's some kind of mysterious, arcane, esoteric conversation that goes on with a lot of wise people. Not at all: They eat their soup noisily, and they listen, and sometimes at the end they come up with something that's pretty intelligent. Sometimes they speak without thinking. Lots of people think while they're speaking. Sometimes they'll spark somebody's idea, and then something may happen. The emphasis is on action rather than argument, and there is minimal time available for anything petty."

"The tone of the meetings? Generally serious, but not mournful," said Arthur Houghton. "There was a lot of good humor and some flashes of real wit. We were a very compatible group of men. Before we were finished, we all knew each other very well. One of the most important things about this group is that they were all flexible."[1]

The artistic boundaries of the proposed center was the first issue the committee had to resolve. Music, in the forms of opera and symphony, was fundamental. Ballet, or the art of dance, was recognized as musically based. But what other arts, visual or performing? On these issues John Rockefeller wrote:

A basic question which first absorbed our attention was how far—if at all—the center should go beyond the musical arts.

Painting and sculpture? Our conclusion was that we should limit
our enterprise to the performing arts because we recognized that
the visual arts were well accommodated in New York, and we
were concerned with how much a single center could wisely
include.[2]

Inclusion of spoken drama was discussed. Commercial theater
might be a near neighbor in the Lincoln Square Project, for Moses
was close to commitments with Roger Stevens to sponsor a commercial theater area north of the opera and concert hall sites. But
repertory theater had, as yet, no permanent home in New York.
There were visions of an American equivalent of the Old Vic or the
Comédie Française, and the group saw an opportunity for a major
theater institution alongside the Met and the Philharmonic. ANTA,
the American National Theater & Academy, was obviously an organization to be consulted.

The question of education in the arts was raised on December 13,
1955. The thinking turned not only to the training of young artists, but
to sources of research in the musical arts. The outstanding music
collection of the New York Public Library, inadequately housed at the
main 42nd Street building, might be included. Musical instrument
collections, such as the large one owned by the Metropolitan Museum
of Art and the ethnic musical collections of the Museum of Natural
History, were considered. Rockefeller pressed for a reaction to the
possibility of including a school, and Spofford, who was also a trustee
of Juilliard, thought it might be interested.

A number of very practical questions were also raised. Access to
and from the center was recognized as a public aspect of great interest and concern. There was a feeling that a survey should be made of
parking facilities and that traffic engineers should be brought in to
study existing traffic patterns and the probable changes in those
patterns that would be caused by large crowds coming to Lincoln
Square. These ideas led to the realization that factual information was
needed on the makeup of audiences for opera, symphony, and ballet.

The relationship of a performing arts center to the mass audience
of radio and television was to be explored. Rockefeller conferred with
Robert Sarnoff and William S. Paley, the heads of RCA and CBS;
both advised that no separate studios or stages for TV productions
need be planned. However, looking ahead to future technological
advances, all stages in the center should be so designed that they
could be used for live telecasts.

Moses was pressing for a preliminary site plan to include in a
brochure he had scheduled for February publication. Harrison's first

plans for the site indicated that the allotted four acres would be hopelessly inadequate. Could the site be enlarged to the north, to take in the block between 64th and 65th Streets? Rockefeller brought up the need for site enlargement in his first detailed discussion with Moses and his staff. Moses explained his plan for the northern block as part of the Roger Stevens commercial theater area, but this plan was not yet final. In the next several weeks Moses and his planners found it possible to accommodate the commercial theater area in the triangle north of 65th Street between Broadway and Amsterdam Avenue and thus free the 64th to 65th Street block for the musical arts group. In the course of these discussions, with help from Harrison, the idea was further developed to close both 63rd and 64th Streets and to create a super block from 62nd to 65th Streets.

Another problem was the omission from the Lincoln Square project of the 12-story Kennedy building on the eastern end of the block running from 62nd to 63rd Streets. (In contrast to the surrounding slum area this was a serviceable building rented by its owners, the Joseph P. Kennedy family, to the federal government for several agencies including the U. S. Immigration Service.) The building was a barrier standing between the new cultural buildings and the Broadway entrance to the project. If retained, it would always be incongruous and would occupy badly needed space should any of the ideas pertaining to other buildings materialize. Moses had omitted it from the project because its purchase would use up too much of the allotted federal and city urban renewal funds. But he was sympathetic to the idea of taking the Kennedy building if it could be done without adding to the city's financial burden. Rockefeller had several talks with Joseph P. Kennedy concerning the sale of the building and its inclusion in the Lincoln Square project. By the first of March, Kennedy had agreed to sell at a price of $2.5 million. Moses was willing to have it included in the project property if the sponsor, Lincoln Center, would pay $1.5 million thus limiting the city and federal obligation to a land write-down of $1 million. Moses conditioned his agreement on help from the musical arts leadership in persuading the Federal Housing and Home Finance Agency to include the Kennedy building in the project.

As the real estate aspects of a possible center assumed greater clarity, Rockefeller and his committee felt a need for wider advice on the artistic and conceptual nature of the project. To this end, a group of individuals, chosen for their knowledge and experience in the performing arts and in varied types of civic projects, was asked to respond to ideas already developed and to suggest other ideas for activities or facilities.[3] A two-day conference was held on February 17 and 18, 1956 resulting in endorsement of the concept of a center, stressing inclusion of ballet and drama, as well as music. There was a strong interest in the inclusion of advanced training for talented young professionals. They urged that the new center encourage creative work, stating that "no matter how beautiful the buildings of the new center may be, or however complete the technical equipment, the center would not meet its challenging possibilities unless opportunities on the creative side were adequately provided."[4]

These conclusions confirmed the judgment of the Exploratory Committee that a center would be desirable. They reached agreement that the composition of the center should include the performing arts of dance and drama, and it should include education, "if the appropriate instrument can be found." In the search for an "appropriate educational instrument," discussions continued with officials of Juilliard, Columbia, and New York University. It soon became clear that training for professional performing was not central in the thinking of those at Columbia or NYU. Training at Juilliard was already focused on artistic professionals, but it was linked with a sizable preparatory school.

The search for an organization to represent the spoken drama began with conversations with officers of ANTA, the American National Theatre & Academy, and Robert Whitehead became their spokesman. Soon the Actor's Studio asked to be considered, and Cheryl Crawford made inquiries of Rockefeller. Discussions followed by Elia Kazan, Lee Strasberg, and Miss Crawford with Rockefeller and Young. They presented their approach to theater as the one most typically American. They were eager to be sponsors of drama performances at the new center and felt that their training technique, commonly called The Method, would be the ideal basis for this training.

The situation regarding ballet seemed initially less puzzling. The New York City Ballet had established itself in the first rank of ballet companies. Lincoln Kirstein was already a member of the Exploratory Committee, and it was assumed by the committee that, in due time, this company would become a part of the center. But the New York City Ballet had no independent institutional existence. It was a part of the City Center of Music and Drama. True, it had full artistic independence; it had its affiliated American School of Ballet, and its Ballet Society provided some support. But its financial control, union agreements, and other business matters were handled by City Center. In the spring of 1956, Rockefeller initiated talks with Newbold Morris, chairman of City Center, who was not enthusiastic. He could see little or no benefit to City Center in leaving its 55th Street theater and taking on a new set of obligations at Lincoln Center.

Photo by Marianne Barcellona/New York Philharmonic

Photo by Heffernan/Metropolitan Opera

Photo © 1980 Paul Kolnik/New York City Ballet

Photo by Diane Gorodnitzki/The Juilliard School

Arts included in the center.

Discussion of the City Center matter with Moses found him definitely opposed. As a result of the lack of any affirmative interest by City Center and opposition by Moses, the Exploratory Committee directed Rockefeller to advise Morris that "it is not possible to include City Center in present planning." Two weeks later Rockefeller reported that Morris was upset and wished to keep alive City Center's potential interest.

The Day & Zimmerman staff, retained by the Exploratory Committee, assembled from each of the potential participating organizations the space requirements for their homes at Lincoln Square. Audience surveys were underway to determine from where and by what means of travel audiences came to performances. Inquiries were made into the economic and educational status of members of the audiences. Existing traffic and parking patterns in the Lincoln Square area were studied with projections of possible future congestion resulting from the proposed development. Improvement of mass transit facilities in the area was explored with the Board of Transportation.

By March, 1956 the Metropolitan and the Philharmonic had signed binding obligations for the purchase of their respective parcels of land. On April 15, Moses publicly announced plans for the Lincoln Square development, a 17-block urban renewal project including the three blocks for the opera house, concert hall, and possible related activities. The project was also to include two blocks for educational purposes with Fordham as the probable sponsor; a plot for the New York headquarters of the American Red Cross; a cooperative housing project and the massive Lincoln Towers (4,000 units) middle-income housing project.

In late April, 1956, a group including Bliss, Harrison, Fowler, and Rockefeller traveled to Europe for discussion with European leaders in the performing arts. They observed the design and technical aspects of new concert halls and opera houses and explored relationships between educational activities and performing groups.

From a design standpoint, they gained practical ideas from the new opera houses in the Rhineland. Also they found the recently completed Festival Hall in London of interest architecturally but were warned of some of its acoustical and functional problems. Rockefeller's talks with Michel St. Denis at Strasbourg about experience there in professional artistic training confirmed his belief that an educational institution was essential in the concept of a center and that it should embrace training in all the performing arts.

Concurrently with the clarification of the concept and artistic limits of the proposed center came a series of major organizational decisions. From the start, it was understood that the old and well-established institutions of the Metropolitan Opera Association and the New York Philharmonic-Symphony Society were and would remain independent corporate entities. Each jealously guarded its artistic autonomy; each had its own prestigious board of directors and its groups of loyal subscribers and contributors. Each would continue to be responsible for running its own fund-raising campaigns for annual operations and for meeting its own deficit. Each was, in fact, a sovereign state with strong historic and emotional attachments to its independence.

The Juilliard School of Music, the New York Public Library, and the City Center of Music and Drama were similarly independent institutions with similar pride in their independence and defensive reactions to any hint of loss of sovereignty. Therefore, the principle of autonomous constituents was firmly established, and it was decided that any organizations that might later become a part of the project must be independent and self-supporting. The common need for new homes, however, assured their cooperation in a single capital fund drive and their acceptance of some form of joint, or overall, ownership of the proposed buildings.

Clearly a new corporation would be required, and each of the participating institutions should have representation on its governing body. There were strong feelings that the board of the new corporation should also represent the broad interests of the public. A possible course of development for the new corporation would be to limit it to the tasks of planning, financing, and building the new center, leaving it after construction was finished responsible only for maintaining and operating the buildings. But such a course would make it no more than a real estate operation. Beyond the real estate aspects the committee saw a need and an opportunity for an artistic and educational agency to foster quality in the performing arts and to enlarge the public enjoyment and appreciation of those arts. From the many sources of artistic and critical advice, one comment struck an especially responsive chord: "It would be of no real use just to re-pot the Metropolitan and the Philharmonic."

There gradually emerged an organizational concept that would make the new corporation a beneficent landlord with the constituents favored tenants, that would recognize the constituents as the project's artistic endowment and place the new corporation in a coordinating role. It would enable the new organization to encourage innovations, to foster the new and experimental, to search for ways to reach an enlarging public, and to encourage international exchange in the performing arts.

Basic to all consideration of concepts, organization, and building was the fundamental question facing the Exploratory Committee, "What can be financed?" All early financial planning was done against two historic facts of life in the performing arts: one, recognition that the arts are inherently a deficit operation and require a substantial subsidy beyond any reasonable expectation of income from ticket sales. Second, American tradition expected this subsidy to come primarily from private, voluntary contributions, and not from government.

The arts of live performance operate inevitably at a deficit because of fundamental features in their economic structure. A clear analysis of this fact was made by the economists, William J. Baumol and Willian G. Bowen. Brief excerpts will summarize their line of argument:

> Performing organizations typically operate under constant financial strain . . . an inescapable result of the technology of live performance. . . . The playing of an instrument or the acting of a role remains today largely what it has been for centuries. From an engineering point of view, live performance is technologically stagnant.

> . . . the work of the performer is an end in itself, not a means for the production of some good. . . . Unlike workers in manufacturing, performers are not intermediaries between raw material and the completed commodity—their activities are themselves the consumers' good . . . .

> Human ingenuity has devised ways to reduce the labor necessary to produce an automobile, but no one has yet succeeded in decreasing the human effort expended at a live performance of a 45 minute Schubert quartet much below a total of three man-hours . . . .

> The central point of the argument is that for an activity such as the live performing arts where productivity is stationary, every increase in money wages will be translated automatically into an equivalent increase in unit labor costs—there is no offsetting increase in output per man-hour as there is in a rising productivity industry.[5]

Faced with the inevitability of rising costs and deficits, the entrepreneur could in theory raise his ticket prices enough to cover costs of productions. However, in addition to this economic consideration, the institutions sponsoring these arts feel a social obligation to make the arts available to as wide an economic spectrum of society as possible rather than to a limited, wealthy group. Hence, they keep their ticket prices below costs and seek subsidies to make up the difference. The result is that nearly every ticket purchaser to a performance of these arts is to some degree a recipient of charity.

The second historic fact in the American performing arts relates to their form of sponsorship and their source of subsidy. In this country the arts were, and still are, largely sponsored by private, nonprofit institutions. Their subsidy came in the 1950's almost entirely from the voluntary private contributions. The American tradition of private sponsorship and privately contributed support has been in sharp contrast to the pattern in most of the rest of the world, especially in Europe, where governmental sponsorship and public subsidy has long been the rule. At the time of the Exploratory Committee, this American tradition was firmly established, and most trustees of arts institutions feared and strongly resisted any form of governmental subsidy. Their apprehension centered on the risks of political interference, particularly in artistic matters. Similarly, in governmental circles, especially among legislators, there was strong resistance to spending tax money on such "frills" as the arts.

Against this background, the Exploratory Committee began to formulate its plans under an assumption that the project would be entirely private and would rely on no public funds except for the federal and city moneys involved in the write-down of land costs in urban renewal. The justification for this form of public subsidy, as expressed in the federal legislation, was for the purpose of eliminating slums. It was not looked upon as a subsidy to the developer, whether it was a housing real estate operator, an educational institution, or a cultural center.

However, the realization of the very large space requirements for the new constituent homes and the expanding organizational concept of the musical arts center soon raised doubts about the feasibility of doing the job solely with private, contributed capital. There was talk of a mortgage repayable over a period of years. But the interest payments and amortization of mortgage debt would place an intolerable burden on the constituents. A decision was reached to hold the mortgage possibility in reserve as a last resort.

The Metropolitan Opera and the Juilliard School owned valuable real estate which they would almost certainly sell if they were to move to Lincoln Square. Their equity in these investments amounted to as much as $4 or $5 million and might conceivably be applied to the costs of new homes. However, their enlarged programs at Lincoln Square would be so demanding that these assets could be used most advantageously to increase their endowment or reserve funds. The Exploratory Committee concluded that every effort should be made to finance the new project without calling on the equity reserve funds of any of the constituents.

In spite of the prevailing bias against governmental funding, the specter of expanding capital costs soon led to a reexamination of possibilities for help through governmental capital funds, especially from the city. There were several helpful precedents. The city of New York had evolved a pattern of limited support for some of its cultural institutions. It had, on several occasions, matched private funds with city capital funds for construction when the buildings were to be owned by the city. The city had provided land for the Metropolitan Museum of Art and for the New York Public Library, both private institutions. The major museums and the library also received annual city appropriations for building upkeep. The trustees of these institutions felt it was safe to receive such city support so long as they retained full control of their artistic functions through the use of their private funds for professional and curatorial activities.

There was a growing realization on the part of Exploratory Committee members that the potential significance of the evolving center related not only to the future cultural life of the city, but also to the city's economic well-being and to its general prestige. Comparisons were made with the significance to New York of the United Nations headquarters. That project evolved with strong city support, which took the form of large appropriations of capital funds for nearby street and highway improvements and for park and landscaping developments. There was a widespread consensus that those public expenditures had been justified through the economic stimulus of the United Nations to the redevelopment of the East Side of New York and to the wide range of new economic activities that the presence of the United Nations brought to the city. When Rockefeller brought the policy question of possible city support to the Exploratory Committee on February 4, 1956, the response was open-minded and generally affirmative. (David Keiser also suggested that the committee should explore the possibility of federal funds. Later, state support was considered as well.)

Several studies of ways it might be possible for the city to aid and support Lincoln Center were undertaken by the committee's legal advisers, the law firm of Milbank, Tweed, Hope and Hadley. They were led by a senior partner, John E. Lockwood, who was also an associate in the Rockefeller family office.[6] The report indicated that, under the state constitution, public capital funds could be used only for facilities that would be owned by the city or state government; however, in the proposed center, a number of such opportunities existed or could be created.

On April 30, 1956, Rockefeller and Harrison discussed with Moses various ways the city might contribute to capital financing. No conclusions were reached, but the subject of governmental support remained under active negotiation, with significant progress during the next six years.

The primary source of capital to create the center remained in the private sector. From their first meeting the planning of a campaign for private contributions had been a top priority. Their case for contributions would have to be a sound one; their budget must be solidly based on factual information; their goal must represent a challenge but not be so high as to seem unattainable.

Notwithstanding their own experience in campaign strategy, the group sought professional judgment on money-raising. In March, they turned to H. J. Seymour a fund-raising adviser who had helped plan several of the most successful university fund-raising campaigns. Their May meeting was devoted entirely to consideration of his counsel. Seymour, emphasized the crucial importance of receiving a few very large gifts at the beginning of the campaign. He urged that at least $25 million be assured before launching a public money-raising effort. When succeeding phases of the campaign reached special categories of donors, such as banks or insurance companies, he advised care to secure initial, large, pace-setting gifts from donors whose participation would represent endorsement to others. These "Bell Cows" were to be leaders in a giving parade.

A capital budget for the project was a prerequisite to setting a campaign goal. But capital budgeting was dependent on numerous other decisions and planning assumptions. On May 14, 1956, in order to provide a basis for budgeting, the committee adopted six major assumptions:

1. The new corporation will be a membership, non-profit, tax-exempt organization.
2. The corporation will own all structures and basic facilities within the center.
3. Operating costs will be prepared on two bases: (a) year-round tenancy for constituents and (b) part-time preferred tenancy for constituent requirements leaving the corporation responsible for renting the halls during other times.

4. There will be four auditoria, an educational building, a library, a garage, and a restaurant.
5. Auditoria will be designed for multipurpose use and year-round operation.
6. Capacities will be approximately:

Opera House	3,800
Concert Hall	2,800
Theater	2,200
Recital Hall	1,000
Garage	700 cars

The D & Z staff assembled information on constituents' space needs, and these requirements were reduced to a common denominator of cubic feet. A cost of $2.00 per cubic foot was accepted as the basis for construction estimates. This figure was higher than prevailing costs in New York for apartment and office construction in recognition of the unprecedented and nonrepetitive nature of the center's buildings, but it proved to be a serious underestimate. The buildings, when completed, worked out to an average cost of nearly $4.30 per cubic foot.

Early in June, the first estimates of costs were ready. They added up to the staggering sum of $90 million for land and buildings. This was considered far in excess of the amount that could be raised for building purposes; the architect and staff were asked to prepare a budget reduced to $40 million. They came back with a $45 million estimate, but this had been achieved only by eliminating the education building and the library. The committee was unwilling to cut out these crucial elements, so the search for other financial solutions was continued.

By May, the planning for incorporation had reached the stage of needing a name. The staff prepared a list of 24 possible names ranging from "The Center for the Advancement of Musical and Performing Arts" to "The Music Drama and Dance Concourse." After considering these and other possible names, the committee felt that the geographic place name, Lincoln Square, would inevitably be associated with the project, so they chose "The Lincoln Center, Inc." as its name. Lawyers checked this name and found that it was not available but that "Lincoln Center for the Performing Arts, Inc." could be used. This became the official name of the corporation.

All members of the Exploratory Committee, with the exception of Harrison, were the initial incorporators. Harrison was not included because it was assumed that he would have a key professional role in the design of the project and should not be placed in the position of being his own client.

On June 22, 1956, the certificate of incorporation was officially filed in the office of the secretary of state in Albany, and Lincoln Center for the Performing Arts, Inc. was formally established. Rockefeller and his colleagues had made themselves responsible for a new non-profit corporation with no financial assets, with no traditions or history, with no contributing constituency, and with formidable obligations. By changing the Exploratory Committee for a Musical Arts Center into the new corporation, they had given resounding, affirmative answers to the questions of desirability and feasibility. They had embarked on their long venture.

CHAPTER 3

Urban Renewal

In the nineteenth century, the area that became Lincoln Center had developed rapidly as the growth of the city pushed northward on Manhattan Island. After the Civil War, expansion assumed boom proportions around Lincoln Square. Developers built brownstones designed as individual luxury homes, and, near the elevated railroad, they built walk-up, "old law" tenements. But the Lincoln Square area never became fashionable as did that of Riverside Drive farther north. With overbuilding, the boom burst. Single homes were broken up into small apartments; a number of apartments and former small hotels were converted into crowded rooming houses. Maintenance of buildings was neglected, building code violations were numerous, and fire hazards were great. By 1955, the entire area was in an advanced state of decay.

The initiative to deal with this blighted area was taken by Robert Moses, acting in his capacity as chairman of the New York City Committee on Slum Clearance. Moses wore this hat along with numerous others that had already given him a well-earned reputation as New York's master builder. His Slum Clearance Committee was, in the mid fifties, the principal planning and administrative mechanism of the city to handle governmental urban renewal.

35

Without a governmental urban renewal program, Lincoln Center could not have been built, and the national policies of urban renewal in the fifties should therefore be recalled. In cities, especially the older and larger ones, many areas that housed the poor were unsanitary, overcrowded, and degrading. They were slums, and slums were to be "cleared"—that is, eradicated. A fresh start was wanted to create a totally different urban area, in many cases to serve different purposes and different segments of society.

Significantly, there was not at that time any widespread public outcry for preservation of either neighborhoods or buildings. A few voices were raised, forerunners of attitudes and public policies that became the preservation movement a generation later. But in the fifties the bulldozer psychology prevailed. Dispersal of the concentrated poverty of slum areas was generally viewed as socially desirable. There was, however, public and official concern for what would happen to residents and small businessmen forced to move from these slum areas. To meet this concern, urban renewal policies required that "safe, decent, and sanitary accomodations" must be found for all residential tenants at rents within their financial means and in localities reasonably convenient to their places of work. Modest compensation for business losses was provided.

Renewal could take many forms, though new housing was predominant. The new housing to be built in a particular project was not necessarily intended to replace the housing lost in slum clearance. Some of it might be subsidized low-income housing, but equally possible some could be built for tenants of a higher income level. It was expected that the total housing stock of the city would be increased by the project and that this, in turn, would tend to make available dwelling units elsewhere in the city for displaced tenants. In addition to housing, slums could be replaced with stores and office buildings, parks, schools, firehouses, hospitals, and a great variety of nonprofit institutions.

The Federal Housing Act of 1949 was the official expression of these policies and attitudes, and Title I provided the federal financial incentives for municipalities to carry out these policies. It established standards for large-scale federal grants to cities for these urban renewal purposes. Grants were available to induce cities to buy up slum land (by condemnation, if necessary) and to resell it at a lower "fair re-use value" to developers, who would then erect the new buildings. The difference between the city's land acquisition costs and its "fair re-use value" was the "land write-down," which was financed two-thirds by the federal grant and one-third by the municipality. New York State also provided an additional subsidy which could be used to pay half of the city's one-third. This "land write-down" was regarded as the cost of achieving the public purpose of slum clearance. A second form of federal grant was available for construction costs of public projects in urban renewal areas. The same formula of two-thirds federal and one-third municipal funds prevailed. In order to be eligible for a federal grant, a project had to be primarily (that is, 80 percent) for the benefit of the public that would live in or use the specific project. Local parks, schools, or branch libraries would qualify. A new city hall for the benefit of an entire municipality would not.

By the spring of 1955 renewal of the Lincoln Square area had become definite and appeared to be feasible in official circles. While it lacked the finality of public hearings and formal votes in the City Planning Commission and in the Board of Estimate, Moses had carried his planning far enough to assure that the area would qualify for federal urban renewal funds, that funds would be available, and that a number of renewal sponsors were seriously interested. The total area of 17 blocks might provide as many as 5000 new high-rise apartment units, a two-block university campus, retail shopping areas, a new public elementary school, commercial theaters, and an opera house.

The site for a new Metropolitan Opera house first offered by Moses was, geographically, only a very small part of the project, not more than one block. Obviously if the Opera were to build near Lincoln Square, it would add luster and prestige to the whole area. But the Opera was not seen as essential to proceeding with the Lincoln Square project. On the contrary, it was presented merely as a possibility that the project planners might be able to accomodate. Had the Opera not become a part of the project, the slum would have been cleared, and a new area of the city would have been built without either an opera house or any of the other Lincoln Center buildings.

However, as the project actually developed, what began as one block for the Opera was expanded first to three blocks and eventually to four for the present Lincoln Center for the Performing Arts. The areas for housing were defined and scheduled for development under two separate sponsors, Webb and Knapp and the Lincoln Guild Housing Corporation, a cooperative. Moses' negotiations for a university center ended successfully when Fordham became the sponsor of the two southern blocks of the project for its schools of law, business education, social service, and general studies. The New York Chapter of the American Red Cross became another sponsor and built its headquarters on the northwest corner of Amsterdam Avenues

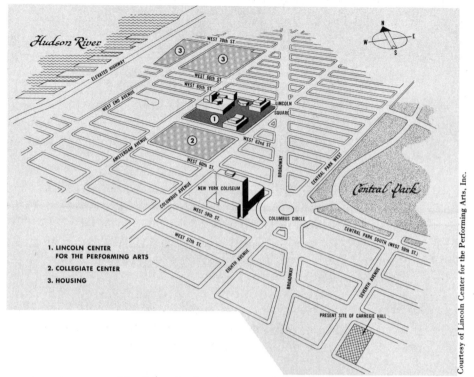

The Lincoln Square urban renewal area.

and 66th Street. The original plan for a commercial theater area in the triangle between Broadway and Amsterdam Avenue, with Roger Stevens as the principal sponsor, remained part of the project, until May of 1957 when it was dropped by the federal agency on grounds that the plan for that area did not meet all the federal requirements. [1]

Moses announced the Lincoln Square plans publicly on April 16, 1956. Opposition to the project arose at once. Harris L. Present, an attorney who was chairman of a recently formed Council on Housing Relocation became the spokesman for tenants in the project area. Early opposition centered on the hardship that would have to be borne by residents and businessmen who would have to move.

The official procedural course that had to be followed in any urban renewal project was at best a complicated one with a series of sequential steps which had to be taken. Along the way one after another obstacle had to be overcome. Lincoln Square had to run that course. Moses was the coach and timekeeper. In all of his successes as master builder, he set deadlines, sometimes arbitrary, made public pronouncements, sometimes abrasive, and issued memoranda in multiple copies. Without his drive and persistence the time span might have dragged on much longer, and the project might never have reached completion.

After the fanfare of public announcement of the project, summer dragged on without action on Lincoln Square by the City administration. Moses' patience had worn thin when, in September he wrote Rockefeller, charging that lack of support by Mayor Wagner and the Board of Estimate had brought the Lincoln Square project to a standstill. A few days later, Rockefeller had a private meeting with the Mayor to seek his cooperation in securing city financial support in a variety of ways. He urged prompt official action on Lincoln Square for he was as eager as Moses to get on with the project and as impatient with delays.

Finally, the Board of Estimate unanimously gave its preliminary approval of the Lincoln Square Project on September 30, 1956. Harris Present responded by filing a petition with the Federal Housing and Home Finance Agency to block the project. The basis of the petition was an alleged violation of the constitutional guarantee of separation of church and state. The inclusion in the project of Fordham University, a Jesuit institution, was alleged to make it a recipient of a federal subsidy and thus to invalidate the whole of the Lincoln Square project. The case received national publicity, and because of strong feelings held by many citizens on the church and state issue, it stimulated a number of emotional and, at times, vituperative, letters to Rockefeller and to others associated with Lincoln Center. Lincoln Center was, of course, in no way involved directly in the constitutional issue, but in the public mind, the separate identity of Lincoln Center from the other sponsors in the Lincoln Square project was easily ignored.

The Directors of Lincoln Center remained publicly silent until a few months later, faced with ever more troublesome delays in the start of its project, Lincoln Center intervened in the case with an *amicus curiae* brief filed by its counsel. The position taken was that Federal and state contributions in Title I proceedings do not constitute a subsidy to any sponsor, but are for the public purpose of eliminating the blighted slum area; if the court should determine otherwise, it should avoid action which would prevent the city from proceeding with other parts of the project not involved in the question. The complaint reached the Supreme Court in June, 1958, which dismissed it. An appeal in a second case came to the Supreme Court in May, 1959 and was again denied. The end result of this litigation was a favorable clarification of the legal status of the project.

The primary concern of Rockefeller and his colleagues at that time was to maximize the governmental financial contribution to the project. This effort focused on two items, the reuse price to be paid for the land and the possibilities for obtaining public capital funds through either urban renewal construction projects or other forms of city aid.

The starting point for land-price negotiations had been the price of $8.00 per square foot, set by Moses in his first offer to the Metropolitan. Fordham was asked to pay only $5.00 per square foot. There was no ready justification for this price differential, and renegotiation of the $8.00 Lincoln Center price became one of the first subjects of Rockefeller's discussions with Moses and with Albert A. Cole, the Federal Housing Administrator. After looking into the matter, Cole reopened the valuation of the land. Then, on January 10, 1957, with Moses' consent, Lincoln Center offered to bid $5.00 per square foot for its land. Simultaneously, the Metropolitan and the Philharmonic withdrew their previous offers of $8.00 per square foot.

Within four months a new conflict had arisen between Moses and the federal agency over the total of urban renewal funds available to New York City and specifically for Lincoln Square. In the face of this crisis over federal funds, Moses reverted to his earlier position, calling for $8.00 per square foot for the performing arts part of Lincoln Square.[2]

While the leaders of Lincoln Center recognized the city's problems over urban renewal funds, this turn of events caused them to question the degree of the city's interest in and support of the project itself. Moses' reactions to their pleas for financial help seemed to be influenced by a belief on his part that Rockefeller philanthropic funds represented a virtually inexhaustible source, and that the Rockefellers would not let the Lincoln Center project fail. But this attitude on Moses' part was of grave concern to Rockefeller, for he had joined the Exploratory Committee and had become president of Lincoln Center with a conviction that it was not and must not become a "Rockefeller Project." He saw it as a cultural and civic opportunity that could succeed only if it were able to command widespread community support.

Therefore, Rockefeller and his colleagues persistently sought to find ways to reduce the price they were asked to pay for land. At the time, Major General (Retired) Otto L. Nelson, Jr., then vice president in charge of housing of the New York Life Insurance Company, was serving (at $1.00 a year on a part-time basis) as special assistant to the president of Lincoln Center. He had become an expert in government subsidized housing; he had learned the intricacies of the procedural steps in Title I projects and had effective contacts in the housing bureaucracy in both Washington and New York.

With Nelson's help, in addition to direct renegotiation of the re-use price, a variety of other approaches to the land-price question were tried. The largest item for negotiations related to the Kennedy building. The initial agreement, worked out between Moses and Rockefeller, represented a price of about $62.00 per square foot. Since that building was included in the Lincoln Square project, its land could qualify for the Title I land write-down exactly as other parts of the project would qualify, and it could be sold for redevelopment at the same low re-use price placed on the rest of the property. The federal officials were willing to have it so treated, but Moses remained unchanged in his initial agreement.

Greater success came from efforts to find other ways that public urban renewal funds might be used to meet some of the capital burden. The proposed undergroud parking garage readily qualified for a project-related Title I construction grant. Its budget, initially set at approximately $3 million, grew in early planning to over $5 million.

An effort was also made to secure a federal grant for the library and museum. But this building failed to meet the legal requirement that its function be 80 percent related to the project. The federal officials reasoned that the reference and research functions related to city-wide and, indeed, to national usage. Eventually it was worked out that this building would be built largely with city capital funds and be owned by the city.

A credit for the costs of tenant relocation and demolition was sought, but never achieved. On this point, Moses was adamant on the basis of consistency with his other New York City projects. New York practice in this regard was an exception to national policy, which placed responsibility for relocation and demolition on municipalities rather than on redevelopment sponsors. Donation by the city of land in the streets to be closed was also sought but could not be secured.

After all of these efforts and protracted renegotiation of the basic land price, the federal officials insisted on securing several new, impartial appraisals. The final land price was worked out at an average of $10.62 per square foot, representing $1.5 million (or $62.86 per square foot) for the Kennedy building and a reduction to $7.04 per square foot for the remainder of the three-block site.

The official progress of the Lincoln Square Urban Renewal Project is marked by public hearings and by the subsequent decisions of various officials or agencies. The first notable public hearing was held before the City Planning Commission on September 11, 1957.[3] Because of the great public interest in the project, the hearing had been scheduled in City Hall's largest room—the Board of Estimate chambers. Even so, its adjoining corridors were jammed with citizens and representatives of the press. Both the proponents and the opponents of the project were "wearing their colors." Green lapel labels read "For Lincoln Square"; the opposition was labeled with red tags reading "Against Lincoln Square." There was an unmistakable air of high emotion and expectation of controversy in the room.

The Planning Commission was represented by its full membership with its chairman, James M. Felt, presiding. Felt was a respected public official and private citizen of New York. He patiently but persistently worked to make New York a more livable city. He had a well-earned reputation for fairness, and at this hearing, he announced a plan for equal time for those "for" and "against" the project; he scrupulously kept those testifying to the prescribed time limits.

Moses started the hearing with a brief description of the entire Lincoln Square project and an indication of his vision of its importance to the City. Rockefeller reviewed the origin and concept of Lincoln Center. He dealt forthrightly with the problem of sponsor responsibility for relocation of tenants, fully accepting that responsibility on behalf of Lincoln Center for its area and giving assurances that it would be carried out considerately and compassionately. Keiser, for the Philharmonic, and Jackson, for the Metropolitan, followed with testimony on the importance and urgency of the project for their institutions. Harrison gave a brief description of the physical aspects of the new center and its meaning to the City. William Schuman, then president of Juilliard, stressed the educational aspect of the project and its importance to aspiring young artists. Father McGinley, the president of Fordham, told of his institution's plans for its Lincoln Square campus, emphasizing the need for additional facilities to meet the rising tide of students seeking higher education. Spokesmen for the other sponsors outlined their plans, pointing to the stimulation the project would give to the economic revival of the whole West Side. The opponents, in their turn, were led by Harris Present. There were numerous emotional and pleading statements by residents and small businessmen who had lived and worked for many years in Lincoln Square and whose primary wish was to be allowed to remain there undisturbed.

The official report of the Planning Commission came three weeks later, unanimously urging the Board of Estimate to give its final approval to the project.[4] They saw the project as "a rare opportunity which, if not availed of now, may never again present itself." They characterized the existing slum area as "clearly substandard and unsanitary . . . a blighting and depressing influence on surrounding sections contributing to gradual deterioration of the Upper West Side." They called the proposed performing arts center "outstanding . . . an unparalleled cultural opportunity that will almost certainly make New York City the musical capital of the world now and for many years to come."

The Board of Estimate held its public hearing on October 24, 1957, a marathon affair which went on until 4:30 A.M. the next day, to give opponents full opportunity to be heard. Because the proponents of Lincoln Center had already presented their plans before the Planning Commision, only a brief summary was made by Rockefeller before the Board of Estimate. At the conclusion of the hearing, the Board again deferred final action. On November 26, the Board finally approved the Lincoln Square Urban Renewal Project. The *New York Times,* in an editorial, stated: "November 26, 1957 may well be recorded in the New York calendar of Important Events as the day when our finest single civic improvement was initiated."[5]

Two weeks later, the contract between the city and Lincoln Center was signed by Mayor Wagner and by Rockefeller. January 31, 1958 was set for public auction of the land and for vesting of title. However, further legal actions by the opponents succeeded in delaying the auction date. Near noon on Friday, February 28, 1958, Supreme Court Justice Owen McGivern signed the condemnation order transferring title to the land in the Lincoln Square project to the city of New York. At 2:00 P.M. in the office of the city's Real Estate Bureau in the Municipal Building, the four major parcels of land in the project were placed on the block for public auction. Each of the redevelopment sponsors presented their bids; the auctioneer called for other bids, and there were none; the properties were sold to Lincoln Center, Fordham University, the American Red Cross, and Webb & Knapp, Inc. Lincoln Center paid $3,993,667 for its 13-acre site, and then in the mayor's office, Wagner signed and delivered the deeds to the property.

Lincoln Center had become a landlord of 188 buildings, housing 1647 families, with all the immediate responsibilities of property management and the larger task of tenant relocation. Administratively, these functions were under the direction of General Nelson with policy guidance provided through a committee, chaired by Josephs. The real estate firm of Braislin, Porter & Wheelock, Inc. had been retained as relocation agent, with an office in the neighborhood. Badly needed fuel oil and coal deliveries were made immediately. Also, because the residential buildings now owned by Lincoln Center had been built prior to 1901, there were numerous building code violations, nearly 400 in all, and many repairs were urgently needed. In an effort to keep these structures habitable until their occupants could be moved, over 9000 maintenance work orders were issued. Special problems existed regarding obsolete heating systems. Under a city ordinance, kerosene room heaters in 130 apartments had to be replaced by new gas heaters, even though the buildings were to be demolished in less than a year.

Actual relocation of tenants could not begin for several months until the pending litigation was resolved in the Supreme Court. Nevertheless, Lincoln Center's relocation policies were promptly made known to all tenants, and each family was interviewed to determine its housing needs and preferences. Cash bonuses ranging from $270 to $500 were offered by Lincoln Center to each family that relocated itself, and finder's fees were paid to brokers who located satisfactory apartments. In cooperation with the City Housing Authority, a system of priority applications was evolved for public housing elsewhere in the city; a list of 6500 vacant apartments was provided.

Of inestimable help to the project and a credit to the tenant families is the fact that over half moved themselves. So quickly did they accept the inevitability of the renewal project that 112 families moved out before the final court order had been handed down to dispose of the legal questions. Moves into public housing elsewhere in the city accounted for 12 percent of the total, and nearly a third found new homes through the listing service. A majority (55 percent) of the moves were to other locations in Manhattan with over 900 into other West Side neighborhoods. Over one-fourth moved to other New York City boroughs and one-tenth left the City. A study of the first 742 families relocated showed that, on the average, they moved to larger quarters, from less than one room per person on the site to more than one room per person in their new homes. They paid an average of about $10.00 a month more in rent, but their payments per room were down by nearly $2.00. In all cases their new quarters met the legal requirements for "safe, decent, and sanitary" accommodations.

In addition to its residential tenants, Lincoln Center became landlord to 383 commercial tenants. These ranged from the Atomic Energy Commission to the Cuban Revolutionary Movement and included many small retail establishments. Under federal law, each commercial tenant was eligible to receive from federal funds up to $2500 for moving expenses and tangible loss.

The tenant in the Kennedy building, the U. S. Immigration and Naturalization Service, presented a special situation. General Nelson negotiated successfully for the building to be vacated in time for the construction schedule, but within that time frame, to retain the tenancy as long as possible for its income-producing value.

The timing of all relocation and demolition effort was carefully related to the construction timetable. The area was divided into three zones, and the site of Philharmonic Hall was the first to be cleared. Award of demolition contracts and actual demolition of buildings were timed to follow immediately after tenant removal.

Lincoln Center's progress in clearing the site was consistently ahead of the scheduled dates, thanks to the cooperation of tenants and the effectiveness of its relocation agent. In the first six months, 48 percent of the tenants had been moved; eight buildings had been demolished, and 26 more were scheduled to go down in the next month. By the end of the year, Nelson reported that "Area #1, the site of the concert hall, will be cleared and ready for construction by March 1, 1959."

The relocation and demolition program was completed (with the exception of the Kennedy building) by March 31, 1960, a full nine months ahead of the schedule established by the Slum Clearance Committee. In the course of the program some eviction notices were filed, but in only three cases was it necessary to evict tenants by action of marshals.

The site for Lincoln Center was not complete with the acquisition and clearing of the main three-block area. Before its purchase was accomplished in February, 1958, preliminary architectural planning had gone far enough to indicate that the site would be overcrowded. The planners hoped to use a portion of the southwest corner of the site which Moses had reserved as a public park. But Moses refused to make any change in his plans for the park. Enlargement northward into the block between 65th and 66th Streets seemed a more likely possibility. Moses agreed to support an amendment to the Lincoln Square project to include that half-block to the north, and in an expansive planning mood, he suggested that a pedestrian bridge or a tunnel could link this site with the three-block area of Lincoln Center. On March 12, 1958, Lincoln Center made a formal offer to buy the half-block if it could be made available under Title I urban renewal procedures.

Progress was rapid in the official consideration of this offer. Rockefeller discussed the Lincoln Center addition with Administrator Cole in Washington, and Cole approved the proposal in principle. Meanwhile, the Committee on Slum Clearance had approved the project. General Nelson pressed other city officials for prompt action to secure the commitment of federal funds before June 30 when an appropriation would lapse. On May 22, the Board of Estimate gave its preliminary approval. Within a week, Rockefeller had conferred again with Administrator Cole, seeking federal help in establishing the re-use price for the addition. By letter of June 24, Cole advised Rockefeller of authorization to proceed with the plan for the additional half-block. Appraisals were made to determine the minimum re-use price for the land; in view of the Broadway frontage, a price of $15.03 per square foot was established. The Board of Estimate held a hearing on August 21, 1958, and formal approval was voted. On October 1, Spofford, representing the center at public auction, bought the half-block between 65th and 66th streets for the agreed minimum purchase price of $850,000.

With the Lincoln Center site expanded to an area of three-and-one-half blocks, it was at that time considered to be complete. Much later, in 1965, the northern half block was further enlarged through another urban renewal proceeding.

The story of urban renewal is not complete without an accounting of the long-range stimulation the Lincoln Square project has had on the renewal of the west side of Manhattan. New housing within the project itself created a large new residential neighborhood. Lincoln Towers, a cluster of high-rise middle-income apartments provided over 4000 new dwelling units which were occupied as rapidly as they were completed. The Lincoln Guild cooperative created 400 more units, individually owned. A new retail shopping area was created along Amsterdam Avenue. These commercial parts of the project provided the city with a new assured tax revenue more than offsetting the loss of former taxpaying properties in the tax-exempt sites for the nonprofit sponsors in the project. The activities of Fordham University, the Red Cross, and Lincoln Center bring thousands of people daily into the neighborhood. This concentration of people has created a sustained demand for many new eating establishments, ranging from fast-food chains to gourmet restaurants. A variety of new retail stores and services have located in the neighborhood.

In the generally accepted theory of urban renewal, as it existed in the fifties, it was hoped that public intervention in a specific renewal project would encourage a succession of private investors to build in the surrounding neighborhood, resulting in a snowballing effect of widening renewal and economic vitality in the city. In the case of Lincoln Square, this hope was realized.

In the surrounding area from Columbus Circle to 72nd Street, west of Central Park, the stimulating effect of the Lincoln Square project is evident in a continuing succession of large-scale investments in new apartments and commercial buildings. Notable are the Gulf & Western office building, the American Broadcasting Company facilities, and a number of luxury apartments. Other institutional buildings

Photo: Susanne Faulkner Stevens

Photo: Susanne Faulkner Stevens

New buildings in the Lincoln Square area.

were constructed by such organizations as Roosevelt Hospital, the American Bible Society, and the Jewish Guild for the Blind. Several fine old buildings received landmark designation, and numerous rehabilitation projects were undertaken by private investors. On the side streets, a gradual process of renovation of brownstone homes has upgraded many blocks.

One measure of the magnitude of these renewal developments in the surrounding area is its impact on city tax revenues. An aggregate commercial investment of over $700 million in the Lincoln Square area has increased the city's annual tax receipts by more than $30 million.

The city itself has contributed to the renewal momentum with new low- and moderate-income housing developments and with several new public schools. The city also adopted a Lincoln Square Special Zoning Ordinance in 1969, designed to give developers floor-area bonuses in return for amenities such as street-level arcades and public spaces.

In a quarter of a century, the Lincoln Square area of New York City has undergone profound change. In the mid-fifties it was a neglected, impoverished, and degrading area, one of the city's worst slums. From an area regarded as one to be avoided, it has become a desirable location for home or work. Once an obscure part ot New York, it has become, through its centerpiece, Lincoln Center, a place of world renown.

PART II

From Incorporation to
Ground Breaking
1956-1959

Photo by Bob Serating

CHAPTER 4

Development of the Institution
1956-1959

During the three years leading up to ground breaking, the evolution of the organization of Lincoln Center for the Performing Arts involved the creation of the new agency to build and to coordinate the center and the development of the federation of autonomous artistic and educational institutions that were to have their homes in the center.

Lincoln Center was incorporated on June 22, 1956 as a nonprofit institution to sustain and encourage the musical and performing arts. It was authorized to own real estate in the Lincoln Square project, to erect its buildings on that site, and "to encourage, sponsor, or facilitate performances and exhibitions, to commission the creation of new works, and voluntarily assist the education of artists and students of these arts."

The small group that made up the initial board of directors was drawn from the membership of the Exploratory Committee for a Musical Arts Center. At their first meeting, held on June 25, by-laws were adopted, John D. Rockefeller, 3rd was elected president, Devereux Josephs, vice president, and Robert E. Blum, treasurer. Soon after incorporation, Edgar B. Young was named secretary, and the board was enlarged by the election of three additional directors,

Laurence J. McGinley, S.J., Dr. George D. Stoddard, and Frank Weil.

Father McGinley, president of Fordham University, was a leader in both educational and religious circles. He had already worked closely with Lincoln Center's leaders in the urban renewal phase of the project. He became one of the center's most active and valued directors, remaining on the board to the present time. Dr. Stoddard was then dean of the School of Education of New York University; formerly he had been president of the University of Illinois and then commissioner of education of New York State. He took the leadership in early development of the center's general educational role and in expanding its constituent composition. Weil was well known in business and financial circles, and in nonprofit affairs he had been particularly active in the Federation of Jewish Philanthropies. He became the first chairman of Lincoln Center's Finance Committee and provided helpful insights into matters of fiscal planning and management as the organization began to take shape. His service was abruptly ended by his death on November 10, 1957.

To fill this vacancy, Frank Altschul, who had a wide range of business, cultural, and international interests, was elected a director. He succeeded Weil as Finance Committee chairman and took special interest in the development of sound personnel policies for the new organization. He remained a Lincoln Center Director until 1961. Lincoln Kirstein, one of the original directors, resigned from the board in May, 1959.

The principle of a loose federation of constituent institutions was controlling in the development of Lincoln Center. The Metropolitan Opera Association and the Philharmonic-Symphony Society of New York, on coming into the Center, were to retain absolute artistic and financial autonomy. It was agreed that any other institutions that might join the center must have a similar independence. The possibility of financial subsidy by Lincoln Center to the operating needs of the constituents was considered but was rejected for consistency with the principle of autonomy and for pragmatic fiscal reasons.

The role of the constituents in the governance of Lincoln Center, Inc. was specific in a by-law provision for constituent representatives to serve as directors of the new corporation. The Metropolitan, as the first and largest of the constituents, was to designate three directors; the Philharmonic was to designate two; subsequent constituent institutions would be entitled to such representation as would later be determined by the board. These original arrangements have been continued and have, throughout the evolution of Lincoln Center, given the constituents a significant voice at the highest policy level. But the constituents have not been in control, for directors not designated by constituents are in a majority.

The relations of the constituents to each other and to Lincoln Center, Inc. were more nebulous. There was a general expectation that the constituents would benefit from association with each other and that innovations would lead to enlarged services to the public. A constructive relationship between artistic professionals was anticipated; interplay between young people in training in the educational arm of the center and the artists of the performing companies would benefit both.

The primary relationship between Lincoln Center, Inc. and the constituents would be that of landlord and tenant. However, in the total operation of the center, especially through its Fund for Education and Artistic Advancement (see Chapter 5), the directors expected Lincoln Center, Inc. to assist but not to control the development of the performing arts through the constituents.[1]

The importance of these underlying concepts of the center and of inter-constituent relationships was emphasized in a response from the Rockefeller Foundation, which conditioned its further participation in the project

> upon the development in the Center of a satisfactory educational activity, upon the inclusion of various forms of dramatic art and upon the achievement of cooperative arrangements among the several groups, thereby ensuring that the undertaking will be, in fact, a Center and not simply a collection of more or less isolated activities.[2]

This condition of the Rockefeller Foundation underscored a concern felt by some of the leaders in Lincoln Center that a number of these ideas related to a center were not fully understood or accepted by the constituents. The official representatives from their boards had been parties to the long series of explorations, discussions, and agreements undertaken by members of the Exploratory Committee. But a gap in communication and understanding had developed between them and their colleagues in constituent management.

Rockefeller began to question the degree of constituent support for the entire performing arts project, especially for the inclusion of an educational institution. To improve understanding and support, Bliss suggested that the professional leaders of the constituents get together to share ideas and information about the new center. (A year later his proposal evolved into the Lincoln Center Council.) But at the time, Houghton, Spofford, and Rockefeller felt that something more definite than informal consultation was needed.

By November 29, 1956, Houghton had brought the issue to the board of the Philharmonic-Symphony Society, and they had adopted a resolution endorsing the concept of the center as a whole and pledging their participation and cooperation. Their resolution expressed

> Full recognition by the Philharmonic of the benefits accruing to the Society through being a part of the Center and thereby in close association with the other component organizations.

> Realization by the Philharmonic of the great importance of the educational aspects of the Center and of the responsibilities of the component organizations to the musical world and to the public in the furtherance of these educational goals.

> Understanding and approval by the Philharmonic of the broad basic philosophy of Lincoln Center as a national and international center providing a relationship and exchange among the several fields involved; and readiness by the Philharmonic to take an active part in promoting the great benefits to be derived therefrom.

Spofford took similar steps with the board of the Metropolitan Opera Association, and on February 21, 1957, they adopted a resolution officially approving the participation of the Metropolitan in the proposed center,

> . . . enthusiastically believing that the broader aspects of the center concept involving opportunities afforded for closer association with the other participants and the possibilities of expanded service will result in its maximum contribution to the cultural life of the community and the nation.

Refinement of the role and function of Lincoln Center, Inc. and of relations between constituents occurred gradually through 1957. By November of that year ideas were sufficiently clarified to be expressed in the major grant request submitted to the Ford and Rockefeller foundations.

> The Center, as the overall body in this aggregation of cooperating performing arts institutions, will serve them all through its phys-

ical facilities, will provide the environment and the mechanism for artistic interplay of ideas, and for the interacting stimulus of professional upon student and of talented youthful vigor on mature artistic temperament. In addition, the Center will be a constant force at work on its constituent institutions to encourage them in creative artistic advancement and in the enrichment and enlargement of their artistic services to the public.

With a nod to the difficulty of realizing these hopes, the statement added:

The realization of these goals, and indeed the validity of the concept of the Center, depends in part upon the sound and imaginative management of the Center itself, but even more upon the nature of the constituent institutions and the readiness of their leaders to cooperate fully within the framework of the Center.

The directors moved ahead in the months after incorporation to select and establish other constituent members of the center. First on the agenda was a final determination of an educational unit. Professional training of talented young artists, including a workshop approach to bridge the gap between formal training and performance, was desired. It was hoped that a single educational institution would provide training in all the performing arts—in dance and drama as well as in vocal and instrumental music.

When these principles were discussed with officers of the Juilliard School, they were reluctant to accept all of this concept. The school was already focused on professional training in musical arts, but its board was hesitant to give up their sizable preparatory school. Moreover, income from the Juilliard Musical Trust, their principal source of endowment, was strictly limited to music training. It could not be applied, for example, to a drama program. Since negotiations with Juilliard seemed to be at an impasse, the possibility of forming a new school was considered, but was dropped.

Subsequently, Rockefeller and Stoddard were invited to meet with the Juilliard directors. Schuman, the president of Juilliard, urged his board to endorse the concept of concentration on advanced training of persons with exceptional talent.[3] He also advocated expansion of the Juilliard program to include training in dance and drama. After long consideration, the Juilliard directors accepted Lincoln Center's invitation to come into the center; public announcement was made on February 7, 1957. Schuman was added to the Lincoln Center Council, and John W. Drye, Jr., who was chairman of both the Juilliard School and the Juilliard Musical Foundation, was elected a director of Lincoln Center. He served continuously until he became a director emeritus in 1972.

Drye was a native of Texas. Although he had spent all his adult life as an attorney in New York, he retained his Texas drawl and an earthy, realistic approach to all problems. Drye was general counsel and a director of Union Carbide Corporation and served on numerous other corporate boards. Reflecting his lifetime love of opera, he was also an active member of the board of the Metropolitan. As chairman of its New House Committee, he was fully informed about the origins and development of Lincoln Center.

The decision to include the art of spoken drama in Lincoln Center had been relatively easy to make. To find an appropriate institution to sponsor the drama proved far more difficult. The center needed an organization that would become, in its field, a counterpart to the Metropolitan Opera Association and the Philharmonic-Symphony Society. In drama, there was no lack of organizations with aspirations to become a constituent. Both the American National Theater Association and the Actors' Studio made overtures. Each had prestigious professional leaders with records of successes as Broadway producers. But neither had a permanent performing company or the institutional necessities of strong and active boards of trustees with a record of sustained fund-raising capability. There was a careful exploration of other organizations in the drama field; none had both an institutional framework and a stable financial base.

Late in 1956, a Committee on Drama was formed under the chairmanship of George Stoddard. He was a trustee of the American Shakespeare Festival Theatre and Academy, had participated in its formation, and was deeply interested in repertory theater. His committee was asked to continue the search for a drama constituent and to recommend policy and a program. Stoddard continued talks with both ANTA and Actors' Studio. The discussions with ANTA were led by Mrs. H. Alwyn Innes-Brown, who headed the New York chapter, and by Robert Whitehead, who became its professional spokesman. Whitehead proved especially helpful in thinking through the artistic concept of a possible theater company at Lincoln Center. He saw it as an opportunity for quality presentations of great works of American dramatic literature as well as English and other European classics. And he saw it also as an opportunity for the encouragement of contemporary American playwrights. Mrs. Innes-Brown understood the financial necessities of any lasting theater development at Lincoln Center, and she suggested a possible donor (later disclosed to be Mrs.

Vivian Beaumont Allen) who might make a major contribution toward the capital need for the theater building and might later give annually to help subsidize a repertory company.

The Stoddard Committee also had been asked to establish criteria to serve as guidelines for constituency in any field. On October 7, 1957, the board approved Stoddard's recommendations for Standards for Constituents, as a basic policy guide. The term "constituent" was defined as "An associated, self-managing, non-profit institution, chosen as the responsible agency or instrument for one part of the total artistic program." The general standards that had to be met to be considered for membership included:

1. The constituent must be able to provide a needed service in or to the performing arts.
2. It must set and maintain artistic standards of the highest quality.
3. Its professional leadership must gain and hold the respect of experts and of the public.
4. A constituent must have an institutional framework designed to assure continuity and financial stability, a commitment to public service, and a dedication to artistic advancement.

None of the proposals from existing theater organizations, including ANTA, met these standards fully, and the Stoddard committee decided to recommend the creation of a new drama institution. The drama critics, Brooks Atkinson of the *Times* and Walter Kerr of the *Herald Tribune*, encouraged this approach. Whitehead supported it and took the lead in formulating the nature of theater needed in Lincoln Center.

In April, 1958, an Advisory Council on Drama was formed, from which it was hoped that a new constituent institution would emerge.[4] Whitehead was retained as Lincoln Center's drama consultant, anticipating that he would become professional manager of the new theater organization. The Advisory Council explored various approaches to the formation of a performing company, considered the relationship of a company to the future drama training program contemplated at Juilliard, and defined the functional needs of a theater building at Lincoln Center. But it made no progress in finding leadership for a new organization. This essential step in the formation of a drama constituent was not taken until after ground breaking.

The search for a dance constituent proceeded concurrently with the movement toward a drama constituent, but this proved to be a more intractable problem. In the early days of 1956, the Exploratory Committee had expected the New York City Ballet to join, but the company was a part of the City Center of Music and Drama, not an independent institution. The early overture to City Center had been rebuffed by its chairman and by Moses.[5] Lincoln Kirstein, managing director of the Ballet, was open-minded about sponsorship through a separate institution.

In 1956 the New York City Ballet was not alone on the American ballet scene. The American Ballet Theater, under the leadership of Lucia Chase and Oliver Smith, had established itself as a major company with a well-deserved reputation in the United States and overseas. In the latter part of 1956, Miss Chase indicated her strong desire for American Ballet Theater to be included in Lincoln Center on a basis of equality with the New York City Ballet. The possibility of more than one resident performing company in the same art form precipitated a searching policy discussion among the directors. The representatives of the Metropolitan and the Philharmonic insisted that only one institution sponsoring each art should be brought into the center with constituent status. For the time being, their view prevailed, although two years later this principle of exclusivity was modified into a doctrine of primacy.

Following this policy decision, in January, 1957, Stoddard was appointed chairman of an "Exploratory Committee on the Dance," to which the dance critics, John Martin and Walter Terry were consultants. As a first step, Stoddard explored with Lucia Chase and with Kirstein the possibility of a merger of their two companies. On both sides he encountered rigid opposition and fears of an artistic disaster. After weighing the strengths and weaknesses of the existing dance companies to determine which one best met the criteria for inclusion in Lincoln Center, the committee concluded, in April 1957, that the New York City Ballet Company should be so considered. The board took no action at that time, but Kirstein was encouraged by the recommendation and proceeded to lay plans for his company's possible future under independent sponsorship. In an effort to bring the matter of a dance constituent to a conclusion, the subject was again on the board agenda for June 17, 1957. It could not have come to the board at a more inopportune moment. Urban renewal affairs were in a state of crisis, with Moses embattled with City Hall and Washington over available federal Urban Renewal money and threatening to increase Lincoln Center's re-use land price. The matter of dance sponsorship received no consideration and was deferred.

Meanwhile, American Ballet Theater insisted that it would be severely handicapped if it did not become a part of Lincoln Center.

Stoddard then tried again to find a corporate framework within which both ballet companies could be accommodated with a guarantee of artistic independence for each. Lucia Chase was ready to cooperate in some such plan; Kirstein, on the other hand, could see no advantages in Stoddard's plan and rejected it. The situation in the field of the dance was no nearer resolution and remained at a stalemate for another year.

In the autumn of 1958, developments in capital financial planning (see Chapter 5) altered the approach to determining the dance constituent. Lincoln Center proposed to request the city to provide half the cost of the dance theater under a plan to make it a new home for City Center of Music and Drama. This possibility would involve the whole of City Center rather than a dance constituency alone. Kirstein favored this larger participation, for he was, by this time, resolved to keep his ballet company under the sponsorship of City Center.

The key individual for negotiation with City Center was Morton Baum, chairman of its Finance Committee and the most influential member of its board. Baum wielded a power far wider than his title suggested. He shunned the spotlight and ruled by the force of his tight grip on the purse strings. He was a frugal manager, a stern taskmaster, and in negotiations, as hard as nails. A respected member of New York's legal community, he had been an advisor to Mayor Wagner and his predecessors on city financial matters. Moreover, he loved music and ballet, and he held an incontestable belief in the low-priced ticket policy of City Center. As a result he had achieved a supportive attitude toward City Center on the part of a succession of mayors and their administrations.

As Baum saw the evolving plans for Lincoln Center assuming greater certainty he began to question whether the future of his organization would be better assured outside the new cultural center or whether the possibility of joining Lincoln Center should be reopened. On the initiative of Kirstein and Baum in early December, meetings occurred between Baum and Young to analyze the basis on which it might be feasible and mutually desirable for City Center to become a part of Lincoln Center. In a working paper outlining a possible City Center constituency, the pattern paralleled that being developed with the Metropolitan, the Philharmonic, and Juilliard. In addition, it anticipated city financial aid and ownership of the building, with Lincoln Center as the city's tenant and City Center as a sub-tenant. The draft pledged both organizations to a continuation of City Center's policy of low ticket prices.

The talks with Baum were conducted on the premise that all of City Center's activities were under consideration. City Center would become the primary constituent for ballet and operetta. With respect to opera and drama, City Center would recognize the primacy of the Metropolitan and of the new drama organization in process of formation and would work out its program in those fields in consultation and agreement with the primary constituents. However, the inclusion of the City Opera in Lincoln Center stirred deep misgivings among the leaders of the Metropolitan. Rudolph Bing, the general manager, and Anthony Bliss, the president, both felt that the Metropolitan should be solely responsible for opera at Lincoln Center. Spofford and Rockefeller felt that the issues between the Metropolitan and the New York City Opera were reconcilable, and patiently and persistently kept the discussions going. Spofford interceded to bring about direct negotiation between Baum and Bliss.

By January, 1959, the newly elected governor of New York, Nelson Rockefeller, entered the discussions concerning City Center. On January 9, he convened a meeting of Mayor Wagner and other city officials with Lincoln Center officers, primarily to consider financial problems related to Lincoln Center. (See Chapter 5.) One topic dealt with the financing of the theater for the dance as a home for City Center. John Rockefeller's memorandum of the discussion reported:

> If Lincoln Center and the New York City Center agree that it is to their mutual advantage and to the advantage of the community for the City Center to move outright to the Dance Theater in Lincoln Center, the City will give favorable consideration to its joining with Lincoln Center in paying half the cost for land and construction after applying the proceeds of sale of the City Center's present home. (Estimated cost of land and construction is $11 to $12 million.) It was agreed that the City would continue its current support of the City Center project and that it would join with City Center in requesting enabling legislation to make the transfer possible.[6]

Moses, who was opposed to most of the suggestions that had been made in the conference, reacted on the City Center matter in his memo to the Mayor sent two days later:

> Bringing City Center to Lincoln Square I gathered seemed to you to be a sensible proposal which would provide programs of proven popularity but it was not even remotely suggested that the City would pay the cost. Governor Rockefeller said something about a *pro rata* sharing but this was neither defined nor discussed. The details and division of construction and mainte-

nance costs should be worked out between the City Center and the City.[7]

It was clear that no agreement had been reached on crucial financial matters. As a result, not long after the meeting with the governor, Newbold Morris, chairman of City Center, took the position that there was no reason to talk further about becoming a constituent until capital funds for a building were assured. As the date for ground-breaking, May, 1959, approached, the issue of City Center participation and the question of a dance constituent were still unresolved.

The Exploratory Committee had recommended inclusion of a reference and research library of the performing arts as a part of the educational services of the center. The New York Public Library possessed the world's most extensive reference sources in the fields of music, dance, and drama. Its collections in these fields were housed at the main library building in badly overcrowded quarters and were only partially accessible. The New York Public Library was therefore a natural prospect, and indeed the only prospect, to be considered seriously as the library unit in the center. In discussions of the library possibility, various kinds of exhibitions related to the performing arts seemed attractive, and the library idea was expanded to include a museum. Houghton took the lead in this development since, among his many interests, he was a trustee of the New York Public Library, the Morgan Library, and the Metropolitan Museum of Art. On March 11, 1957, the board adopted his statement of policy regarding the inclusion of a library and museum in the center. It stated, in part:

> The Center, to be a true cultural center for the performing arts, must embrace the trilogy of education, creative scholarship, and performance. The reference material in the organized collections of the proposed library and museum can serve as a tool for education and as a creative stimulus for new performance. . . .

Although the New York Public Library is a private institution, it has long been supported with municipal capital funds for buildings and operating funds for maintenance and for the branch library system. Since the library at Lincoln Center could be considered a branch of the New York Public Library, it could qualify for such aid. When Rockefeller and Spofford met with the mayor on February 10, 1958 to discuss general financial relationships, they specifically mentioned their hope for both capital funds and operating support from the city for the library and museum. The mayor made no commitments, but was sympathetic.

Early in 1958 the library trustees elected a new president, Gilbert W. Chapman. Trained as an engineer, Chapman had a successful business career and was currently president of Yale and Towne Manufacturing Company. The new president expressed keen interest in Lincoln Center developments, and the board invited him to develop specifications for library facilities and program at Lincoln Center. Soon Chapman and Edward Freehafer, director of the library, proposed a thorough study of a library and museum of the performing arts. The library trustees were prepared to finance half the $25,000 needed to conduct the study and asked Lincoln Center for a grant of $12,500. The directors approved the grant, the first allocation from the center's Education Fund. This study, conducted by Dr. Davidson Taylor, director of the Arts Center Program of Columbia University, produced a detailed prospectus for the proposed library and museum and indicated the scholarly and public services it could provide. By February 1959, planning had moved to the point that Chapman wrote Mayor Wagner that the proposal for a branch at Lincoln Center would probably be approved by the Library trustees. Following such approval, a request would be made to the city for capital funds, estimated at $8 million for the building, and for annual operating funds following the existing policy of city support of the circulating library system.

Concurrently with the efforts to complete the initial constituent composition of the Center, the organization of Lincoln Center, Inc. was gradually developed. At the time of incorporation, there was neither an office nor a staff. The group of able volunteers had been working together in the months of exploration and continued to give unstintingly of their time and judgment. The pattern of biweekly luncheon meetings continued. Rockefeller, as president, was chief executive officer of the corporation. The vice president, Josephs, carried a heavy load of responsibility, particularly in the relations of the new corporation with agencies of government. On November 20, 1956 the board elected Houghton and Spofford as additional vice presidents, recognizing their key roles in the development of the center. Young, as corporate secretary and by reason of his position as an associate of Rockefeller, functioned as an unofficial coordinator of the new enterprise in a close working relationship with other directors.

The board recognized that Lincoln Center would need a staff, but was determined from the start to keep it small. The first staff appointment was made in April, 1957 when General Otto L. Nelson, Jr., (on part-time loan from the New York Life Insurance Company) was named executive director for construction. Concurrently Reginald Allen was employed with the parallel title of executive director for operations. Allen had been manager of the Philadelphia Orchestra, had been associated with major producers in the film industry, and came to Lincoln Center from the Metropolitan Opera where he had been assistant manager and secretary to their board of directors. Both Allen and Nelson reported directly to Rockefeller as president. Nelson's responsibility was related to building the Center; Allen's to developing the long-term operational pattern in cooperation with the constituents. In February 1957, office space was rented in the Coliseum building on Columbus Circle for Nelson and Allen and their gradually expanding staffs and to serve as fund-raising headquarters. Public relations counsel was needed to assure successful fund-raising and for action by governmental bodies. In June 1957 Paul Garrett, who had recently retired from the position of vice president for public relations at General Motors Corporation, was retained on a part time basis. By 1959, as planning moved rapidly toward the ground-breaking event, Garrett felt the time had come for Lincoln Center to have a full-time person for public relations. On his recommendation John W. McNulty, one of the fund-raising staff members who had worked closely with Garrett, was appointed Director of information.

Anticipating the eventual operation of the center when the constituents would be residents in their homes, their professional heads needed a channel for consultation among themselves and with the operating officers of Lincoln Center, Inc. To meet this need, on May 20, 1957, the board established the Lincoln Center Council. The Philharmonic was represented initially by Bruno Zirato, then by his successor, George Judd. William Schuman represented the Julliard School; Rudolf Bing, the Metropolitan Opera; and Reginald Allen, Lincoln Center, Inc. The chairmanship of the council was rotated among the members at three-month intervals, and the individual currently serving as chairman represented the council at meetings of the Lincoln Center board of directors.

A formal expression of the relations between the constituents and Lincoln Center, Inc. required legal contracts covering the terms of the leases of their buildings. While the broad outlines of these relationships were understood from the earlier discussions in the Exploratory Committee, details had to be resolved before contracts could be drawn. In the spring of 1958, Olds was appointed chairman of a committee with Drye and Keiser to negotiate constituent contracts. These three, representing the three major constituents and the Lincoln Center board, were asked to work out a common set of official relationships applicable to all constituent contracts. Allen worked with the committee to provide for the operating needs of Lincoln Center, Inc.

The initial approach of the Olds committee was to ask the president and legal counsel of each constituent to outline the provisions they considered essential in their contracts. Their response troubled Olds, for he felt they were taking an excessively protective approach to their contracts, similar to that a corporate client might take in negotiation with a real-estate developer, rather than an approach for a cooperative venture. After six frustrating months, Olds concluded that his membership on both the Metropolitan and the Lincoln Center boards placed him in a conflict of interest position which he proposed to resolve by resignation from the opera board. His resignation startled his opera colleagues who countered with a leave of absence for the duration of the negotiations. Olds' stand helped to clear the atmosphere in the contract discussions. His committee's position was further strengthened by the addition of Josephs and Father McGinley. In the few months remaining before ground breaking, considerable progress was made in clarifying the substantive features of the contracts, but no final agreements were reached.

In the three years between the decision to create Lincoln Center and its ground breaking ceremony on May 14, 1959, the new institution had been organized. With the association of the Metropolitan Opera and the Philharmonic-Symphony from the beginning and the commitment of the Juilliard School to participate, half of the planned units were in place. The arts of dance and drama and the library and museum were under consideration; pending negotiations gave promise of success. The functions of the central coordinating organization had been clarified, and the key executive positions had been filled. Lincoln Center was no longer merely an idea. It had become a living institution.

CHAPTER 5

Toward Financial Reality
1956-1959

In the evolution of Lincoln Center, financial feasibility limited all the hopes and aspirations. But there was no simple answer to the question of "What is feasible?" As a nonprofit corporation, Lincoln Center had no accumulated financial reserves, no customary corporate or commercial means of financing, no power to issue stock or bonds. Nothing in the future operation of the center or its constituents could be expected to produce an excess of earned income over current operating expenditures. All the educational and artistic activities of the institutions comprising the center are nonprofit in nature. Since they are inherently deficit operations, they require subsidy in some form to meet their operating needs. This leaves no cushion for debt service or for capital accumulation.

In the light of these fundamental economic facts, the Exploratory Committee had determined that a fund sufficiently large to pay for the entire cost of building the center must be raised from voluntary contributions. The basic question then became "Realistically, how much money can we expect to raise?"

There was no formula available to determine the center's fund-raising potential, for there was no defined group of prospective donors, whose contributing potential could be gauged. The fund-raising experience of other institutions was not helpful, for the concept of Lincoln Center was unprecedented.

The financial feasibility of Lincoln Center became, for the directors of the center, a question to be answered by their collective judgment. They would have to depend on their own experience derived from a gradually evolving fund-raising effort. This account traces first the course of capital budgeting, then the development and progress of the campaign itself.

Lincoln Center was under pressure from Moses in the latter part of 1956 to move rapidly in the preparation of a contract to formalize its relations and commitments with the City of New York. The contract, when executed, would obligate the new organization for its land purchase and for millions of dollars of construction expenditure.

These considerations put immediate pressure on the directors to determine a capital budget and a fund-raising strategy. At the board meeting on November 5, 1956, Rockefeller pressed for decisions regarding the total amount to be raised for the center. Based on the studies done for the Exploratory Committee, on preliminary design work by Harrison, and on rough construction cost estimates, the need for land and buildings was established at $55.4 million. Additional funds would be required to support the educational and creative artistic plans of the new center and for contingencies. For these purposes, the board adopted the figure of $19.6 million. Thus a goal of $75 million was set for the campaign. The breakdown of that first capital budget expressed in estimated space requirements as well as in building costs is shown in the table on page 67.

This budget reflected the original assumption that the project would be entirely financed from privately contributed funds. However, the magnitude of the fund-raising task and the probability that costs would increase during planning and construction led the Lincoln Center officers to continue their negotiations, with Moses and with the federal agency, to secure public financing for some parts of the project. While they expected the private sector to provide the bulk of the needed funds, they began to seek a variety of ways that government could participate in the project. (In the final accounting of sources of capital funds, there were four dollars of private funds for every dollar of public taxpayer's money that went into the project.) In the early months of 1957 these efforts began to bear fruit. Moses agreed to recommend that the city, with a federal grant-in-aid, finance and build the garage and the plaza at Lincoln Center. Although this would relieve Lincoln Center of an expenditure budgeted at $3.5 million, the private fund-raising goal was not reduced. The estimated

	Space Required (in Cubic Feet)	Estimated Cost
Constituent Homes:		
Opera House	11,312,000	$23,600,000
Concert Hall	1,750,000	4,000,000
Theater for Dance	2,297,000	5,000,000
Drama Theater	1,256,000	2,900,000
Education Bldg.	2,451,000	5,500,000
Library-Museum	1,400,000	2,800,000
Sub-Total	20,466,000	43,800,000
Common Facilities:		
Garage	4,000,000	3,000,000
Restaurant & Cafeteria	460,000	750,000
Stores	1,130,000	1,700,000
Common Property (Plaza, etc.)		1,000,000
Total Buildings	26,056,000	50,250,000
Land	11.5 acres	5,150,000
TOTAL—Land and Buildings		$55,400,000
Reserve for education, artistic advance and contingencies		19,600,000
CAMPAIGN GOAL		75,000,000

cost of clearing and preparing the land for construction had increased by $1.2 million. The cost of the concert hall had been raised by $2 million, due largely to an increase in the height and overall size of the building, which further study of acoustical requirements indicated to be necessary. One new item was added to the budget—an allocation of $300,000 for a small hall for chamber music, debuts, or recitals.

As preliminary plans became more definite, the adequacy of the revised budget figures came under serious question. On April 7, 1958 the architect warned Young that the concert hall as then proposed might cost as much as $15 million. The Building Committee's reaction to this disturbing news was a reaffirmation for the time being of the $55 million budgeted ceiling on all construction costs. To bring the concert hall into line, the committee (with Houghton participating on behalf of the Philharmonic) instructed Abramovitz to make drastic cuts by reducing the seating capacity to 2400 and eliminating the rehearsal hall, a special boardroom, and a V.I.P. facility. Within a few weeks Philip Johnson warned that his design for a 2600-seat ballet theater would require five million cubic feet of space, more than twice the original calculation. At $2.50 per cubic foot, the theater would cost $12.5 million against a $5 million budget. The Building Committee told Johnson to cut seating capacity to about 2000 and see what could be built for less than $7 million. Two weeks later, the Building

Committee was told that the opera house would cost $30 million, in comparison with its budgeted figure of $23.6 million. The committee's response was still the same: bring the space and facilities in line with budgeted construction money. The one bright spot in this overrun was that, proportionately, it was less than had occurred in the estimates for other buildings.

The gap between financial feasibility and the desire for perfection, as expressed in the constituent's functional requirements, had been drawn. Those Lincoln Center directors who represented the constituents took the lead in negotiations with their own professional staffs and with the architects to find compromise solutions.

For example, the scenery storage space in the opera house was reduced from that needed for a full season to that required for half a season, which brought a significant saving in the cost of construction. On October 6, 1958 Harrison came back to the Building Committee with a revised opera scheme he estimated could be built for $27 million. The committee, with Bliss, Bing, and Krawitz from the Metropolitan participating, accepted this plan for development to the point that more detailed and complete estimates could be made by the Joint Venture Contractors, recently retained by Lincoln Center. Concurrently, revisions in the plans for the concert hall and the theater for the dance also were made.

On October 15, 1958 the secretary prepared a report to reflect all the commitments of the corporation, its contracts with the city and policy decisions previously made. Land costs had risen to $6,900,000, including the estimated price of $850,000 for the purchase of the additional half-block to the north. The reserve for educational and artistic purposes and for contingencies remained unchanged at $19 million. The library and museum would have to be financed outside the goal, probably from city funds, and the garage and plaza were to be financed by the city and federal government as an urban renewal project; student housing for the Juilliard School and commercial facilities such as stores, restaurants, or office space were to be built only if they would be economically viable on a mortgage-financing basis.

From the goal of $75 million, these commitments and policy decisions left $48,500,000 to build five major institutional homes, now allocated as shown in the table.

After these budgetary revisions, but before the estimates were complete, it was evident that there would be a substantial overrun. Already, the estimate for the dance theater had risen to $10,618,000. The gap between inevitable costs and anticipated funds had to be resolved. Young analyzed the alternative approaches. In summary form, they were:

1. To reduce the cost of the buildings
2. To use for construction some portion of the $19.6 million allocated in the campaign goal to educational, artistic and contingency purposes
3. To defer construction of one or more buildings
4. To increase the campaign goal above $75,000,000
5. To mortgage the property
6. To utilize the equity in property owned by constituents
7. To attempt to secure additional city support

A discussion by the board led to no conclusions. The directors were beginning to realize that, up to that time, they had tried to whittle. Now they had to chop—or get a bigger log.

The urgency of the problem was underscored by the imminent need for construction commitments of at least $31 million to build the concert hall and the opera house. The $42 million then raised would be reduced by the land purchase and by donor designations. Moreover, large parts of the major foundation grants were not immediately available. The net result left only $15 million available to apply to the cost of the opera and concert hall. Only when an additional $12 million had been raised would certain of the foundation grants be released to bring the total available for construction up to $43 million.

A month later, the preliminary estimates were in hand for all buildings and totaled $79.4 million, a staggering 64 percent more than the construction budget of $48.5 million. A consensus was reached among the directors that each constituent group would review its plans again with the architect and the contractors in the light of the total Lincoln Center financial situation. Any specific rebudgeting would have to await the results of such a review. The feelings at that December 15, 1958 board meeting were captured by Jackson in his concluding comment, "this has been our first trip together to the cold shower."

Opera House	$24,000,000
Concert Hall	7,000,000
(including Chamber Music Hall)	
Theater for Dance	7,000,000
Drama Theater	3,000,000
Juilliard School	5,500,000
Lincoln Center—Mechanical and	
Maintenance Facilities, Office	
Space, etc.	2,000,000
	$48,500,000

The officers explored more intensively ways that the city might increase its financial participation in the project. Three major areas of help were considered: first, an enlargement of the scope of the urban renewal grant-in-aid for the garage and related construction; second, complete city financing of the library building; and third, a 50 percent financing of the cost of the Theater for the Dance. This last possibility was linked to a reopening of the proposal to bring City Center into Lincoln Center.

The atmosphere for city aid was improved following the election in November, 1958 of Nelson Rockefeller as governor. He was familiar with the plans for the new cultural center and shared his brother's belief in the potential importance of the project in the lives of the people of the city and the state. He wanted Lincoln Center to succeed. But he shared his brother's worries about the feasibility of raising, entirely from the private philanthropic sector, the capital sum required. In his philosophy of government, this was the kind of civic project that should receive encouragement and financial support from all levels of government. Shortly after his inauguration, the governor therefore brought together Mayor Wagner and Moses, with several of their aids, and John Rockefeller 3rd, Houghton, and Harrison. Discussion covered the numerous specific ways that the Lincoln Center officers thought the city might help to bring the center's aspirations to reality. At the end of the meeting John Rockefeller and his colleagues felt there had been a substantial meeting of minds. Two days later Moses, in comments to the mayor, opposed many of the proposals for city help, especially the capital financing of the library, but he left several of the additional grant-in-aid possibilities open for later discussion with federal officials. The issue of city financial participation in Lincoln Center was far from resolution, but the governor's affirmative attitude toward Lincoln Center had been clearly established. (See Chapter 4, p. 60.)

On January 26, 1959, the board reached decisions affecting its capital budget and its fund-raising from nongovernmental sources. On recommendation from the campaign leaders, the board decided not to increase the $75 million goal,

> without prejudice to reconsideration of the matter at a later date when achievement of the $75 million goal may be more immediately in sight.

At the same time, the board reaffirmed its determination

> to complete the entire center and to reject the possibility of elimination or the indefinite deferment of any of the buildings

contemplated in the center. It was also the consensus of the board that the emphasis on qualitative standards must be maintained in the buildings of Lincoln Center.

The entire $75 million budget was reviewed to search for ways to increase the allocation of funds for construction. The Fund for Education and Artistic Advancement was set at $10 million—a floor below which the goal of the fund would not be reduced. Estimated land costs were $7 million. This left $58 million that could be budgeted for construction. The Building Committee then apportioned that sum among the several buildings.

Opera House	$24,500,000
Concert Hall	8,500,000
Chamber Music Hall	1,000,000
Juilliard School	6,500,000
Drama Theater	3,500,000
Theater for the Dance	3,500,000*
Library-Museum	— *
Central air conditioning	3,500,000
General expenses for plaza and underground	2,000,000
Building contingencies	5,000,000
TOTAL FOR CONSTRUCTION	$58,000,000

*Additional funds for these buildings were expected from public funds outside the campaign goal.

At a joint meeting on April 20 of the Lincoln Center and the Philharmonic Building Committees, the results of the review and redesign of Philharmonic Hall were presented.[1] Economies totalling $757,000 had been agreed upon. Nevertheless, the estimated cost was $9,840,000, an overage of $1,340,000 beyond the revised budget. The Building Committee was satisfied that the efforts to reduce costs had gone as far as could be accepted, that excavation could start, and that the approved scheme should move into the detailed design and engineering stage. It accepted the fact that the cost of Philharmonic Hall would exceed its budget by nearly 15 percent. The design review and estimating process was proceeding for the opera house and for the theater of the dance, but no definite reports or budgetary action was possible until after ground breaking.

In the fall of 1956, concurrently with cost estimating, the directors made definite plans for the fund-raising campaign. On November 20, 1956, C. D. Jackson was appointed chairman of a committee for fund-raising planning, with representatives of the constituents and of the Finance Committee serving as committee members. Jackson's group addressed itself first to matters of organization and retained the professional firm of Kersting, Brown & Co. to serve as campaign staff.

The directors also took action to handle the first large financial obligation the corporation would have to meet. Over $5 million would soon be required to buy the land, to relocate tenants and demolish buildings, and to pay for preliminary planning. The best prospects for contributions toward those needs were the Ford and Rockefeller foundations, whose officers had already shown interest in the project. A specific request was made to each foundation for a grant of $2.5 million for land acquisition and preliminary planning. Before the end of the year, the Rockefeller Foundation made its grant of $2.5 million, conditioned on assurance of additional funds sufficient for the land purchase and on formal action by the boards of the Metropolitan Opera and the Philharmonic committing their participation in the project. Similar affirmative response came from the Ford Foundation on January 11, 1957. Additional funds designated for land purchase came from a transfer, from the Metropolitan Opera Association, of the $1.5 million it had raised to fulfill its initial offer to Moses to purchase a site for a new opera house at Lincoln Square.

Lincoln Center received gifts from several other sources prior to the official opening of its campaign. Before the end of 1956 the first unsolicited pledge came from a director, anonymous at the time, but later revealed to be from David M. Keiser. In February, 1957, the Avalon Foundation granted $2.5 million to Lincoln Center.

Leaders of ANTA, in discussions with Rockefeller, referred to Mrs. Vivian Beaumont Allen as a possible contributor. Rockefeller contacted Mrs. Allen and on April 22, 1957 reported to the directors that a possible donor (anonymous at her request) was considering a contribution for a major portion of the cost of the theater building in Lincoln Center. It required over a year for Mrs. Allen's interest to become a firm pledge. Rockefeller had several conversations with her, and she told him that she might be able to contribute $2 million. On May 3, 1957, in a long letter, he reviewed the facts about Lincoln Center and its hopes in the field of drama. He asked her to consider giving the entire cost of the theater, then estimated at over $3 million, and offered to name the theater in her honor.

In the months following this specific appeal, Rockefeller had more conversations with Mrs. Allen and with her lawyer. A number of points were troubling her. She felt that the drama theater should not have to take a secondary place in the center concept, in building location, or in timing of construction. She wanted assurances that "her theater" would be as important as the one for dance.

In another letter in January 1958, Rockefeller assured her that "the repertory theater is an important and integral part of the overall development." He described the approach to the creation of a drama constituent and reported the retention of Whitehead as a consultant "with the expectation, as plans develop and become more concrete, that he would become the permanent leader of the whole (drama) undertaking." Rockefeller's letter concluded with a specific request that Mrs. Allen make a pledge at that time, saying,

> We feel that it is extremely important for the success of our fund-raising effort to have a major gift from an individual donor reported soon. It would be a particular satisfaction to us if this could be the contribution from you for the repertory drama theater.

Mrs. Allen's response came within a few days. Again she had reservations which she wanted cleared up before she made a firm commitment. Her letter then stated, "I shall consider it a privilege, when I receive satisfactory reassurance on these three points, to send you my firm pledge in the sum of three million dollars." Rockefeller reassured Mrs. Allen on her three points of concern: that the repertory drama theater would be primary in its field at Lincoln Center, that every effort would be made to open it on schedule, and that the site was positively assured. His concluding hope was "that you will give further consideration to our request that the theater bear your name." Finally, on April 26, 1958 Mrs. Allen made her pledge of $3 million. She did not live to see the completion and opening of her theater. But between the time of her gift and her death in 1962 she took an active interest in the plans for the building and had frequent meetings with the architect. Before her death she decided that she wished the theater to bear her maiden name, the "Vivian Beaumont."

During early 1957 steps were taken to organize and launch the Lincoln Center Campaign. In June, Clarence Francis consented to serve as campaign chairman and, later in the year, was elected a director. Francis was the retired chairman of General Foods Corporation. His lifetime career had been in the food industry, and he liked to refer to himself as a "prune peddler." In civic and philanthropic life he had been chairman of the Ford Foundation's Fund for Adult Education and of the National Committee for the Hoover Report. He was challenged by the civic and cultural importance of Lincoln Center, undertook his task with boundless enthusiasm, and brought to it his abilities for problem solving, for persuasion, and for initiating novel ideas.

By early October 1957, 25 civic leaders had agreed to serve on the Campaign Committee. Its roster included four Lincoln Center directors, who were also directors of constituents. Other prominent members of constituent boards agreed to serve, including Mrs. August Belmont who had founded the Metropolitan Opera Guild and Benjamin J. Buttenwiser from the Philharmonic board. Banking and business leaders included Thomas d'Arcy Brophy, James A. Farley, G. Keith Funston, Harold H. Helm, John J. McCloy, Howard C. Sheperd and Thomas J. Watson, Jr. This distinguished group provided astute advice and guidance, but their most important function was agreement by each one to see several major prospects personally. The Campaign Committee decided to seek 10 percent of the goal, or $7.5 million, from the banks and corporations, although the business community had never before been asked to give any such sum for a cultural purpose.

At this time, progress in the urban renewal project and in institutional developments were such that the time was ripe to go back officially to the major foundations. In making their first grants of $2.5 million each for land and preliminary planning, the Ford and Rockefeller foundations had avoided any commitments but had indicated their willingness to consider future requests. On October 22, 1957, the directors authorized preparation of requests, in addition to their earlier grants, for $12.5 million from the Ford Foundation and $7.5 million from the Rockefeller Foundation. The requests assured each foundation that

> the Lincoln Center board of directors is . . . committed to the objective of achieving a fully rounded and operating center of all the performing arts, including its educational and cultural program.

A Report of Progress accompanying the requests showed a total of $13.8 million had then been raised and presented a tabulation of the way the campaign leaders thought the $75 million goal could be reached.

The Rockefeller Foundation officers promptly advised that they were prepared to recommend a favorable response to their trustees but felt that a grant would have to be subject to certain conditions. They proposed to designate $2.5 million to the Fund for Education and Artistic Advancement and to make $5 million available for construction, but only when $40 million for construction had been raised from other sources. They explained that the foundation trustees felt that their first $2.5 million grant expressed their interest in a new opera house and concert hall and that their further interest was in the

No. of Gifts	Potential Sources for Lincoln Center Campaign		
	Sources	Average	Amount
5-10	Major Foundations (Grants of $1,000,000 and above)		$35,000,000
	Large Individual Donors & Private Foundations		
5-10	$1,000,000 and above	$2,000,000	10,000,000
85	$100,000-$1,000,000	170,500	14,500,000
300	$5,000-$100,000	10,000	3,000,000
	Corporations		
40	$100,000-$1,000,000	137,500	5,500,000
200	$5,000-$100,000	10,000	2,000,000
	Public Campaign		
50,000	Gifts of less than $5,000	100	5,000,000
	TOTAL		$75,000,000

success of the concept of the center as a whole. The directors were concerned over prospective cash flow problems and asked Spofford and Francis to seek a relaxation in the proposed conditions. Two weeks later they reported continued insistence by the foundation officers on the conditions as the basis for their proposed grant. The trustees of the Rockefeller Foundation, at their meeting in December 1957, made the grant of $7.5 million, conditioned as recommended.

The first response from the Ford Foundation was a decision to defer consideration of the Lincoln Center request until a meeting of their trustees in March 1958. They also made it clear that the amount of a grant would be greatly influenced by developments between December and March in Lincoln Center's effort to secure major contributions from other sources.

This word from the Ford Foundation acted as a spur to the campaign organization. Francis appealed to the directors and their families to make commitments as soon as possible in amounts that could reflect their interest and their ability to give. He proposed a consolidated "Insiders' Fund" as a way to preserve anonymity in amounts of pledges and at the same time to indicate a total amount large enough to encourage and reassure outside donors. In the discussion of this proposal, the directors agreed that the matter required immediate and serious consideration by each one. But they emphasized their desire to refrain from financial pressure on any individual board member, recognizing wide differences in their giving ability and acknowledging that contributions by directors in time, ideas, and judgment were as needed and valuable as money.

━━━

At the end of 1957, two gifts came from Rockefeller sources. Mr. John D. Rockefeller, Jr., father of Lincoln Center's president, contributed $5 million, but public announcement was delayed for another six months until other major gifts from non-Rockefeller sources had been announced. John D. Rockefeller, 3rd pledged $1 million as a part of the Insiders' Fund. (Over the years of development of Lincoln Center, in a succession of gifts, he contributed more than $12 million.)

In rapid succession, a number of other gifts were reported early in 1958. First National City and Chase banks pledged $250,000 each. All other major New York banks were approached for contributions related in size to those from the two leaders. A pledge of $150,000 was made by Standard Oil of New Jersey and of $50,000 by Macy's. The appeal of Lincoln Center to a wide variety of large donors was working.

In March the Ford Foundation trustees acted on the Lincoln Center request and authorized a grant of $10 million with conditions to stimulate other contributions. When Lincoln Center had raised $45 million from other sources, $7.5 million would become available. The remaining $2.5 million would be on a one-to-five matching ratio after $60 million had been raised.

Also in March, Francis reported $100,000 from the Corning Glass Foundation. An anonymous donor, pledged a substantial gift toward the cost of a Chamber Music Hall. Eventually this donor was revealed to be Miss Alice Tully. She was herself a musician, especially enjoyed chamber music, and wanted to help create for that art form a more important place in the musical life of New York. Her desire for anonymity was respected until, a number of years later, she increased her gift and agreed to have the hall she had made possible named for her.

During April, three banks pledged $100,000 each and other lesser contributions from banks brought the total pledged by financial institutions to over $1 million. The James Foundation made a grant of $250,000 and indicated it would make additional grants later. The $3 million pledge from Mrs. Allen was publicly announced on May 5, bringing the total raised in the campaign to $38 million.

Notwithstanding the progress indicated by this campaign total, Francis was unhappy with its pace. For some weeks he had worked to strengthen his volunteer organization. Mrs. Robert Hoguet, a director of the Philharmonic-Symphony Society, agreed to chair a

Women's Special Gifts Committee, and Lauder Greenway, chairman of the Metropolitan Opera Association, accepted a similar responsibility for a Men's Special Gifts Committee. Within a month they had enlisted 42 members of their respective committees. Mrs. Hoguet and Greenway constituted, with Francis, a Campaign Strategy Committee.

The board received additional encouragement and stimulus at the May 5th meeting when it was announced that the Insiders' Fund totaled $1,767,000. Also pledges for $500,000 each came from the Winfield Foundation, the Goelet Family, and the Alfred P. Sloan Foundation. Corporate pledges came from such companies as Texaco ($300,000), U.S. Steel Foundation ($250,000), Metropolitan Life Insurance Co. ($200,000), Equitable Life Insurance Company and New York Life Insurance Company ($100,000 each), Consolidated Edison ($150,000), American Telephone & Telegraph Co. and Lazard Freres Company ($125,000 each), International Business Machines, Joseph Seagram & Sons, Ltd., and Union Carbide Company ($100,000 each).[2]

The Campaign Strategy Committee decided to establish a donor category of "Patron" to recognize gifts or pledges in amounts of $100,000 or more. Francis suggested a goal of 100 Patrons, who would be granted special perquisites. A "Patron's Desk" was staffed in the Lincoln Center headquarters to provide special service in securing tickets. Also, their names were listed on a Patron Plaque in each building and in house programs.

This plan for patron gifts of $100,000 or more became a central feature of Lincoln Center fund-raising throughout its capital campaign. It was expanded to include a separate listing for corporate and foundation patrons. By 1969, the total number of individual patrons reached 134 and of corporate patrons, 66. The patron category has been continued beyond the capital campaign into the planning of Lincoln Center's appeals for annual support and for endowment.

During the winter of 1958 and 1959, the momentum of the campaign increased. A succession of public announcements of large individual gifts and of the total raised in campaign subgroups kept the Lincoln Center drive before the public. The campaign office was moved from its crowded location at Columbus Circle to space, contributed by Houghton, in the newly completed Corning Glass Building on 5th Avenue. Francis' leadership within the campaign organization and its staff was dynamic. His own personal commitments of time and energy set an example for all associated with him. He maintained constant pressure and encouragement.

The annual meeting of the board on April 28, 1959 provided an opportunity to review all aspects of the evolving Lincoln Center.

Members of the campaign committee attended as guests, and Francis reported a total of $46 million raised to that date through 203 gifts and pledges. From 62 corporations, $4,130,000 had been raised. Sixteen foundations had given $27,522,000; 123 individuals had pledged $4,104,000, and two estates had provided bequests of $110,000.

CHAPTER 6

Preliminary Architectural Planning 1956-1959

In the choice of architects for Lincoln Center, two decisions had been made before the Exploratory Committee for a Musical Arts Center was formed. Wallace K. Harrison had been designing opera houses for the Metropolitan since 1930, and the firm of Harrison and Abramovitz was recognized by the opera leadership as their architect. When the Philharmonic decided it must have its own home, their leaders turned to the same firm for preliminary design, and soon Max Abramovitz was recognized by them as their design architect.

The Exploratory Committee had named Harrison coordinating architect for the proposed center, and this appointment was confirmed by the Lincoln Center board at its first meeting after incorporation. The Exploratory Committee also had decided that the center would be a group of freestanding buildings in a setting of plazas and parks and that each of its buildings would have a separate design architect. These decisions reflected the conscious desire of the committee, including Harrison, to encourage an architectural variety within a framework of harmony and unity.

Two weeks after Harrison's appointment as coordinating architect, he invited a group of eminent architects to serve as advisors on the project. This group was composed of Ālvar Āalto from Finland, Sven

Markelius from Sweden, and three Americans: Pietro Belluschi, Marcel Breuer, and Henry R. Shepley. Stuart Constable' met with the group as representative of Robert Moses. At the same time there was recognition of the need for technical expertise on problems of acoustics and stage design. Hugh Bagnell, who had just completed the acoustical design of the London Festival Hall, and the American firm of Bolt, Beranek and Newman were invited to advise on acoustics. Walter Unruh, the German designer of stages for several of the new German opera houses, and George Izenauer, an American innovator of automated light boards and electrical stage equipment, were the first technical advisers.

The panel of architectural and technical advisers met with Harrison and Abramovitz in October 1956. While discussing sight lines and acoustics in theater design, they agreed that the opera house should be shorter and wider than the traditional horseshoe-shaped auditorium of the old Met and of many old European opera houses. Differences arose among the consultants in the acoustical approaches to the concert hall. Bagnell advocated a traditional approach based on rectangular-shaped halls and opposed experimentation. Bolt, Beranek, and Newman wanted to experiment.

The most significant result of this first series of meetings was their review and revision of the site plan for arrangement and location of buildings. The tentative site plan, as it was shown to the consultants, had emerged from the first proposals from the city's Committee on Slum Clearance, as worked out by their architects. Its key feature was a north-south mall, running midway through the three blocks of the Lincoln Center site. The mall linked Fordham University on the south and the proposed commercial theater complex on the north, and it provided a frontage for the concert hall. The park between Fordham and the opera house had also become a feature of the plan, and it was assumed that the opera would face the park.

The panel of architects, in reacting to this first plan, posed a fundamental question: Was the performing arts center to be isolated from the city or related to the city? The group strongly urged the latter and recognized Broadway and Lincoln Square as the focus of activity in this area. A regrouping of the buildings around an east-west axis would provide an approach to the opera house from the Broadway side. In December 1956, Harrison brought to the Lincoln Center board a new site plan based on this concept. The opera house remained on its original site, but faced east at the head of the new entrance plaza. The concert hall was proposed for the northeast corner of the site, fronting south on the new plaza. The dance theater was placed on the southeast corner, across the plaza from the concert hall. The Juilliard School, the drama theater, and the library and museum crowded the northwest corner of the site. The Lincoln Center board accepted this site plan as a basis for proceeding, but it asked Harrison to advise Moses that Lincoln Center reserved the right to ask for reconsideration.

In the spring and summer of 1957, following the adoption of a preliminary site plan, the designers shifted their attention to specific buildings. Each architect had to deal with a dual client—the owner, Lincoln Center, Inc., and the user, the constituent institution. This fact complicated the entire design and decision-making process.

On fundamentals of design, there was agreement between the leaders of the constituents and of Lincoln Center. Both were dedicated to the highest quality. Both shared the dual objective of service to the arts and encouragement of wider public enjoyment of the arts. Both hoped that these buildings, designed in the 1950s, would have a timeless enduring quality so that throughout their potentially long lives of use they would appear to be vital and appropriate homes for the arts they housed. Direct communication was established between each architect and the constituent representatives to determine the functional requirements for each building. In the case of the opera, Harrison dealt as needed with Rudolf Bing, general manager, and on a continuing basis, with Herman Krawitz, the opera's business and technical manager. For the concert hall design, Max Abramovitz dealt with Arthur Houghton and David Keiser, chairman and president of the Philharmonic-Symphony Society, and on a continuing basis with George Judd, then general manager of the orchestra. Similar contact was established later between the architects for the other buildings and their respective constituents.

While this involvement of the constituent leadership in the design process was essential and, on the whole, worked admirably, it often created its own problems. There was a natural tendency on the part of the constituent professionals to seek perfection, to desire the most advanced technology, the most generous spaces for storage, rehearsals, and offices, among other features. Lincoln Center, equally wished to maintain a high qualitative standard, but, as owner, it had to face the reality of paying the construction bills. It had to work within budgets and exercise financial control. Often the problem was to reconcile constituent desires with available funds.

In the design of the auditoria for the concert hall and for the opera, optimum acoustical properties were paramount. It was understood that no matter how beautiful and comfortable these buildings might be, the buildings would be judged to be failures if symphonic music and opera were not heard to their best advantage. Bolt, Beranek and Newman, consultants for the concert hall, were soon at work on a research project to study the relationship between acoustical properties and size and design of auditoria. They assembled a mass of information on the design features of numerous opera houses, concert halls, and theaters throughout the world. The judgment of musicians and music critics concerning the musical success or failure of these halls was tabulated. Correlation of the most successful halls with certain design features was established.[1]

In the design of all the Lincoln Center halls, facilities for live performances and natural—that is, unamplified—sound were required. Despite the technological advances in high-fidelity amplification systems, all major singers and symphony conductors insist on halls without sound reinforcement. Music critics and regular audience members are equally strong in their aversion to amplified music. New homes for the Metropolitan and the Philharmonic would have no chance for public acclaim if they required amplification. This meant that there would be a limit to the size of the halls and hence to their seating capacities, beyond which any expansion could be made only at the peril of acoustical excellence. Although economic factors and a public clamor for more seats argued strongly for larger halls, every shred of musical judgment and of scientific evidence warned that any plan for halls larger than the old Met and Carnegie would involve high risks of acoustical failure. In fact, the old Met with 3600 seats was larger than most satisfactory opera houses of Europe. And Carnegie Hall with nearly 3000 seats was slightly larger than those great and universally admired halls in Boston, Amsterdam, and Vienna. During much of the early design stage the seating capacity for the concert hall was set at 2200. What was finally built at Lincoln Center was an opera house seating nearly 3800, and a concert hall seating 2800.

When public announcement of building plans was made, there was an outburst of public criticism for failure to provide for larger audiences. But the leaders of Lincoln Center and of the constituents firmly supported their architects' designs. With patient explanations, the protests eventually subsided.

An indication of a few fundamentals of the science of acoustics that the laymen learned from the experts may help an understanding of the considerations required of the architects during this design stage. The science of acoustics relates, in building design, to matters of sound insulation and isolation as well as to the acoustical properties of a performance hall. It was necessary that all of the Lincoln Center halls be completely insulated from external noises. Subway rumble, which can be heard faintly in Carnegie Hall, was to be avoided, as was sound from jet planes or fire sirens. Various rooms within a building might require complete sound isolation from each other. Adjacent rehearsal rooms might be quite unusable if one room registered sounds from another. Practice rooms in the Juilliard School would present special problems of sound isolation.

These types of acoustical considerations were not new and the acoustical advisers were able to specify materials of a necessary density, walls of a required thickness, sound traps in air-conditioning ducts, or door gaskets to provide tight seals. On these matters of sound insulation and isolation, the design of Lincoln Center was successful.

But the acoustical properties of auditoria were soon recognized to be an immensely complex subject. How music or spoken words sound in a hall depends on a complex mix of such factors as the size of the hall, reverberation time, and sound distribution. The size of the hall directly affects the intensity or loudness of sound. (Reverberation time means the length of time a sound emanating from a stage is heard in the hall by reason of its reflection from one surface to another and on to others before the sound is finally absorbed. As expressed by a mathematical formula, reverberation time is a function of the ratio of cubic volume of a room to floor-area seating space. Hence, the larger the seating capacity of a concert hall, the higher must be the ceiling if a desired long reverberation time is to be obtained.) The optimum reverberation is different for each art form. Symphonic music is generally considered to be heard at its best in a hall with reverberation of 1.8 to 2.0 seconds at the mid-frequencies. However, a reverberation time of that length makes the spoken word sound mushy if not unintelligible. For theater, a short reverberation around 1.0 second is desired. Since opera is a combination of orchestral and vocal sounds, it needs intermediate reverberation. Sound-absorbing surfaces deaden sound and shorten reverberation. Hard, sound-reflecting surfaces lengthen reverberation; they bounce sounds around. People themselves, and especially their heavy winter clothing, absorb sound and shorten reverberation. There is also a direct relationship between vast spaces and long reverberation. The best example is a huge cathedral with a high vaulted ceiling. Pipe organs sound most glorious in such rooms where reverberation may be as long as three seconds. But in such a place a speaker must slow down his delivery significantly if his speech is to be understood.

The distribution of sound depends on many factors, but chiefly on sound reflecting objects and surfaces. Sound reflects from a surface as light reflects from a mirror. Parallel wall surfaces can cause echos, which must be avoided. Concave surfaces tend to focus sound in a localized area; convex surfaces distribute or diffuse sound widely. The even distribution of sound can be greatly affected by balcony overhangs. Although the direct sound from a stage may reach a listener seated under a large balcony, much of the reflected or reverberant sound will be lost. It was for that reason that all the auditoria of Lincoln Center were designed with shallow balconies.

Many concert halls built in the nineteenth century or earlier were outstandingly successful acoustically. The architecture and decorative arts of those periods favored the requirements for even sound distribution and for desired reverberation. Coffered ceilings, marble statuary, the cupids and curlicues of baroque decoration all serve an acoustical purpose. Contemporary architectural design tends visually to favor large plain surfaces. The architect's acoustical task today is to find ways to break up those surfaces with smaller units set at varying angles.

In the early design stages of the concert hall, it had been assumed that it would be a single-purpose hall. But that assumption was challenged by several potential donors, in particular staff officers in foundations, who urged consideration of the relative merits of a multipurpose hall. The leaders of the Philharmonic wanted a hall designed exclusively for orchestra and other concert purposes. They wanted it to hold a place in the concert world equal to the prestige associated with Boston Symphony Hall or the Amsterdam Concertgebouw. They feared that a fully equipped stage with a movable orchestral shell might require such compromises with the ideal for concerts that the resulting hall would be second rate. They were also concerned over the operational costs of putting up and taking down a shell. Keiser reminded the directors that the early resolution of the Philharmonic board expressing their enthusiasm over participation in Lincoln Center had been based on their understanding that the concert hall would be a single-purpose hall. He warned that the support of the Philharmonic board was linked to this assumption. However, since the Philharmonic would be only a part-time tenant in the concert hall, those in Lincoln Center who were anticipating full-time, year-round usage wanted as much flexibility as possible. The Philharmonic was expected to schedule four concerts a week in a season of about one-half year duration. Other orchestras and concerts would fill some of the free time, but if the hall were designed for a number of purposes with a fully equipped stage, the variety of the possible attractions that could be booked would be increased.

The more this issue was discussed with the acoustical advisers, the more persuasive became the arguments for a single-purpose hall. The directors, on March 11, 1957 concluded that acoustical considerations were controlling, that the concert hall should therefore be designed expressly for concert purposes, that there should be no fully equipped stage, that limited facilities for visual presentations might be included on the stage, but only with the assurance that the acoustical properties for concerts would not be adversely affected.

With this firm decision, Abramovitz could proceed with an idea desired by the leaders of the Philharmonic, to emphasize a feeling that the audience and orchestra were together in one room. They wished to avoid any vestige of a proscenium arch that would frame the orchestra and seem to separate it from the audience.

While these design criteria for the concert hall were being resolved, Harrison had frequent conferences with the Metropolitan Opera leaders. Clarification and refinement of the opera requirements began to emerge. First attention was paid to the backstage facilities, that huge complex of shops for scenery building and costume making, ranging in scope from a wig shop to a forge. For the stage itself, the objective was to provide the new Metropolitan with the most advanced technology and facilities for opera presentation. The specific mechanical and electrical equipment and the space requirements were developed in consultation with Walter Unruh, the German expert on stage technology.

During late 1956 and 1957, Harrison and Abramovitz were also engaged in the design of the garage, the underground roadways, and the plaza and park areas. At this time, negotiations with the city and federal governments for public financing of these areas were sufficiently certain that Moses had decided the Park Department (of which he was also commissioner) would be the city agency to build and operate these facilities, and he had retained Harrison and Abramovitz as architect. Preliminary design for the concert hall and opera indicated that these buildings would utilize all of their underground space. Hence, the garage and related facilities could be situated only below the plaza and park areas, placing limitations on the size of the garage. The size also was restricted by the solid rock underlying the entire site, making deep excavation excessively costly. Studies suggested the feasibility of building a garage on two levels with a capacity for about 750 cars, a number that was considered adequate based on surveys of the travel habits of audiences.

The complex design interrelationships are illustrated by a practical problem that arose in the backstage design of the opera. The truck-loading dock, where large units of scenery would be transferred, had to be at street level on Amsterdam Avenue. Ideally, the platform level for truck loading should be at stage floor level. Stage level, in turn, would determine the level at the rear of the auditorium that would dictate the entrance foyer levels.

For an early design for the opera house, Harrison had placed the entrance foyer at the plaza level, but, as a result, in the backstage of the opera house the stage floor and the truck-loading dock were at different levels. A costly and space-consuming elevator would be required. Harrison solved the problem by lowering the entire complex by five or six feet. But this created a new problem. The garage entrance from 62nd Street would have insufficient headroom and excessive slope due to a slight hump in the grade of that street at the middle of the block. Harrison's solution was to regrade 62nd Street. This would involve city agencies, affect a Consolidated Edison power line, and influence the design of Fordham University, the neighbor across 62nd Street. Cost-benefit analyses were made that favored Harrison's plan. Also, because Fordham's design was not yet developed, it could be planned with this change in mind. Negotiations undertaken by General Nelson with the city and with Consolidated Edison were successful, and the city eventually regraded the street.

In the autumn of 1957, when the schedule for public hearings indicated that the Lincoln Square project was on its way to final approval, Moses exerted pressure to build the concert hall and opera concurrently and as soon as possible. Lincoln Center could not agree to such a schedule, for it felt it must time the commitment for construction of each building to the availability of assured funds. Its money-raising campaign had scarcely begun. While there were confident hopes for enough capital to start the concert hall as soon as land could be cleared, a longer time, a year at least, would be required to raise the $24 million then estimated for the opera.

The increasing pressures for design and construction planning were demanding more detailed attention than the Lincoln Center board as a whole could give. A decision to appoint a building committee came in October, 1957. Rockefeller served as chairman and Drye, Houghton, and Jackson were designated committee members; a year later Spofford was added to the committee. Young and Allen attended committee meetings to coordinate its actions with other facets of the rapidly evolving Lincoln Center organization. General Nelson, executive director for construction, was responsible for implementation of Building Committee decisions.

At the end of October 1957 Harrison convened a meeting of his panel of consulting architects. The panel recommended confirmation of the basic site plan so far as it defined the east-west axis and the placement of the opera, concert hall, and ballet theater, although they could not agree on the location for the other three buildings. They also gave a great deal of attention to means of access for both pedestrians and vehicles and recommended a pedestrian plaza and roadways below the plaza for taxis and private cars. These views prevailed in the final design.

When the panel of architects concluded their meetings they had forcefully registered their dissatisfaction with the crowded northwest corner of the site. This area was too small to contain the buildings for the Juilliard School, the library and museum, and the repertory theater; expansion of the three-block Lincoln Center site was essential. Citing the precedent of locating library and museum buildings in city parks, they urged a reopening of the question of placing such a building in the small park planned by Moses for the Lincoln Square project. They also strongly encouraged the idea of expanding the site northward into the block between 65th and 66th Streets.

Moses remained adamant in his opposition to any encroachment on the park. However, he encouraged an expansion to the north and suggested a broad pedestrian bridge over 65th Street. Architectural planning proceeded on the assumption that this half block would be available. Early proposals located the library and museum, housing for Juilliard students, the restaurant, a complex of banks, stores, and a performing arts club in this area.

Harrison felt an immediate need for more intensive consideration of the design for all buildings contemplated and urged action to select the other architects. On February 10, 1958, the board confirmed Philip Johnson as design architect for the dance theater. Four months earlier, he had accepted an invitation to do preliminary design studies. Johnson was co-architect with Mies van der Rohe of the Seagram building in New York. He was a trustee of The Museum of Modern Art with a long professional relationship to that organization. Among the Center's architects, Johnson was the most articulate, and in group meetings, he played a vocal as well as a creative role.

Also in 1958 Harrison recommended Pietro Belluschi as the design architect for the Juilliard School. The Juilliard officers considered several possible candidates, then chose Belluschi with enthusiasm. Belluschi was the Dean of Architecture at Massachusetts Institute of Technology. Born and trained in Rome, he had come to the United States in 1924. Most of his architectural practice had been on the west coast, with numerous school and college buildings among his credentials. He had designed a highly successful small concert hall on the Berkeley campus of the University of California. Belluschi is a patient, soft-spoken person, but with firm, even stubborn, convictions. More than any of the others on the Lincoln Center architectural team, he seemed to focus on human considerations in architectural design.

In conferences with Schuman and members of the Juilliard faculty, it soon became evident to Belluschi that the initial space estimates for the educational unit had been grossly understated. The bulk and mass of the Juilliard School was growing to the point that it became even more difficult to accommodate it in the northwest corner of the original three-block site. The solution was to move the Juilliard School to the addition to the north and to consider consolidation of the school and the proposed student housing in a single structure.

Before an architect was chosen for the drama theater, significant design ideas had emerged from discussions among theater professionals on the Advisory Council on Drama. There was a widely shared desire to break away from the restraints of the typical Broadway house. Robert Whitehead was strong in his view that there should be no proscenium. Jo Mielziner, a theater designer, urged "enormous flexibility," and he suggested elimination of the traditional theater fly loft. Walter Kerr urged that the theater in Lincoln Center should not have a proscenium but should have a stage with the audience seated around it on three sides. Mielziner supported this thought, suggesting an amphitheater-type seating with the auditorium steeply tiered. There was strong emphasis on the importance of audience sight lines and on intimacy between audience and stage. The advisers quickly reached a consensus that the theater should seat between 1100 and 1200 people.

For theater architect, Eero Saarinen was strongly recommended by Harrison and Whitehead and was approved by the Building Committee on September 8, 1958, subject to concurrence by the theater donor, Mrs. Vivian Beaumont Allen. After meeting with Saarinen, she promptly sent word that she was pleased with the architect chosen.

Saarinen was recognized as one of America's most creative and distinguished architects. He was especially noted for his free-form concrete structures. Son of the renowned Finnish-American architect, Eliel Saarinen, Eero was a person of great intellectual and physical force, a large man with a warm personality. Saarinen felt a need for an expert on theater matters, technical and operational; after consulting Whitehead, he chose Jo Mielziner as his collaborating designer.

By late 1958 only the designer for the library and museum had yet to be chosen. Harrison proposed Gordon Bunshaft, a partner in the firm of Skidmore, Owings & Merrill. He was approved on October 20, 1958, subject to clearance with the president of the New York Public Library, Gilbert Chapman, whose approval was given promptly. Another partner, Edgar J. Mathews, was designated managing partner, and Bunshaft was named design architect.

At that time Bunshaft was best known as the designer of Lever House, one of the first new office buildings on Park Avenue. He had pioneered in bank architecture with the design of the Fifth Avenue branch of the Manufacturers Trust Company—the first bank building with a glass facade. Both of these buildings had been considered bench marks in contemporary architecture. Bunshaft proved to be forceful in a group and sometimes justifiably stubborn in his convictions.

—————————————————————————

Rockefeller felt the weight of the ultimate responsibility for design approval that would rest on the board of directors. He also sensed that the artistic importance of the center and the public nature of the enterprise placed on the directors a particular requirement to exercise sound artistic judgment. Since neither he nor any of the directors had professional expertise in this field, he proposed that a small panel of individuals with recognized artistic competence be invited to serve as informal advisors to the board. Some directors, especially Houghton and Spofford, feared that such a group of advisors would undermine the responsibility for design which they felt must rest upon the architects. The outcome was to invite one person, René d'Harnoncourt, director of The Museum of Modern Art, to meet with the architectural team and to advise the Board of Directors. d'Harnoncourt proved to be an ideal choice for this difficult and delicate task. He enjoyed the respect of all the architects, and he regarded each of them with similar respect. Yet he was independent of them in his artistic judgments. He was a towering person, both physically and intellectually, a born diplomat and a highly sensitive human being. In subsequent meetings he contributed significantly to the architects' deliberations and to the Board's decisions.

Although each of the architects was responsible for his own building, Rockefeller insisted that there be a general design for the center as a whole before the start of construction. Therefore, in November, 1958, Harrison, as coordinating architect, convened a series of meetings with the other five architects and d'Harnoncourt, Rockefeller, and Young. Harrison asked Rockefeller to chair their meetings. Rockefeller, a nonprofessional, could deal with all the architects as a respected layman. He persistently drew out ideas from each architect until consensus was achieved.

The architects first reviewed the site plan, accepting the entrance plaza leading up to the opera and with the concert hall to the right (or north) of the plaza. But there was much discussion over the precise location of the other units in the center. While the primary purpose of acquiring the additional northern half block had been to accommodate the needs of Juilliard, the architects wanted to try other possible arrangements.[2] There was jockeying among the architects, each trying to place his building in that block, the only space with a Broadway frontage. If adopted, any of their proposals would have placed Juilliard on a smaller site, creating problems for Belluschi, who had to deal with the much larger space requirements for the school. Finally, by mutual agreement, Juilliard was restored to the northern block, the ballet theater to a site south of the entrance plaza, and the repertory theater was placed on the northwest corner of the original three-block site. The library and museum was left, under this arrangement in a long narrow building running just south of 65th Street between the west side of Philharmonic Hall and the east front of the repertory theater. Although this plan was not yet wholly satisfactory to Saarinen and Bunshaft, at this stage it seemed to be the best that the architects could develop.

The members of the architectural team then addressed themselves to questions of unity in the overall design. They first considered the use of a common exterior building material. Belluschi suggested Roman travertine, from the same quarries near Tivoli that provided the marble to build ancient Rome. Agreement was enthusiastic. Of all decisions required of them this was the quickest one they would make.

A second question concerned the treatment of the facades of the three buildings facing the entrance plaza. Harrison, Abramovitz, and Johnson all urged glass because they wanted those approaching the halls to be able to see interiors and to see other people moving about. They wanted those within the foyer areas of the halls to be able to look out, to be aware of the life on the plaza and in the other buildings of the center. Glass facades facing the plaza were approved.

Other important elements of unity emerged from these meetings. The concert hall and the ballet theater, facing each other and framing the approach to the opera, were to be of identical height and mass, with differences in the designs of their facades. Outside balconies at promenade levels on these buildings and on the opera house at the same elevation were approved to extend the opportunities for interaction and to relate all buildings to their common plaza.

The architects worked with clay models representing the mass and location of each building. Shapes of clay were changed and moved around, and the interrelationship among the several buildings was

René d'Harnoncourt meets with six architects in search of a center. From left to right: d'Harnoncourt, Harrison, Belluschi, Johnson, Bunshaft, Abromovitz, Saarinen.

constantly scrutinized. There was one tense but humorous moment when, with a sweeping slash of a modeling knife, Saarinen struck off the stage-house projection of Johnson's ballet theater. Saarinen had perceived a visual problem with its exterior as viewed from the plaza. The solution came when acoustical considerations raised the height of the concert hall, and then, to conform, the height of the facade of the ballet theater as the visual balance; its stage-house projection thus was masked by the higher facade.

In February, 1959, the results of the architects' deliberations, both as to site plan and unifying design elements, were approved by the Building Committee. Board approval came a week later, when d'Harnoncourt summed up the architects' approach. They had recognized two alternatives; either a system of unification or a "World's Fair" atmosphere representing a group of six individual and unrelated buildings. The architects strongly recommended the former and in their discussions moved from diversification to unification. He said further that

> this does not mean monotony or the submergence of individual buildings, but it does represent an effort to create Lincoln Center as a unified whole to house six separate institutions.

In an article entitled "Six Architects in Search of a Center," Harold Schonberg, Music Critic of the *New York Times*, described the efforts of the architects to arrive at the best possible site plan and to agree on overall design elements. He compared the situation to an imaginary occasion when

> six great pianists . . . all mighty executants, all overpowering personalities, were locked in a room and ordered not to come out until they had decided on the correct interpretation of Beethoven's 'Hammerklavier' Sonata. How many eons would pass? How many wounds would be inflicted? How much blood would be shed?[3]

Describing each architect as "a fierce individualist," he found them "resolved to succeed as a group."[4]

A problem related to the site plan arose from discussions among the governor, the mayor, Moses, and John Rockefeller regarding help from the city for financing the capital cost of both the ballet theater and the library and museum. Were that to be provided, both of those buildings would be owned by the city, rather than by Lincoln Center. General Nelson felt an exchange of the sites for the ballet theater and the drama theater (which also would please Mrs. Allen, who was discontented with the planned location of the drama theater) would place the ballet theater adjacent to the library and museum, thus joining the sites for the two city-owned buildings. But this suggestion had practical architectural problems. The ballet theater would be a considerably larger building than the drama theater and would make the northwest corner even more crowded. Moreover, the drama theater alone would not be a suitable match in size to the concert hall across the plaza. These considerations were weighed by the Building Committee at its meeting on April 13, and the site plan as recommended and approved on March 2 was again confirmed for the time being. (The problem with Mrs. Allen remained unsolved.)

To design each of the buildings, the architects had need for mechanical, electrical, and structural engineering expertise. Harrison had selected the firm of Syska and Hennessy as his mechanical and electrical engineers for the design of the opera, and Abramovitz turned to them for the concert hall. Their early engineering studies indicated that air conditioning, steam distribution, and perhaps other services could be provided more efficiently from a central source rather than by separate installations in each building. The Building Committee and the architects approved this and retained Syska and Hennessy as the engineers. In order to assure coordination between the central services and the engineering planning for the several buildings, the committee decided that the same firm should also be used for mechanical and electrical engineering in each building. However, they decided that each architect would choose his own structural engineer, and each was to be fully responsible for the coordination of all engineering design with his architectural design.

The Building Committee emphasized that the architect alone was to be in charge of all design aspects of his building. The principle of full design responsibility applied to all other consultants and advisors that might be needed by each architect. In recognition of the special interest of each organization in the acoustical success of its new home, the architects were directed to select their acoustical advisors in consultation with the constituents. Abramovitz retained Bolt, Beranek and Newman as acoustical advisors; that firm was also chosen by Saarinen in the design of the drama theater. Johnson, in his early design studies for the ballet theater, turned to a Danish acoustician, Wilhelm Jordan. Needing an American associate, Jordan used Cyril Harris, a professor at Columbia University.[4] Johnson's success in working with Jordan and Harris led Harrison and the Metropolitan Opera to choose them as well. For the Juilliard building, Belluschi and Juilliard chose a German acoustician, Heinrich Keilholz.

The requirements for optimum acoustics frequently interfered with clear sight lines to the stage. To cope with these and similar problems each architect needed a theater seating specialist. The one preeminent expert in that field was Ben Schlanger, and all of the architects turned to him for advice and seating design detail. Schlanger understood and respected acoustical principles and in addition had developed his own system for designing the layout of individual seats to provide as nearly ideal sight lines as possible.

In determining both the overall design and the seating detail of modern halls, the architects had to take into account the fact that, in the period since World War I, the average American had grown taller and heavier and translate this into more knee room and wider seats. This resulted in fewer seats in a given space.

The pressures to start construction were mounting. Clarence Francis and his campaign leaders were urging a start of construction as a prerequisite to expansion of their campaign efforts to reach a larger public. While progress had been made in raising money from foundations and from several substantial donors, they felt that a more general campaign needed the impetus of visible signs that the proposed center was becoming a reality. In addition, those responsible for financial planning were pressing for more definitive designs so that costs could be accurately determined.

The Philharmonic was living under threat of its eviction notice. (They had been able to negotiate an extension for their lease of Carnegie Hall, but only for the one season of 1959 and 1960.) Houghton and Keiser therefore resisted every proposal that might cause further delay. Moses pressed for the start of construction. He was anticipating construction interrelationships between buildings to be built by Lincoln Center and the adjoining plaza, park, and garage complex to be built by the city, and he hoped the same general contractor could be employed for both the private and the public work. If Lincoln Center would engage a joint venture of several builders, he thought he could persuade the city to utilize the same group of contractors for its work.

In response to this urging from Moses, a group of four major construction firms, the Turner, Fuller, Walsh, and Slattery companies, proposed in October, 1958 that they form a joint venture to build the center. On December 5 the Board approved retention of this joint venture for cost estimating during the remainder of the planning stage and to serve as Lincoln Center's general contractor.

The plans for Philharmonic Hall were still incomplete in early 1959, and there was no way the ground-breaking date, already set for mid-May, could be met with the protection of a guaranteed construction cost for the completed building. The directors insisted, however, that ground breaking be an actual start of construction, not merely a public relations event. Nelson, Abramovitz, and the joint venture proposed that excavation and foundation work be authorized as a part of the eventual total job and at a cost not to exceed $800,000. This would permit the start of construction; the architectural and engineering work for the design of the completed building could be carried on concurrently. This procedure involved the financial risk of a start before total cost could be determined and assured. But there was a counterbalancing risk of rising building costs involved in delay. The board accepted the first risk, and, on March 23, 1959 approved the contract for excavation and foundations.

As the date for ground breaking (May 14, 1959) approached, all was not yet neat, tidy, and final in the realm of design; but solid progress had been made during the three years of preliminary planning. The architectural team was complete; major features of the site plan were firm; agreement had been reached on the unifying elements of overall design; the architectural scheme for the concert hall was well advanced; substantial progress was evident in opera plans; and a start had been made on the design of other buildings.

Rendering by Hugh Ferriss/Photo courtesy of Lincoln Center for the Performing Arts, Inc.

A rendering of Lincoln Center at the time of ground breaking.

CHAPTER 7

Ground Breaking
May 14, 1959

The importance the directors attached to ground breaking was underscored by an invitation from Rockefeller to President Dwight D. Eisenhower to attend the ceremony and turn the first spadeful of earth. C. D. Jackson was a presidential adviser and used his good offices to urge acceptance of the invitation. Clarence Francis knew Eisenhower well and was, at that time, a special consultant to the President. On March 9, after a personal conference with the President, Francis reported that Eisenhower would plan to be present, that he would make a brief address, and that the event could be scheduled for 11:00 a.m. on May 14.

Keiser and Allen worked out the program for the occasion. Leonard Bernstein would conduct the Philharmonic Orchestra; Rise Stevens and Leonard Warren would represent the Metropolitan; the Juilliard chorus would participate. Spofford issued invitations to city and state officials. Governor Rockefeller would be out of the country, and the state would be represented by Lt. Governor Malcolm Wilson. Mayor Robert Wagner, Manhattan Borough President Hulan Jack, and Commissioner Robert Moses would attend on behalf of the city.

General Nelson synchronized the schedule for demolition of build-

97

ings with the ground-breaking date and was responsible for security arrangements with the Secret Service. The campaign director, Alan Holding, served as general coordinator of arrangements, emphasizing the relationship of the occasion to fund raising. Over 6000 special guests were to be invited, and he estimated that one-third of them might attend. The response to invitations exceeded all expectations; over 6000 individuals accepted. The public also was invited, and a crowd of thousands was expected.

The physical arrangements on the site became the first responsibility for Col. William F. Powers who joined the staff as Deputy Director of Construction on April 1, 1959. A small pavilion with a raised and covered platform was built for the honored guests. On one side a large tent was erected over a stage for the orchestra and chorus. An elevated platform was built at the rear for the equipment for television and radio broadcast, and for press photographers. Audience areas were clearly marked with ropes and stanchions and nearly 7000 chairs were rented.

As "G" Day approached, several days of soaking rain produced a sea of mud, and there was no possible alternate plan for foul weather. But the morning of Thursday, May 14, dawned clear, the green-striped tent over the musicians' area gleamed in the sun, the prepared areas drained and dried quickly, and all was ready to receive the guests. They came early, as had been requested, so that the program could begin precisely at 11:00 A.M.

President Eisenhower arrived on "Columbine III" and was met by Clarence Francis. Distinguished guests took their places on the podium as Bernstein led the Philharmonic in Aaron Copeland's "Fanfare." After "Ruffles and Flourishes," to the orchestral strains of "Hail to the Chief," Rockefeller and Francis escorted the President to his seat. Brief talks by Rockefeller, Mayor Wagner, Commissioner Moses, and Lt. Governor Wilson alternated with musical numbers, and then the President was introduced. The highlights of his remarks pertaining to Lincoln Center were:

Lincoln Center for the Performing Arts symbolizes an increasing interest in America in cultural matters as well as a stimulating approach to one of the nation's pressing problems—urban blight.

Here in the heart of our greatest metropolitan center men of vision are executing a redevelopment of purpose, utility and taste. It is a cooperative venture in which Federal and local governments, artistic groups, large foundations and private citizens are joining forces. . . .

The beneficial influence of this great cultural adventure will not be limited to our borders. Here will occur a true interchange of the fruits of national cultures. From this will develop a growth that will spread to the corners of the earth, bringing with it the kind of human message that only individuals, not governments, can transmit.

Here will develop a mighty influence for peace and understanding throughout the world.

At the end of his talk, Eisenhower, accompanied by ranking public officials and by Rockefeller and Keiser, came down from the podium. With a polished shovel he dug into the ground while the strains of Handel's "Hallelujah Chorus" came from the Philharmonic and the Juilliard Chorus.

Before the President walked to his nearby, open-top car, he greeted

Photo by Bob Serating

President Dwight D. Eisenhower breaks ground for Lincoln Center. Behind the President: John D. Rockefeller 3rd, David Keiser, Robert Moses, Borough President Hulan Jack, Mayor Robert Wagner, Lieutenant Governor Malcolm Wilson.

the participating artists while, at the same moment, power equipment began the serious business of excavating for Philharmonic Hall.

The *New York Herald Tribune* caught the spirit of the ground-breaking occasion in an editorial the following day.

The site was bounded on the north by a factory building devoted to "Sportswear, Corsets and Gloves," and on the west and south by rows of crumbling tenements. Some were hollow shells, already vacated; others were still occupied, for the morning's wash fluttered on their clotheslines.

The site itself consisted of two city blocks that had been leveled, as if by a bomb, their only touch of color an orange steam shovel. There was nothing beautiful about the scene, and yet for the 12,000 assembled people it had a special beauty of its own. For

President Eisenhower greets Mrs. Vivian Beaumont Allen. In background: Mayor Robert Wagner, Commissioner Robert Patterson, Mrs. Rockefeller, and John D. Rockefeller 3rd.

amid the rubble they could imagine the shiny new buildings that will rise there soon. . . .

Off to one side, under a striped tent, Leonard Bernstein led the New York Philharmonic in the first of hundreds of performances that it will give from that spot when its hall is ready in 1961. . . . On a long dais, surrounded by men mighty in government and the arts, the President of the United States made a graceful speech, and there was drama in the thought that he was the first of many Presidents who will visit Lincoln Center. . . .

This was the real beauty of yesterday morning's occasion—the fact that a great vision suddenly took shape, a first audience was convened, a first performance given.[1]

After the event, Rockefeller and many of the participants received letters of appreciation. Robert Moses wrote:

The Performing Arts ceremony was not only a success, it was damn near perfect. I have never seen a thing of this kind run more smoothly and with more dignity and inspiration. I believe it made a deep impression and that support is assured. There remain many problems, not insoluble, if good will among the numerous participants is maintained.

Referring to Rockefeller's leadership of the project, a *Times'* "Man in the News" profile cited two of his qualities:

Tact is one of the chief gifts needed by a coordinator. It is something John Davison Rockefeller has in abundance. . . . Another characteristic needed by a coordinator is the largeness of vision to accommodate the ideas of many people. Mr. Rockefeller has this vision both by inclination and by accumulation. . . .[2]

The *Times* referred to the center as "the grasping of an opportunity made by necessity" and concluded with a forecast: "It will be a beacon to the world, revealing that Americans know how to build the life of the spirit on its material bounty."[3]

PART III

To the Opening of Philharmonic Hall 1959-1962

CHAPTER 8

Evolution of the Organization
1959-1962

The immediate result of ground breaking was a substantial increase in public awareness and understanding of the Lincoln Center project. Over 12,000 people attended the ceremony, and they left with high expectations of events to follow. An estimated 500,000 witnessed it locally on television. Press attention brought more than the physical fact of the beginning of the center into public view; it also called attention to the evolving institutional developments with commentary on what these might mean to the state of the performing arts and to their public enjoyment. The citizens of New York, or many of them, now knew that something unprecedented and exciting had been started at Lincoln Center.

To sustain this public interest, the time had come to adopt a more open public relations policy. In rapid succession, news stories were released concerning architectural developments, the prospect that the New York Public Library would become a part of Lincoln Center, relationships to the rapidly developing field of educational television, and the possibility that the city-wide High School of Performing Art might become a near neighbor of the center. In September, 1959, Lincoln Center issued a Report of Progress, covering its first three years of corporate existence, and distributed it widely to public officials, libraries, donors, and the press. It still stands as an authoritative public statement of the origins, early policies, and initial development of the center.

The strongest manifestation of the new policy was a "Public Participation Campaign," organized under the volunteer leadership of David Ogilvy and a committee of 31 major advertising executives. A survey, conducted by the Ogilvy group in July 1959, indicated that 75 percent of the people of New York had never heard of Lincoln Center in spite of its wide news coverage. In response, they planned an intensive public relations campaign for which a volunteer staff was assembled from leading firms in the field. Their purpose was not to get millions of people to send in dollars; the objective was to make the center more widely known and to develop a recognition by a large cross section of society that it would serve their interests.

Their campaign was launched early in 1960 by the exhibtion of a model of Lincoln Center, with an audio explanation, in public places such as City Hall and Grand Central station.

A school program featuring essay contests and art projects was conducted in over 800 schools to make children and their parents aware of Lincoln Center. A series of six full-page advertisements was run in the daily papers and in several magazines with national circulation. Television and radio spot announcements were taped by well-known artists who contributed their talent. A direct mailing was sent out to a list of 100,000 names. A second survey in September indicated that public awareness of Lincoln Center had increased from 25 to 67 percent, and it was estimated that information had reached at least 5,500,000 people.[1]

Lincoln Center began to seek a closer relationship with the city administration. Rockefeller suggested that the mayor and the commissioner of parks be invited to join the Lincoln Center Board as ex-officio directors of the corporation. Some of the directors and the legal counsel were opposed, for this would bring Mayor Wagner and Commissioner Moses directly into the policy guidance and management of the center and might complicate action on many matters still to be negotiated with governmental officials. But Rockefeller argued persuasively that it would be mutually helpful for these city officials to participate as insiders; the board adopted the proposal on June 15, 1959. Mayor Wagner and Commissioner Moses both agreed to serve, but sent representatives to most of the board meetings.

By the fall of 1959, the tasks of management were becoming increasingly demanding. More and more of Rockefeller's time was required on major fund-raising matters and on the evolving relationships with governmental agencies. He felt that executive leadership had to be shared and strengthened in some manner. Accordingly, with board approval, Spofford was given a more active role, and he arranged partial leave of absence from his law firm. He was already vice president and was designated chairman of the Building Committee, succeeding Rockefeller in that post.

The most urgent organizational problem was the structure of the Building Committee. For each of the Lincoln Center buildings, Spofford formed a subcommittee to function as a decision-making body, composed of board-level people representing the constituent concerned and others representing interests of the center as a whole. The Executive Director for Construction, Col. Powers, devised a system for careful agenda preparation and follow-up for each subcommittee meeting. The lines of communication with the architects were greatly improved, and the roles of the owner and the user were clarified.

Progress was made in analyzing the specific functions that Lincoln Center, Inc. would later have to perform. These included the operation of Philharmonic Hall and the chamber music hall, of central air conditioning, maintenance facilities, guided tour services, and concessions for restaurants, gift shops, and coat checking rooms. Anticipating the operation of the concert hall, Allen developed a policy to guide the booking of attractions to fill dates not required by the Philharmonic Orchestra. The board approved his emphasis on the highest quality in concerts and the exclusion of political meetings and conventions, but debated his proposal to exclude jazz. After consideration by the Lincoln Center Council, booking of jazz artists was authorized.

Allen concentrated first on a transfer of the major symphony orchestra series and concert artists from Carnegie Hall. He succeeded in his negotiations with the Boston and Philadelphia symphonies.[2] But full attainment of his objective was complicated when, in the fall of 1959, a group of artistic and civic leaders, led by Isaac Stern and Harold Riegelman, formed a citizen's committee to "Save Carnegie Hall." They received considerable public and press support, but the Philharmonic and Lincoln Center were placed in a dilemma by the proposal. If Carnegie were to remain an active concert hall, that fact would remove the compelling need of the Philharmonic for a new home, a primary factor in the creation of Lincoln Center. The Philharmonic leaders sustained their commitment for their new home, but they had serious doubts that audience potential could support two major concert halls in New York.

The save Carnegie movement rapidly gained political popularity and created a public relations question for Lincoln Center. Support would risk creating a future deficit operating problem for Philharmonic Hall, and some directors advocated a position of open opposition. Garrett, public relations counsel, cautioned that Lincoln Center could not win on such an issue in a public fight, and a policy of public silence was maintained.

The city eventually acquired Carnegie Hall and leased it to the new Carnegie Hall Corporation. This action was of immediate benefit to the Philharmonic Society and to Lincoln Center, because completion of the new hall was delayed and the orchestra was permitted to remain at Carnegie until its new home was ready in the fall of 1962. The long-term result has been far from disastrous to the operation of Philharmonic Hall. Some bookings that might otherwise have come to the new hall went to Carnegie, but the availability of the two concert halls has expanded musical services in the community.

The New York World's Fair, scheduled for the summers of 1964 and 1965, although initially unrelated to Lincoln Center, had a significant influence on its evolution. The first suggestion for Lincoln Center to seek a relationship to the fair came from Rockefeller in November 1959. On March 1, 1960, Moses became president of the World's Fair Corporation. During the summer, he proposed that the performing arts activities of the fair be presented at Lincoln Center rather than in special buildings at the site of the fair in Flushing Meadow Park. Such an arrangement had direct advantages for Lincoln Center. It imposed a useful deadline for construction; it presented a challenge to develop festival programs; moreover, the expected fair attendance of 50 million offered an opportunity to influence, in a short time, the pattern of summer operation with respect to both audiences and artists. The board accepted Moses' proposal and the responsibilities incident to its participation as the performing arts segment of the fair.

Soon after Moses became World's Fair president, his ex-officio position on the Lincoln Center board was taken by his successor as city Parks commissioner, Newbold Morris (who was also chairman of City Center). Rockefeller recommended, and the board approved, election of Moses as a director in his own right. He continued to serve until his retirement in 1969 when he became a director emeritus.

By the summer of 1960, administration of the rapidly evolving Lincoln Center was becoming increasingly complex and time consuming. Looking ahead, mounting management pressures were inevitable as the construction program would become fully active, as the fund-raising campaign would reach its peak, and as the dates approached for Lincoln Center operation and programming for the World's Fair. It was time to strengthen the organization. Rockefeller, Spofford, and Young met for an all-day conference on July 12, 1960. Analysis of the organizational and executive needs expected during the next four years indicated that the center needed a full-time president. Rockefeller and Spofford could become chairman and vice chairman and continue to give policy direction. A semi-independent organization should be developed to handle the World's Fair program. Another such unit should be formed to administer the Fund for Education and Artistic Advancement. Gradual expansion of the board to a maximum of 30 directors was recommended to broaden community representation. At this size, management, by consensus, would no longer be a feasible way to cope with the expanding range of issues and pressures arising in the development of the center. An executive committee of seven members would be needed. Such a committee could absorb the Financial Policy Committee and continue to meet on a regular schedule every two weeks; the larger board of directors would be convened once each month. Rockefeller reported to the board the conclusions the three officers had reached. The board concurred, and the search was begun for a president.

By September, 1960, the search had focused on General Maxwell D. Taylor, the retired U.S. Army Chief of Staff, who was then serving as chairman of the Mexican Light and Power Company. Spofford had known General Taylor in the Army and had worked closely with him in the formative days of NATO. Taylor's keen analytical mind, his firmness in executive decisions, his ability for clear verbal expression, his reputation for fairness and integrity were qualities needed for the executive leadership of Lincoln Center. His military experience seemed an odd background for preparation to lead a cultural institution. But Taylor was much more than a respected military leader. He was a well-known educator, having significantly broadened the educational approach at West Point during his period of command there. In management and public-administration circles, he was regarded as a careful innovator and a strong executive. General Taylor was ready to return to the United States. He wanted an opportunity for leadership in civilian life and accepted the offer to become president of Lincoln Center, effective January 1, 1961.

In December 1960, action was taken to implement the changes in the board and committee structure. The certificate of incorporation and the by-laws were amended to increase the size of the board; the Executive Committee was created. Rockefeller was elected chairman, and Spofford, Josephs, and Houghton became vice chairmen of the board; Spofford was elected chairman of the Executive Committee, with Francis, Houghton, Josephs, Olds, Taylor, and Woods named as members. Young, the secretary of the corporation, was designated secretary of the Executive Committee as well. Three new directors were elected at this time: General Taylor, Dr. Frank Stanton, and Harry Van Arsdale, Jr.

Stanton, president of Columbia Broadcasting System, was an astute businessman. But his contributions to the center were much broader; he brought important new insights to the center's evolution. He was experienced in the realm of nonprofit institutions, for he was a trustee of the Rand Corporation, the Institute for the Advancement of Science, the Carnegie Corporation, and the Rockefeller Foundation. He was personally interested in architecture and experienced in large building projects. He and his wife were discriminating collectors of art, particularly of contemporary sculpture. Stanton was made a member of the Building Committee and became chairman of the Art Committee when it was formed later.

The addition of Van Arsdale, president of the Central Labor Council in New York City, answered a need felt by Rockefeller for participation by organized labor in the development of the center. He thought of the public to be served by the center as a broad cross section from all economic and social levels. He wanted the involvement of leaders of organized labor to represent the interests of large groups of citizens as well as for the particular viewpoints they could bring.

One final step was taken in the reorganization adopted at that December 1960 meeting. Spofford felt that Taylor's executive role in the construction of the center would be stronger if he were chairman of the Building Committee. Accordingly, Spofford resigned from that post, and Taylor was named to it. The reorganization planned at the all-day conference the preceding July was now complete. Lincoln Center had entered a new and encouraging phase under Taylor's executive leadership.

The new president, already apprised of the status of Lincoln Center, expressed to the board his sense of urgency and his priorities: a firm construction schedule, completion of fiscal planning studies and solution of financial problems related to constituents, a carry-through on operational plans, especially as related to the World's Fair. Close liaison with the fair corporation at executive and board levels was essential. On Taylor's recommendation, a Lincoln Center committee on the World's Fair was created under Houghton's chairmanship, with members drawn from the board representatives of the constituents. This committee was charged with general policy guid-

General Maxwell D. Taylor, new president of Lincoln Center (second from left) visits construction site with Executive Directors Reginald Allen and Col. William F. Powers.

ance for festival planning and for liaison with their counterparts in the World's Fair Corporation.

For management of the festival, Taylor did not feel that a separate organization was required. He expected the operation of the Festival of the Performing Arts to involve an expansion of the same activities that Lincoln Center and its constituents would be undertaking in any case. They were to be conducted under the program leadership of Reginald Allen.

On March 27, 1961 the board approved an understanding Taylor had worked out with Moses. All presentations in the performing arts for the Fair were to be at Lincoln Center, and artistic responsibility was to be carried entirely by the center. Official invitations to foreign governments for participation by their performing groups were to be issued by the fair corporation. The need for subsidy was mutually recognized, but each corporation was careful to disclaim any financial responsibility, and neither could foresee any subsidy funds from their own resources. They agreed to seek independent financing for the festival and to cooperate in requesting grants and contributions to underwrite specific attractions.

Robert Moses, President of New York World's Fair Corp. signs agreement with General Taylor, President of Lincoln Center.

Events in Cuba caused President Kennedy to telephone Rockefeller on April 21, 1961 with an urgent request that Lincoln Center immediately release General Taylor for a two-month period to conduct a special assignment in the aftermath of the Bay of Pigs. Rockefeller agreed at once but with emphasis on the limited duration of Taylor's leave of absence, stressing the national and international importance of Lincoln Center. On Taylor's recommendation, it was agreed that, during his absence, Young should function as acting president and as chairman of the Building Committee. Fortunately, Young had been a close confidant and adviser to Taylor and was familiar with the status of negotiations in each area of executive concern. He already had effective working relationships with all the directors and key staff of Lincoln Center and its constituents, with the architects and contractors, and with city and state officials involved in Lincoln Center matters. The momentum that Taylor had started was also aided by a continuation of the pattern of breakfast conferences for key officers. This early hour and a half without interruption gave Rockefeller, Spofford, Josephs, and Young, with others as needed, opportunity for concentrated attention to the most urgent pending problems.

At the annual meeting of the corporation, held on May 8, 1961, all the officers and directors were reelected and two additions were made to the board. The Metropolitan nominated Anthony A. Bliss replacing Irving S. Olds, who was continued as one of the "public" directors of the corporation. Bliss was not a newcomer to Lincoln Center, having been a member of the Exploratory Committee. Edgar Young was also elected a director, in recognition of his increasing responsibility in the evolution of Lincoln Center.

At this same meeting, the directors considered the long-term role of Lincoln Center, Inc. in educational and artistic matters. Their principle instrument to carry out these purposes was the Fund for Education and Creative Artistic Advancement, with its campaign goal of $10 million. By 1961, more than half the goal, $5.5 million, had been received in gifts specifically designated for the fund. Responsibility for recommending the constructive use of this Fund had been placed in the Committee on Education, under the chairmanship of Dr. George Stoddard. In his report to the board, Stoddard recognized the fact that the $10 million goal, even when fully raised, would be a small resource in relation to the scope of educational and artistic opportunities. He suggested that the principle as well as income be expendable over a period of ten years, with the hope that the program of the fund would encourage new gifts to keep it replenished. To avoid dissipating the fund through grants to a large number of organizations, he urged concentration on the Lincoln Center constituents. However, any such grants had to be consistent with the policy of constituent autonomy and financial independence. Hence no grants should be made in support of the regular programs and activities of the established constituents. But encouragement could be given for innovative and experimental programs, and a special responsibility was recognized for new institutions or new activities created by Lincoln Center. Grants could be made to constituents to commission new artistic works.

The committee also advocated grants to expand those activities of the constituents that exposed young people to the arts of live performance. The well-established performances for students, held at the

Metropolitan and the Philharmonic, were to be encouraged, as were experiments to take the arts into the schools. Financial support already had been granted for innovative programs taken to the schools by the Metropolitan Opera Studio and by Juilliard. Those initial grants were the forerunners of the Lincoln Center Student Program that later involved all the constituents and became a continuing program of artistic and educational outreach. (See Chapter 16, pp. 232-235.)

As possibilities for major grants to support Lincoln Center's initiative in creating new institutions, the Stoddard committee was considering proposals for $.5 million to the repertory theater to launch its performing company and as much as $2.5 million to Juilliard over a period of years in support of its new drama training program. Stoddard suggested possible future support to constituents for Lincoln Center summer festivals. He did not seek immediate authorizations for these large and long-range proposals, but he asked the directors to give thought to the opportunities and the policy implications of such major allocations from the fund. Later, on July 10, 1961, the board appropriated $1 million over a five-year period to Juilliard for its drama training program and, for future planning purposes, an additional $1.5 million. Also, a grant of $.5 million was made for the repertory theater.

Near the end of General Taylor's two-month leave, Rockefeller was advised by President Kennedy and by Taylor that the general would be recalled to active military duty on July 1 for assignment in the White House as the military representative of the president. Taylor had to resign as president of Lincoln Center; the Executive Committee, at its regular meeting on June 26, continued the designation of Young as acting president. The assignment was understood to be a temporary one, and Young participated actively with the chairman and vice chairmen in the search for a new president.

During the early summer, the officers and the Executive Committee analyzed Lincoln Center's future executive needs in the light of progress during the preceding year. There was a consensus that greater emphasis should now be placed on the program functions of the Center. Executive leadership in the construction phase could be met through volunteer and staff assignments. These considerations turned the search for a new president to educators and artists. By late July, 1961 the search focused on William Schuman, president of the Juilliard School. As a composer, Schuman held a recognized place among professional musicians. As an educator, he had built a reputation as a member of the faculty of Sarah Lawrence College, and his standing among professional educators had been enhanced by his leadership at Juilliard. Three Lincoln Center directors, Drye, Keiser, and Spofford, were also on the Juilliard board and spoke highly of Schuman's administrative ability. He had a thorough knowledge of Lincoln Center through his participation in the Lincoln Center Council. Since he had often attended Lincoln Center board meetings as council representative, he was known to all members of the board. Schuman indicated that he was challenged by the position, and when the Executive Committee met again on September 5, 1961, it officially recommended the appointment of William Schuman as president. This recommendation went to the board on September 11, and he was unanimously elected president of Lincoln Center, effective January 1, 1962. He was also elected a director, effective at once, to fill the vacancy on the board created by Taylor's resignation. In choosing Schuman as its next president, Lincoln Center had consciously chosen a composer, and without any rigid part-time schedule, a portion of each week was to be reserved for Schuman, the artist. As he expressed it, Lincoln Center was employing a composer, not a "former composer."

Schuman began immediately to attend board and Executive Committee meetings. He was urged by Rockefeller to focus his attention on long-range planning for the artistic and educational activities of Lincoln Center. In succession during the fall and winter, he worked out tentative plans for a summer festival in 1966 after the conclusion of the World's Fair; for a teachers' institute as a related feature of the student program; for the development of a music theater constituent to be led by Richard Rogers; and for a film festival. He was encouraged by the board to make definite proposals concerning these plans.

Concurrently with Schuman's selection as president, Young was elected chairman of the Building Committee, ending his acting status in that post. He remained acting president until Schuman took office; then, at Schuman's request, he continued in the management as executive vice president.

One other change was made in the roster of directors and officers in the fall of 1961. Gustave L. Levy, a partner in the firm of Goldman, Sachs and Company, was elected a director on October 9, replacing Frank Altschul, who had resigned. Levy was already active in Lincoln Center's capital campaign. He had served as president of the Federation of Jewish Philanthropies. He was a member, and later became president, of the New York Stock Exchange. Levy was immediately named chairman of Lincoln Center's Investment Committee and later became treasurer of the corporation.

By January 1962, Lincoln Center had many legal questions and contracts pending with experts in the Milbank law firm, and a more systematic liaison between legal counsel and the Lincoln Center administration became essential. A member of the firm, John Mazzola, was assigned to the task on a part-time basis and was named assistant secretary of the corporation. A year later, Mazzola came to work full time for Lincoln Center. He has remained with the center and served in increasingly responsible posts of secretary, legal counsel, senior vice president, and managing director. In 1977 he was elected president of Lincoln Center.

Planning for the World's Fair Festival took immediate priority in program developments in 1961. Young met with World's Fair officers on July 17, to review the facts of Lincoln Center's building schedule. Philharmonic Hall and the New York State Theater would be ready. But delays in final plans for the opera house made its use in 1964 impossible. Completion of the Vivian Beaumont theater for 1964 was dubious, because of complications in securing legislative authorization for city financing of the library part of the combined building.

Allen felt that the buildings should be made available rent-free and fully staffed to performing artists taking part in the Fair program. An estimated $2.8 million would be needed to implement such a policy. But sources of subsidy for the festival remained uncertain. In spite of interested response from Washington officials, federal funds could not be assured until Congress acted. Approaches had been made to the Kennedy Foundation but without success. The possibility of television revenues from the Festival was intensively explored, but results were negative.

In spite of these discouraging financial prospects, Allen's contacts with performing groups were continued and were intensified by Schuman after his appointment. Their objective was an international program of 22 weeks' duration in each of the two summers of the Fair. By December 1961, no way had been found to finance the ambitious program. At that point, abandonment of the festival plan would have seemed the prudent course. But that option could not be considered seriously because it would have jeopardized the large-scale capital financial plan already accepted by the state and city administrations.[3] The Executive Committee concluded that Lincoln Center must carry through on its plans for a World's Fair Festival, but on a reduced scale, and agreed to limited deficit financing from its Fund for Education and Artistic Advancement. For the New York State Theater, the committee decided that a full two-year program must be planned with Lincoln Center as the financial underwriter, the deficit not to exceed $250,000. Festival plans for Philharmonic Hall and for the Beaumont Theater would have to be made on a self-supporting basis.

Preparation for the opening and operation of Philharmonic Hall, scheduled for September 1962, was the principal organizational development throughout that year. Allen and Powers filled key staff positions and arranged for personnel training; they conducted labor negotiations with more than half a dozen unions; they concluded contracts with concessionaires.

The attention of the center's top leadership turned to the opening events and to their public relations, a matter of major importance to successful fund raising for the completion of the center and to its long-term program objectives. The occasion was to celebrate the opening of Philharmonic Hall and of the new home for the Philharmonic orchestra, but it was also to symbolize the opening of Lincoln Center for the Performing Arts.

Seeking wide coverage for opening night, early effort was placed on securing nationwide television coverage, an objective achieved with C B S through Stanton's help. Among other advance planning decisions was that of the *New York Times* to prepare, for opening day, a special supplement to the Sunday Magazine section devoted entirely to Lincoln Center. The monthly journal, *Musical America,* also decided to feature the center in its September 1962 issue.

During these three years leading up to the opening of Philharmonic Hall, Lincoln Center had evolved from ambitious plans and high aspirations into a functioning organization. Its relations with its constituents and its coordinating mechanism were still in formation, but its leadership had been asserted and had begun to be recognized.

CHAPTER 9

The Growing Federation
1959-1962

Three institutions, the Metropolitan Opera Association, the Philharmonic-Symphony Society, and the Juilliard School of Music were firmly associated with Lincoln Center for the Performing Arts by 1959. Sponsorship was still pending for the arts of dance and drama and for the library and museum. The search for a constituent for the dance began with the New York City Ballet. In time, this led to consideration of City Center of Music and Drama, its sponsoring organization. City Center was also responsible for the New York City Opera and for presentations of drama and musical comedy. Although explorations of a basis for a City Center constituency had occurred earlier (Chapter 4, p. 58), consideration of including the whole of City Center did not reach the board until June 15, 1959. In Rockefeller's view, the advantages outweighed the disadvantages; he thought such an association would lead to improved relations with the city government and to a broader public interest in Lincoln Center. He raised three specific points and encountered no objection: city ownership of the building, eventual city financial participation in building maintenance, and a constituent committed to a low-price ticket policy. He recognized financial and administrative problems, and especially, the difficult relations with the Metropolitan Opera.

118

The gravity of those relationships, as seen by the Metropolitan, was emphasized by Anthony Bliss, opera president. Anticipating program expansion after its move to Lincoln Center, the Metropolitan considered it essential to have an integrated program for all operatic activities undertaken at the center and on tour. Bliss could foresee difficulties if opera at Lincoln Center were to be developed by two independent companies. Other directors stressed the need for unanimity on the question of whether Lincoln Center wanted City Center to become a constituent, and the board authorized an ad-hoc committee to look further into the City Center question. Rockefeller appointed Spofford, Stoddard, Olds, and Allen, with Josephs serving as chairman. He asked this group to consider "whether, if a satisfactory solution can be found to the problem of financing the building and of relationship with the Metropolitan Opera, it is reasonable and desirable to proceed with negotiations with City Center toward its becoming a constituent in Lincoln Center." They concluded that there would be positive advantages to Lincoln Center from the inclusion of City Center; specifically, this action would bring into the center a popular enterprise and would be a tangible indication that Lincoln Center exists for the benefit of people at large and not for any limited social or economic group. Rockefeller reported official word from Morton Baum indicating that City Center wished to be considered for inclusion in Lincoln Center. Baum's letter was optimistic about resolution of the financial problem. The Lincoln Center board then affirmed its belief in the desirability of bringing City Center into Lincoln Center, assuming solutions could be found to the problems of the two provisos. It authorized continued negotiations with the officials of City Center.

During the remainder of 1959 and into 1960 the focus of consideration of the City Center matter moved to the Metropolitan. Finally, at a special meeting in February the Opera board by unanimous action resolved that

(1) if and when the matter of the inclusion of City Center should come before the Board of Lincoln Center, the Metropolitan Opera Association would be pleased to have City Center join the group; and

(2) The Metropolitan Opera Association feels confident that the detailed questions which will inevitably arise with regard to the scheduling of the operatic portions of City Center's program and the program of the Metropolitan Opera will be satisfactorily worked out between the managements of the two organizations.

The opposition of the Metropolitan Opera had been overcome. The unanimous action by the directors reflected the patient diplomacy of Spofford and the optimistic and influential judgment of Mrs. Eleanor Belmont.

But their affirmative action had not come easily, for the opposition of Rudolf Bing, their General Manager, was well known. Years later he wrote about this situation.

> . . . a great policy dispute over the future of Lincoln Center was triggered by a proposal to move the New York City Center, including its opera company, into what had been projected up to then as "the dance theater." I was furiously opposed. . . .

> I thought it was simply wrong to have two opera companies operating on different systems on the same square. It would upset the box office—people could see *Traviata* for $15 at the Met or $6 only one and a half minutes away. And later people would say they had seen a shocking *Traviata* "at Lincoln Center". . . .

> It now [1972] seems clear to me that I was wrong in fighting the entry of the City Opera to Lincoln Center. There have been no particular difficulties. They have helped us and we have helped them by lending singers, and many of our most valuable artists—like Judith Raskin, Shirley Verrett, Placido Domingo, Sherrill Milnes, Donald Gramm—have been graduates of the City Opera. Productions there have considerably improved (though I hope I am permitted my continuing opinion that they are simply not in the same league as Metropolitan productions), and the company's general manager Julius Rudel has become a major figure in the musical life of America.[1]

A final solution for the financial proviso, did not come until the end of 1960 (see Chapter 10, p. 134). At that time, capital funds for the building both from the state and city seemed probable, and a new pressure was exerted to secure agreement with City Center for its participation, for the expectation that City Center would occupy the building, now referred to as the New York State Theater, was a key to the financial plan.

General Taylor reopened the negotiations with City Center early in 1961. His discussions with Newbold Morris and Morton Baum dealt first with provisions for the eventual lease of the building. The capital financial plan anticipated state ownership of the theater during the two years of the World's Fair and city ownership thereafter. Lincoln Center expected to be the primary lessee of the building under both forms of ownership and to make it available to City Center as a sub-tenant. City Center, on the other hand, wished to lease the building directly from the city as they had done for many years in the occupancy of their 55th Street house. This issue was regarded by Lincoln Center officers as one of major policy importance. They felt that all constituents of the center should be tenants under similar terms of occupancy, including acceptance of the basic Lincoln Center concept. If City Center were to become a primary lessee from the city, it would be a neighbor of Lincoln Center but not an equal participant in the center. However such an independent status was, in fact, as far as Morton Baum and his colleagues were willing to go. City Center officers sought allies for their viewpoint in Albany, at City Hall, and with Moses; Taylor, supported by Spofford and Young, carefully explained Lincoln Center's position and reasons in these same quarters. When the chips were down, the governor, the mayor, and Moses accepted the Lincoln Center position, and the enabling legislation was so drafted.

In the course of these negotiations, Taylor was also immersed in complex financial planning and in architectural issues. He was obviously challenged by the wide-ranging new situations he was called upon to handle, and he seemed to be enjoying each new puzzle or conflict. But on one occasion, when considering these matters with Young, he said, somewhat wistfully, "Ed, nothing in the Pentagon was ever so complicated!"

Concurrently with City Center developments, the search for a drama constituent was continuing. When the Advisory Council on drama was unable to find a leader to head a new organization, Spofford enlisted the interest of George D. Woods. Woods was chairman of the First Boston Corporation and was widely known in philanthropic as well as financial circles. He was a director of several large corporations and a trustee of the Rockefeller Foundation and the American Shakespeare Festival and Academy. Organization plans, developed by Woods and Spofford, in consultation with Whitehead, called for the Advisory Council to be expanded and divided into three separate functional groups: the first would become the directors of the new sponsoring corporation, the second, the professional theater advisers, the third, its fund-raising arm, comparable to the Metropolitan Opera Guild. Early in 1960 legal steps for incorporation were taken, under the name "The Repertory Theater Association, Inc." The initial incorporators and directors were Mrs. Vivian Beaumont

Allen, Howard Cullman, Spofford, Stoddard, Thomas J. Watson, and Woods. They elected Woods the president of the new institution, Stoddard vice president, and appointed Robert Whitehead as their producing director. The Lincoln Center board, on February 15, 1960, designated the Repertory Theater Association as its constituent unit for drama. Woods was elected a director of Lincoln Center, representing the new constituent, and Whitehead became a member of the Lincoln Center Council.

On Whitehead's recommendation the Repertory Theater appointed Elia Kazan as co-producing director. This action brought Kazan once again into the stream of theater planning for Lincoln Center after a year's absence following his precipitate resignation from the Advisory Council on Drama. (He had left in disagreement and anger over plans to place drama training in Juilliard. He felt that such training should be the responsibility of the drama constituent.)

During the next nine months Whitehead and Kazan laid plans for their performing company. They envisaged an acting company of 35 and the presentation of four or five plays "from the whole history of world dramatic literature" and "from the best contemporary work of all countries." They anticipated summer seasons of bookings to present "the outstanding companies of world theater." The small Forum Theater would be their experimental house.[2]

Their plans to create and train a performing company had been based on a schedule for their theater to open in 1963. By April 1962, delays in the Beaumont construction made that opening date impossible, and spring 1964 was doubtful. Woods warned the Executive Committee that delays could mean heavy additional expenses for the Repertory Theater Company beyond those to be covered by the $500,000 grant from Lincoln Center. Woods also questioned the continuing financial viability of the new group. On August 23, he was discouraged over their early fund-raising efforts and alerted Lincoln Center's Executive Committee to "real problems to be faced in the underwriting of the activities of the Repertory Theater beyond its opening night."

At this time Whitehead's greatest concern was to find a way, in view of the building delays, to maintain his schedule for the formation of a company, for its training, and for the start of public performances. By late 1962 he was on the way to a solution for that problem. (See Chapter 17, p. 243.)

Progress toward the library and museum was made as a result of studies undertaken by the New York Public Library with the consulting services of Davidson Taylor. The Library board of trustees, on June 10, 1959, officially expressed their

> desire to promote and approve in principle the establishment of the proposed Lincoln Center Library & Museum and the deposit and maintenance there of suitable portions of collections in the Music and Drama collections under the direction and control for all purposes of the New York Public Library, provided that the New York Public Library assumes no obligation to provide financial support for or incur any expense in connection with the proposed Lincoln Center Library-Museum.

Rockefeller met several times with the Library president, Gilbert Chapman, who became increasingly interested in Lincoln Center. Rockefeller proposed that Chapman be elected a director even though the question of Library constituency was not yet settled. On November 23, 1959, this was done, and Chapman became involved in both architectural and financial planning for the library and museum. Preliminary design studies indicated a building that would cost $9 million if all the library and museum functions were to be accommodated. Chapman believed this sum was beyond any reasonable expectation of financial reality. He also was concerned over the operating costs of the program in such a large building. He suggested that the specialized museum spaces be eliminated and library space be cut to reduce the proposed building by one-third. Several directors, including Stoddard and Rockefeller, were reluctant to lose the features of the museum. The matter was referred for study to the Library and Museum Committee. They reported that, despite the seriousness of the financial problem, it would not be sound to eliminate the museum function in its entirety.

A year later, General Taylor pressed for a conclusion in negotiations for the library and museum and encountered no serious problems. On February 13, 1961, he recommended, and the board approved, an official invitation to the New York Public Library to become the Library and Museum constituent. The Library officers made it clear that they wanted their institution to be a part of Lincoln Center, but they again deferred their official action until the uncertainty concerning capital financing and annual operating support by the city could be resolved.

The involvement of each independent constituent institution in Lincoln Center created new and untried relationships with Lincoln

Center, Inc. The working effectiveness of these relationships could not be established by fiat; that would have to evolve gradually over a period of years. But the legal framework for those relationships was needed at this stage of development as a basis for mutual understanding. Irving Olds and his committee were working to develop a formal contract, including a building lease, between each institution and Lincoln Center, Inc. Progress continued to be slow because of new difficulties encountered in arriving at specific financial terms for the lease of the buildings. The principle had been clear from the beginning, that Lincoln Center would not charge rent but would bill the constituents for operating costs on a breakeven basis. The constituents were to receive the full benefits of nonprofit operation, of real-estate tax exemption, and of freedom from debt-service charges. But the constituent managements wanted their leases to include specific dollar figures on operating and maintenance costs in their new homes. As the design process had evolved, they realized they would be located in buildings that would be significantly larger than their old homes, and they were deeply concerned over the inevitable mounting size of their building operating budgets. It became clear that reliable operating cost estimates would be required before any contracts with constituents could be negotiated. Allen, with some outside consulting help, undertook the task of developing preliminary estimates of the costs for maintenance and day-to-day operations.

In his contract negotiations, Olds continued to be disturbed by the underlying attitude of some of the constituent leaders who were, he felt, taking an adversary position in considering their relationship to Lincoln Center.[3] Olds persistently tried to change that atmosphere into one of partnership and cooperation, but without complete success. General Taylor pursued the same objective when he entered these negotiations in 1961. He met privately and in small groups with many of the officers and board members of the constituent institutions and of those organizations likely to become constituents. He had the advantage of coming into a strained situation as an outsider, who could be a mediator as well as an advocate. He sought to understand the concerns and fears of the constituents and to reassure them regarding the intentions and aspirations of the new Lincoln Center organization.

By the end of March, Taylor, in collaboration with Rockefeller, had worked out a common statement of objectives, understandings, and mutual responsibilities that should underlie each constituent contract. The board endorsed the document, and it was incorporated in each contract. It committed all participants in Lincoln Center "to the highest standards of artistic excellence and to the widest possible service to the public . . ." and to "a cooperative and friendly working relationship." It expressed a set of specific obligations such commitments placed on Lincoln Center, Inc. and on each constituent. The statement became the generally accepted expression of "The Lincoln Center Concept."

Contract negotiations with the Metropolitan improved. However, one sticking point remained. The charges for building use included an amount to cover a pro-rata share of the cost of Lincoln Center's administrative overhead. The Metropolitan and other constituents feared that Lincoln Center's overhead might involve expensive program innovations that they should not be called upon to subsidize, although they readily accepted their fair share of overhead related to building operating and maintenance. Taylor reached agreement by persuading the Lincoln Center board to limit its overhead charges strictly to the costs of building operation. The final agreement with the Metropolitan was signed on April 28, 1961.

This agreement recognized the Metropolitan as the primary constituent in the field of opera and committed it to a year-round lease of its building for a period of 25 years, with renewal clauses, and to full operating and financial responsibility for the building's maintenance and upkeep. Booking of outside attractions was the ultimate responsibility of the Met, with a provision for collaboration with Lincoln Center.

The change in policy with regard to overhead charges helped to expedite the negotiations with the Philharmonic, though it took several more months and some additional compromises before agreement was reached on June 12. The contract with the Philharmonic recognized its primacy in orchestral music but differed from that with the Metropolitan in its lease arrangements. The orchestra was to be only a part-time tenant of its hall, using about 35 to 40 percent of the time available. It would have prior claim on the hall for its concert dates, and Lincoln Center would be responsible for filling the free time. The Philharmonic and Lincoln Center would share, on a basis in proportion to usage, any net profit or deficit in the hall operation. A limit of $200 per concert date was placed on the Philharmonic's potential deficit obligation.

Completion of these two contracts represented more than progress in constituent relations, for they triggered the release of $10.5 million in conditional grants from the Avalon, Ford, and Old Dominion Foundations. This large cash payment immediately eased a problem of cash flow and enabled Lincoln Center to pay the bills for design developments and to make increased construction commitments without borrowing.

●━━━━━━━━━━━━━━━━━━━━━━━━━━━━━━━●

Negotiations were conducted with two other groups—educational television and the professional high schools of music and art—that sought proximity to the new center. In the late 1950s the potential role of educational television was recognized. On a national basis, the educational television headquarters in Ann Arbor, Michigan, was considering a reorganization and a move to New York City. In the New York area, efforts were underway to form an organization to sponsor and operate a public television station, resulting eventually in the creation of WNET—Channel 13. The Ford Foundation seemed willing to make major grants to help in the funding of both developments and inquired about the possible inclusion of educational television as a component of Lincoln Center. After a preliminary architectural review by Harrison, it was clear that the Lincoln Center site was not large enough to include this. The board confirmed this judgment and also decided that Lincoln Center could not assume any financial responsibility for creating a home for educational television.

However, the Board members wanted to encourage the proposed public television center to locate close to Lincoln Center. Moses favored this approach and was helpful in exploring the availability of possible sites nearby. Despite continuing encouragement from Lincoln Center and from the Ford Foundation, the public television headquarters were not located adjacent to Lincoln Center.

The public High Schools of Performing Arts and of Music and Art were natural candidates for consideration in relation to Lincoln Center's educational role. The High School of Performing Arts is located in an old building on West 46th Street. The High School of Music and Art is on the campus of the City College of New York in a building needed for college purposes. The Board of Education had already made plans to consolidate the two schools in a new building.

Juilliard's president, William Schuman, urged that the new high school of the arts be built near Lincoln Center where its faculty and students could benefit from the association with professional artists at the center. The Lincoln Center board went on record officially encouraging the Board of Education in this development and welcoming the proposed high school as a neighbor. In addition, Moses encouraged the plan, as did James Felt, chairman of the City Planning Commission, and Mayor Wagner. But this proposal was repeatedly delayed. It had to compete for funds urgently needed to expand all high school facilities. Eventually, the building was begun but then was halted in its early stage by the city's fiscal crisis of 1974. Construction was resumed in 1980.

During these three and one half years between the start of construction and completion of the first building, much of the time and effort of the leadership of Lincoln Center had been devoted to establishing the constituents. Progress was substantial, but the planned federation of six institutions was not yet final and complete. The two original members, the Metropolitan and the Philharmonic, were firmly established in their relationship to Lincoln Center. The Juilliard School and the Repertory Theater Association were officially constituents, but their contracts had not yet been completed. The New York Public Library was so far along in its planning for Lincoln Center that the absence of a formal constituent status caused no concern. The negotiations with City Center had not yet reached a basic agreement, but planning was proceeding on the assumption that City Center would eventually join. The concept of the federation had been clarified and the relationships with the constituents were beginning to develop.

CHAPTER 10

Higher Goals and Campaign Progress 1959–1962

In its first three years, the Lincoln Center campaign to raise $75 million had produced gifts and pledges of over $46 million. In addition, the city and federal governments had agreed to finance the $7 million estimated cost of the garage and public open spaces. However, a gap was growing between the construction budgets and the probable costs of building. Shortly before ground breaking a careful review of each building plan was begun in a search for economies. Although this review process was conducted with the full cooperation of each architect and of the leaders in each constituent, the results did not produce the substantial construction economies necessary to come within budget limits. In the review of the Philharmonic Hall plans, reductions were minimal, and construction had been started with knowledge that the hall would exceed its budget by 15 percent or more. Only minimal reductions could be made in the cost estimate for the Opera house, for the Opera leaders insisted that elimination of any space provided in the plans approved the preceding April would be unacceptable. Adherence to those plans was certain to bring construction costs to a point at least 15 percent beyond its budget.

Reviewing these financial problems for the board on June 1, 1959,

Spofford stated, categorically, that Lincoln Center could not be built for the $58 million construction budget provided by the $75 million campaign goal. He proposed a careful study to determine more precisely the magnitude of the gap and to appraise possible approaches to closing it. Young undertook that study and determined that the total construction budget gap would be nearly $37 million: $16.65 million was needed for those buildings which were to be financed from private contributed funds; an additional $20 million would be needed for those parts of the total project that might be financed from governmental funds.

In the analysis of possible ways to close the gap, none were found to be adequate, and all were unattractive. Nevertheless, on the strong recommendation of the Campaign Committee, the directors decided, for a second time, not to change the $75 million goal. They rejected the possible elimination of any of the planned buildings, for the opera house and the concert hall were to be built regardless of the plan for a larger center; designated pledges in hand for the repertory theater and for the chamber music hall were not transferable. The ballet theater and the library museum could, theoretically, be dropped from the project, but this would free only $3.5 million of contributed funds. Moreover, any elimination would critically damage the concept of the center and would certainly reduce the interest of major foundations in the project. They decided to explore the possibilities for further governmental support and accepted a possible mortgage of $10 to $15 million on the property.

Because none of the decisions solved the problem of the budget gap, a special Committee on Financial Policy was appointed with Spofford as chairman. Young prepared figures for the committee showing the construction timetable, the amounts needed in relation to it, and the funds that were assured to meet those obligations. The amount that had been raised at that time (September 28, 1959), after excluding designated gifts of $9.5 million, was $38 million. This sum more than covered the obligations already incurred for land and for building Philharmonic Hall and the central air-conditioning plant. Within nine months, by July 1, 1960 when construction of the Opera house should start, an additional $18.4 million would be needed to meet the total land costs and construction commitments by that date.

Clarence Francis and his campaign leaders estimated that, in the next nine months, $12.5 million additional could be raised, leaving a deficit of $5.9 million. Spofford's committee felt this could be handled by borrowing, if necessary. His committee urged that campaign efforts and publicity be placed on this short-term $12.5 million need rather than on the eventual $75 million goal. This represented a change in strategy, reflecting their conviction that concentration on annual fund-raising goals for immediate purposes would be more effective than attention to the eventual cost of the entire project.

While these financial policy studies were in process, the plans for the campaign itself were developing rapidly. A month after ground breaking, the campaign leaders proposed to conduct an enlarged corporate solicitation. Later, gifts down to a level of $1000 would be sought, and eventually a broad campaign for smaller gifts would be conducted with appeals by mail to 100,000 prospects.

The success in the campaign that had raised over $46 million by the May 1959 ground breaking was demonstrably related to the highly personalized nature of the appeals. Rockefeller and Francis had handled 101 prospects and had obtained $37 million in 42 gifts. Other directors had accepted 191 prospect assignments, resulting in 69 gifts totaling $40.5 million. Other volunteers in the campaign had taken 171 prospects, resulting in 77 gifts for a total of $4.75 million.

In the year following ground breaking, a succession of corporate and patron contributions and several foundation grants were recorded in Clarence Francis' biweekly reports to the board. The total of such gifts and pledges amounted to nearly $4 million, including 13 new pledges of $100,000 each from individuals or families and three foundation grants aggregating $1 million.

Two very large contributions came from Rockefeller family sources. One was the result of a trust, created 42 years earlier by John D. Rockefeller, Sr., grandfather of Lincoln Center's president. Formed for the benefit of his granddaughter, Muriel McCormick Hubbard, it provided for termination on her death and directed that, if she should die without "issue," the remainder be distributed to such charities as might be designated by a committee established by the trust instrument. Mrs. Hubbard died on March 18, 1959 without having had children of her own; there were, however, four adopted children. Legal counsel for the Trustee, Chase Manhattan Bank, advised that they could not be considered "issue" under the terms of the trust. The trust committee, of which John D. Rockefeller 3rd was a member, named Lincoln Center as the principal recipient charity, with a designation of the funds for the support of the Juilliard School. Meanwhile, counsel for the adopted children filed suit on their behalf. The judicial proceedings dragged on for five years, and the case was finally resolved in an out-of-court settlement in 1965, under which Lincoln Center received $9 million.[1]

The second gift was an additional $5 million from Mr. John D. Rockefeller, Jr. Earlier he had given $.5 million to the Metropolitan

Opera for its Lincoln Square site and $5 million directly to the Lincoln Center. In December, 1959, the elder Rockefeller wrote to his son, John 3rd, expressing increased interest and confidence in the plans for Lincoln Center and pledging a second $5 million. He designated half of that amount to the Fund for Education and Artistic Advancement, an action that gave financial solidity to Lincoln Center's stated intention to become an educational and artistic force.

Twelve months after ground breaking, the total raised for Lincoln Center had risen to $64.6 million. The short term objective, set eight months earlier had been exceeded. But budget needs had risen again.

* * *

To examine these new financial requirements, the Committee on Financial Policy met jointly with the Building Committee in April, 1959. A need for a larger construction contingency fund was seen. Plan changes for Philharmonic Hall and for the opera house had caused minor cost increases; a major budget increase was inevitable to build an adequate ballet theater. The two committees accepted the necessity for those larger budgets.

On May 23, 1960, in its final report to the board, the Financial Policy Committee explained the increase in capital costs. The report cited

> . . . a natural process of evolution and maturing of concept during a period of nearly five years of careful planning. Lincoln Center has learned that, in order to be modern and adequate, an opera house, a concert hall, or a theater must provide spaces and facilities for both audience and performers far in excess of the traditional provision for these purposes in New York . . . The seating capacity of theaters has remained relatively unchanged but the spaces required both backstage and in the front of the house have grown tremendously. It is this factor of growth in concept, in program requirements that has been the primary cause of the rise in capital cost estimates. The total cubage of the Lincoln Center buildings has increased 72% during its period of planning.

> To summarize, this increase of costs does not stem from extravagance but from a more realistic estimate of what we wish to achieve.

The report rejected the earlier decision to accept partial mortgage financing for any of the constituent homes. In view of the heavy building operating costs anticipated in the large new buildings, the committee felt that there could no longer be an expectation that any interest and amortization charges could be absorbed by the constituents. Any borrowing would have to be on a short-term basis as a form of deferred fund raising or limited to the financing of business or self-liquidating parts of the project.

The committee presented two major recommendations: (1) Approval of an increase to $102 million in the capital budget, to be financed through private contributions. This implied an increase to that amount in the campaign goal. (2) An increase in the governmental segment of the project to $35.2 million, representing the entire cost (rather than half) for the City Center building and for the library and museum. To these amounts was added a mortgage segment of $4.4 million, related to the commercial parts of the project. The sum of these three budgeted amounts was a new project total of nearly $142 million. The Board gave its unanimous approval to the $142 million project budget, specifically stating that "the campaign goal (for private contributions) is hereby increased to $102 million." Francis, who earlier had opposed an increase in the goal, participated in the analysis of the situation and concurred in the conclusion that no alternative course of action was feasible. Moreover, with a total of $64.6 million then raised, the campaign leaders could see that they were within sight of their original goal.

Equally important developments were occurring with respect to governmental financial participation. Until the spring of 1960 the focus had been on winning increased city support. Nelson Rockefeller, now Governor of New York State, believed in the importance of Lincoln Center to both State and City. He had become convinced that the center could not be financed entirely from private contributions even if supplemented by city funds, and he asked his confidential adviser, John E. Lockwood, to explore possibilities for state aid. Specifically, he thought there might be some way the state could, through its participation in the World's Fair, help Lincoln Center. Precedents were found in the state participation in the 1939 World's Fair a quarter century before, and on May 18, 1960, Lockwood met with John Rockefeller, Spofford, and Young to suggest that the theater planned at Lincoln Center for City Center might become a major part of New York State's participation in the 1964 World's Fair. In a few days, encouragement for governmental financing came unexpectedly from Robert Moses, who had by that time become president of the New York World's Fair Corporation. He reversed his earlier opposition and said, in a letter to Rockefeller, that he had slowly come around to the idea that the city and the state must help materially on the library and museum and the City Center Theater.

By September, the state administration expressed serious interest in applying $15 million of its funds for the World's Fair toward the costs of the theater at Lincoln Center, but only on condition that the city government would provide an equal amount toward the completion of Lincoln Center. This matching proposal was receiving support in the city administration not only from Moses, but also from his successor as city parks commissioner, Newbold Morris, who was also chairman of City Center.

The plan for city and state capital financing was crystallized in a letter sent by John Rockefeller to Mayor Wagner on September 14, 1960, specifically asking the city to match the proposed state appropriation by providing $12 million in capital funds and $3 million over a period of six years for maintenance of City Center and the library and museum. The mayor suggested that Lincoln Center invite all members of the Board of Estimate to a luncheon meeting near the center for an inspection of the site and to inform them about the financial proposal. Such a meeting was held on October 5, attended by nearly all Board of Estimate members and by Mayor Wagner and Lt. Governor Wilson. The financial plan was explained, with details

Photo by Bob Serating

Mayor Robert Wagner (center) and the Board of Estimate visit the Lincoln Center site. At left: Col. William F. Powers and Lawrence J. McGinley, S.J. At right: Clarence Francis.

on the proposed $12 million in city capital funds: $7.2 million for the library and museum, $2.75 for the City Center theater to supplement the state's $15 million, and the balance for repurchase from Lincoln Center of the land for both buildings, since they were to be owned by the city. A pictorial presentation described the plans for the entire center, emphasizing the two buildings to be publicly financed. The officials toured the site, and their interest was clearly aroused.

Meanwhile, decisions were made in Albany to channel the state funds through the State World's Fair Commission, a bipartisan group of legislative leaders and citizens appointed by the governor. Lincoln Center invited members of this commission to a luncheon meeting on December 15 to receive similar information and for personal inspection. In particular, the presentation described the proposed usage of the theater for the World's Fair, emphasizing the large foyer as a desirable place to hold state receptions and banquets. Lincoln Center suggested that the theater be named "The New York State Theater" as a lasting reminder of the state's participation.

At the city level, support for the plan came from the comptroller, the president of the City Council, and the chairman of the planning commission. But private discussion in the Board of Estimate highlighted the political pressures felt by the five borough presidents, who saw the Lincoln Center proposal in competition with local needs, such as for schools and libraries. Their hesitancy delayed action.

Disturbed by the city delay, on December 19, the governor brought together top officials of state and city with the leadership of the World's Fair Corporation and of Lincoln Center. Both the governor and the mayor reaffirmed the commitment of their administrations to the financial plan previously submitted by Lincoln Center. Action by the city was promised.

On January 9, 1961, the Lincoln Center board reviewed these developments. Inherent in the plan was the fact that Lincoln Center would have to assume the cost of short-term construction financing, for the state wanted to buy a completed building. Robert Blum, Lincoln Center's treasurer, thought short-term bank loans could be arranged. Spofford reminded the directors that if the cost of these buildings should overrun their budgets, Lincoln Center would be obligated for any excess. Of most importance, he emphasized that acceptance of funds from the city and state would commit Lincoln Center to carry through its other building plans for completion (with the exception of Juilliard) in time for the World's Fair. Woods asked how long talk on these matters could be continued and still have assurance that buildings would be ready for the fair. Spofford replied that "there was no longer any conversation time."

The question of completion of the center for the fair was one of both time and money, and there were heavy risks attached to each. The total amount raised in the campaign at this time approached $67 million. But after accounting for donor designations, an unraised gap of $18 million remained to meet the latest budgets for the opera and the repertory theater buildings. Yet agreement to proceed at once with these buildings was urgent, for the governor required a commitment in writing as a basis for his recommendation to the legislature to appropriate the $15 million.

The directors and the architects met on this issue on February 13, 1961. Though the schedule was tight, the architects thought they and the contractors could meet the time requirement. In the consideration of the financial commitment, Rockefeller voiced his view that the center could not look to its major foundation supporters for further contributions at this time, though he thought they might help later to close the campaign. Then, in an action consistent with his belief that Lincon Center must not be considered a Rockefeller project, he withdrew from the meeting and left the decision to his fellow directors. After a detailed discussion, the directors concluded, unanimously, that they should undertake the commitment requested.

Lincoln Center's firm agreement opened the door to a rapid series of developments which General Taylor pressed with state and city officials and with City Center.[2] In order to carry out the joint state and city financial plan, it was necessary for the state legislature to enact two enabling bills. The first, to authorize the state to participate and to appropriate its $15 million, was introduced in the legislature and was passed on March 24, 1961, the last day of the legislative session.[3] The second bill, to give similar authorization for the city to participate through its capital appropriations, was held up on its way to the state legislature. Since that bill was applicable only to New York City, it was necessary for the City Council to pass a home-rule message indicating city approval before the legislature in Albany could consider it. But a bitter political controversy over the creation of new judgeships had arisen between leaders in the City Council and in the state legislature. As a result, the City Council refused to pass the home rule message on the Lincoln Center bill until this controversy was resolved. The legislature adjourned before the home rule message was received from the city.

When the Executive Committee met on the Monday following, a new set of financial questions had to be faced and resolved. The issue for Lincoln Center was whether to proceed with the building of the NewYork State Theater, knowing that it might have to assume an obligation of nearly $5 million representing the city's part in the aborted plan for the building and its land. Without hesitation the Executive Committee voted to proceed with the building of the State Theater.

A contract between the State Commissioner of General Services and Lincoln Center provided for purchase by the state of the completed New York State Theater bulding for $15 million. Lincoln Center, as owner of the land, would lease it to the state for the two years of the World's Fair. The plan contemplated transfer of ownership to the city after the Fair, but the contract gave Lincoln Center protective options for lease or repurchase if the city should fail to carry out its part of the financial plan.

At the next Lincoln Center board meeting on April 10, 1961, Charles Tenney, the mayor's representative, referred to the "shattering experience" resulting from the failure of the Council to act. His office was exploring what could be done without the special bill. While no authority for the city appropriation toward the costs of the State Theater could be found, there was a definite possibility that capital funds for the library could be appropriated through an amendment to the city's capital budget. Official consideration of city financing of the library and museum was started on May 22, 1961, when Mayor Wagner brought the matter to the Board of Estimate. It took over six months to carry the plan through the succession of hearings and official approvals, but on November 28, the city Council took the final step to appropriate $7,587,000 in city capital funds for the land and building for the library and museum. The contract with the city followed the pattern of the state contract and provided for the city to purchase the completed building, thus enabling Lincoln Center to enter construction contracts.

Also in November, 1961, the effort was resumed to complete the plan for the city's share of financing of the New York State Theater. By then, the political impasse over new judges had been resolved. The draft of legislation to be submitted to Albany spelled out the authority for the city to lease the theater after the fair to Lincoln Center on a long-term basis. It also authorized, but did not require, Lincoln Center to sublease it to City Center. This provision provoked a new controversy with the leaders of City Center. They wanted the legislation to require Lincoln Center to sublease the building to them. While Lincoln Center was firm in its desire to have City Center become a constituent, negotiations to that end were still pending, and there was no certainty as to their outcome. Therefore, Lincoln Center wanted permissive, rather than mandatory, legislation, a viewpoint that was accepted by city officials and prevailed in the legislation.

The City Council adopted the necessary home rule message; the state legislature passed the authorizing bill, and it was signed by the governor on April 24, 1962.[4] Once again, the procedural steps for city funds had to be undertaken by the various city bodies. On August 30, 1962, the City Council gave final approval to an amendment to the capital budget to provide $4,383,000 toward the cost of the New York State Theater building and its land.

Two years of patient and persistent efforts on the part of Mayor Wagner and other city officials and by the leaders of Lincoln Center finally resulted in complete fulfillment by the City of its part in the capital funding for Lincoln Center.

During this period, new approaches were formulated in the campaign for voluntary contributions. Clarence Francis developed a plan to seek contributions from foreign groups and foreign governments, first in Latin America. After a year of effort and no results, he turned toward Europe and secured a major gift from the Federal Republic of Germany. In June, 1961, Chancellor Konrad Adenauer wrote Rockefeller that the German Bundestag had approved a gift of $2.5 million to Lincoln Center, designated toward the completion of the Metropolitan Opera House.[5] Requests for gifts were made to numerous other foreign groups and governments resulting in contributions, at later dates, from Austria, Italy, and Japan. A common theme characterized the rationale for the foreign gifts. Each was an expression of thanks for American generosity in postwar friendship and reconstruction. It was ironic that foreign gifts came only from former enemy countries.

At the beginning of 1960, the general campaign was expanded to a wider public; a plan was developed known as the "Seat Endowment Campaign" with special recognition of gifts of $1000 or more. For each such gift, a small plaque would be placed on a seat in one of the Lincoln Center halls, indicating either the name of the donor or a commemorative name. In the course of the campaign 2558 seats were endowed with gifts aggregating over $3 million.[6] In efforts to broaden the base of giving, the campaign was extended to the suburbs, and a direct-mail appeal for smaller gifts produced 8,848 gifts amounting to a total of a half-million dollars.

However, the campaign continued to concentrate on major donors. In the fall of 1961, Francis announced plans to ask approximately 500 contributors for repeat gifts, as a first step in a gradual move to close the capital campaign. For this effort, the campaign organization was strengthened by appointment, as co-chairmen, of three people deeply involved in the center: Gilbert Chapman, president of the New York Public Library, Mrs. Robert Hoguet, Jr., a member of the Philharmonic board, and Gustave Levy, a director and treasurer. On May 14, 1962 the "Completion Campaign" was officially launched to raise the $28.6 million still needed to reach the private contribution goal of $102 million. Goals were set: $2.5 million would be sought from corporations, $1.5 million from suburban campaigns, $2 million from seat endowment gifts, $9 million from individuals. The balance of $13.6 million would be requested from the major foundations.

At this time, Rockefeller considered his personal relationship as a donor to Lincoln Center. On July 6, 1962, he wrote a confidential letter to Spofford, in which he pledged to give $2.5 million toward the completion needs and an additional $1.5 million as a special gift outside the campaign goal to enable Lincoln Center to take action in relation to essential unbudgeted needs or opportunities. As examples, he said, "I think particularly of the needs of the repertory drama company, and the real estate problems relating to the rounding out of the Juilliard site."

In his pledge letter, Rockefeller expressed again his feelings and concerns about his own and his family's financial relationship to Lincoln Center:

Let me say finally, that I feel somewhat distressed when I occasionally hear of people referring to Lincoln Center as a Rockefeller project. While I am proud and happy to be associated with Lincoln Center, the Center has come about as a result of the efforts of many able and devoted people. The last thing that my family or I would want is that it be considered as a monument to one name.

The Completion Campaign began to build its own momentum, with new gifts and pledges reported at each board meeting. By September 23rd, 1962, the date for the opening of Philharmonic Hall, the total raised in the campaign had been pushed to $76.5 million, comfortably over the original goal of $75 million. The governmental commitments (federal, state, and city) had reached $40 million, completing that part of the capital plan. Of the budgeted need for $142 million, $116.5 million, or 82 percent, was assured. In the three-year period between Lincoln Center's ground breaking and its first opening, these financial goals and results, unprecedented for the performing arts, had been raised in a saga of funds versus need, of political negotiation, and of stubborn confidence.

CHAPTER 11

Construction Underway
1959-1962

In the weeks immediately following ground breaking, the architects began to work on the problem of the crowded northwest corner in the site plan. The breakthrough occurred in a collaboration between Eero Saarinen and Gordon Bunshaft, design architects for the repertory theater and for the library and museum. Their solution was to combine their two buildings into a single structure that placed the major part of the library above the theater auditorium and wrapped it around the higher stage house. As a result, the small open area in front of the theater was doubled in size, the opera gained a green park on its north side as well as to its south, and Juilliard was provided a front on the main campus. The pedestrian bridge over 65th Street, which tied the Juilliard site to the original three-block area, was expanded in width to relate to the larger North Plaza. The combined theater and library building became a more impressive structure than either could have been separately. Its setting at the head of the enlarged North Plaza gave it a distinguished location and assured it an important place in the Center. Saarinen presented the plan to Mrs. Vivian Beaumont Allen, who had earlier indicated strong disapproval of the location of "her" theater. She was impressed by the new plan and accepted it.

Concurrently, Philip Johnson initiated several changes and refinements in the concept of the main entrance area, which was soon

The design architects, Harrison, Johnson, Belluschi, Saarinen, Abramovitz, Bunshaft.

designated Lincoln Center Plaza. He proposed porticoes on the front of both Philharmonic Hall and the dance theater, a change that significantly improved the facades of the two facing buildings and created a visual processional approach to the opera house. The other architects concurred in the proposal, recognizing also that the resulting narrowed plaza provided a better relationship to the opera facade. The architects moved the front of the opera house a few feet eastward to improve the proportions of the whole plaza and of the passages to the park areas flanking the opera. The eastern end of the plaza remained open to Columbus Avenue and Broadway, maintaining the relationship to the city desired by the architects at their first meeting.

Subsequently, Johnson was asked to develop a plan for the plaza pavement pattern. He proposed a series of concentric circles with spokes of travertine and a dark aggregate in the intervening spaces.[1] The panel of architects then recommended that the central feature of the plaza be a fountain, which Johnson designed. The estimated cost of the fountain was $200,000, an item not included in the capital budget of either the city or Lincoln Center. A special gift from the Revlon Foundation permitted it to be built.

The new site plan with its combined building and revised plazas was exciting and architecturally sound. However, it posed new legal problems because, in making their site plan changes, the architects had blithely moved parts of Lincoln Center buildings on to city land. Moreover, the combined theater and library building put into one structure a facility to be owned by Lincoln Center (the theater) and one to be owned by the city (the library.) In spite of these complications, Rockefeller argued that the merits of the plan warrented a major effort to secure its adoption. The board concurred and approved the plan on July 13, 1959. Successful negotiations with the city resulted in a new contract, approved without opposition by the Board of Estimate, that revised the boundaries between Lincoln Center and city land and treated the combined building as a condominium, so that each owned different areas on the several floor levels of the building.

The new site plan also required revision in the detailed plans for the garage complex, including the vehicular and pedestrian covered passages as well as the bridge and the plazas. These changes increased cost estimates from $7 million to $10.15. Since this complex was to be built by the city with two-thirds of its financing provided through a

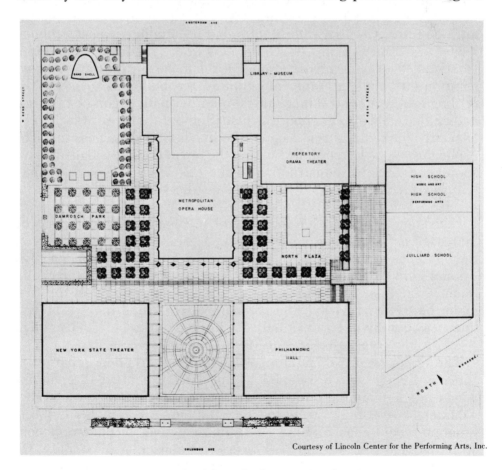

Courtesy of Lincoln Center for the Performing Arts, Inc.

The final Lincoln Center site plan.

federal urban renewal grant-in-aid, an increase in the amount of this grant was essential. Any shortfall in the public financing of this part of the project would become the responsibility of the center. Therefore, negotiations in Washington were undertaken by Rockefeller and Nelson, and in January, 1961, federal approval of the increased grant-in-aid was received.

Planning for heating and air conditioning in the Lincoln Center buildings was an engineering problem with architectural overtones. Three related but separate systems would be required to provide heat, to chill water for air conditioning, and to provide air distribution. The ventilation system involved fans and ducts that could best be designed separately in the engineering for each building. But heat could be supplied most simply and economically by buying steam from Consolidated Edison Company. Their rate structure made it advantageous to have one central steam distribution plant for the entire center. Chilled water could also be produced most economically in a central plant. Its equipment would require two different locations, one at or below ground level to house the large, heavy compressors, and the other atop one of the buildings to house the cooling tower. A central mechanical plant for both steam distribution and chilled water production was placed under the North Plaza to be as nearly equidistant from each of the five buildings as possible. The cooling tower was eventually built on the top of the opera house above shop spaces. Since construction of the opera was delayed, a small temporary cooling tower was placed on the vacant Juilliard site to service Philharmonic Hall in its first two years of use.

Budgetary provision for the central mechanical plant had to be increased as its cooling capacity grew to meet the increased size of the buildings of the center. In the original $75 million campaign goal, a lump sum of $2 million was provided for mechanical and maintenance facilities, and office space. By February, 1959, in the first major budgetary revision, the mechanical plant had its own budget line at $3.5 million. Its eventual cost worked out to be $3.71 million.

The organization for administering the construction program of Lincoln Center was developed by the first executive director for construction, General Otto Nelson, who served on a part-time, volunteer basis. By 1959 he felt that the center's complex building program would soon require a full-time engineer in charge of construction, and Col. William F. Powers was chosen as his deputy. He began to work for Lincoln Center a few weeks before ground breaking and rapidly assumed many of Nelson's responsibilities. But Nelson was so involved in negotiations with the Federal Housing and Home Finance Agency that he was persuaded to continue his official relationship with Lincoln Center until October 1960, when agreements were reached on the grant-in-aid to the city for the garage complex. At that time, Powers was appointed Executive Director for Construction.

Powers was a West Point graduate and a retired officer of the Army Corp of Engineers; his experience had involved supervision of large and complex building projects. He maintained quality standards, prodded to adhere to schedules, and established an effective system to keep track of budget authorizations and construction commitments. He was both fair and firm in his dealings with architects and contractors, and the directors could rely on the accuracy of his reports, whether the news was good or bad.

Powers operated with only a small staff throughout the years of building. A general assistant, Thaddeus Crapster, was employed in January, 1961. He had worked with Harrison and Abramovitz in their early design work for Lincoln Center and became the principal liaison between the Lincoln Center construction office and each of the architects. He also served as secretary of the Building Committee and of its several subcommittees. As each building entered the actual construction stage, a construction engineer was added to Powers' staff to function as the owner's primary liaison with the contractors.

The general contractor to build the center was chosen at the end of 1958 when the joint venture, composed of the Fuller, Turner, Walsh, and Slattery companies, was retained. Philharmonic Hall and the central mechanical plant were built by them. But, in the summer of 1962 when construction began on the New York State Theater and on the building for the theater and library, the relationship with the joint venture came under a critical review, precipitated by its high bid to construct the theater and library building. This situation, aggravated by problems of cost control on Philharmonic Hall, disturbed the officers of Lincoln Center. They felt that construction of the center was suffering from "committee management" on the part of its contractor. Within the joint venture, several of the company executives were questioning the benefits of their own association. Moreover, Moses' original reason for urging Lincoln Center to retain a joint venture was no longer operative, for the city had let its contracts for building the garage complex without using the joint venture.

In considering problems related to the joint venture, impartial advice was needed from someone with a thorough understanding of the New York construction scene. Young sought counsel from Carl Morse, head of the Diesel Construction Company which was then completing the building of the Pan American building. In addition to his responsibilities with his company, he served as a consultant and owner's representative on several construction projects elsewhere in the country. Morse was challenged by Lincoln Center's building and cost control problems. He had further discussions with Spofford, Rockefeller, Woods, and Olds and then offered his services to Lincoln Center. He offered to give 20 percent of his personal time and the expertise of the top people in his organization on a "pro-bono-publico" basis.

Morse was appointed a member of the Building Committee, where he was brought into all the dealings with the architects, contractors, and constituent leaders. He immersed himself in all of Lincoln Center's construction matters and quickly concluded that the center should deal directly and exclusively with a separate contractor for each building. On July 26, the Building and Executive Committees decided that Philharmonic Hall and the central mechanical plant would be finished under the contract with the joint venture. Upon completion of those buildings, Lincoln Center would terminate its contract with the joint venture. The Turner Construction Company would build the New York State Theater and the theater and library building. The George A. Fuller Company would build the opera house, and in the future, Walsh Construction Company would build Juilliard.

PHILHARMONIC HALL

The building of Philharmonic Hall was characterized by pressures to maintain a schedule for opening and successive struggles to contain costs. The plan to demolish Carnegie Hall established 1961 as the target date to open the new hall. At the time of ground breaking, plans were incomplete, and the initial contract had to be limited to rough excavation. This meant that the hall would have to be built while its design and engineering was still in process, and it was impossible to impose a contractual limit on the cost of the completed building.

The effort to meet the 1961 opening date set deadlines for completion of plans, the award of subcontracts, and actual construction. The first deadline called for the architect and his engineers to provide, within four months, the working drawings for finished excavation and foundations. This objective was not met, for Abramovitz proposed significant changes to improve his overall design. Addition of the plaza portico required a major structural change, as did restoration of

12 feet in the width of the building, cut out earlier for economy. The other architects supported this proposal; Johnson especially favored the added width, for it would mean that his building across the plaza, matching the Philharmonic in mass, could also be wider, a change he needed badly for functional reasons. The Building Committee approved the change, although it added $400,000 to the building cost. Another decision was required on the use of glass in the outer walls of the building. Earlier, glass on the walls facing the plaza had been agreed upon. But the amount of glass or stone on the other faces of each building had been left for recommendation by each architect. Abramovitz strongly urged that the side walls of the concert hall as well as the front be entirely of glass. This would increase capital costs by $200,000 and would add operating costs equivalent to $50.00 per concert. Houghton, speaking for the Philharmonic, considered the operating cost differential so minimal that he felt the decision should be an architectural one. The Building Committee was impressed by the architectural considerations and approved the proposal for glass side walls. The added cost of the portico, the wider building, and the glass sidewalls, was just under $750,000, a sum that could be absorbed in the contingency allocation.

The Building Committee was jolted two weeks later when Abramovitz brought in a new cost estimate for the completed hall, as prepared by the joint venture contractors, of $14.2 million, an increase of $3.6 million above the comparable estimate of six months earlier. The volume of the building had been increased by nearly one million cubic feet, or 27 percent. Not only was it wider, but on the recommendation of the acousticians, it was higher. The structure had become more complex, and the quality of materials specified had been raised. With their new estimate, however, the contractors proposed possible economies which, if all were adopted, could save nearly $1.3 million.

Consideration of these and other possible economies required a series of review sessions by the new Philharmonic subcommittee of the Building Committee. After six months, the budget overage had been reduced by $1 million, and on April 18, 1960, the subcommittee recommended a budget authorization of $13.17 million. The Building Committee was satisfied that their standards of quality and of public and artistic service could not be met for less, and they approved the higher budget. Where the money for this increase was to be found was still an unresolved question. The Committee on Financial Policy, also under Spofford's chairmanship, was in the midst of its analysis of Lincoln Center's overall capital cost problem, and it would be another month before that committee would have definitive proposals for the board.[2]

Meanwhile, the Philharmonic review process had again delayed the timetable for working drawings for the completed building. Excavation and foundation pourings were proceeding on schedule, and in order to avoid a halt in construction, commitments of $5.5 million were authorized so that contracts could be let for the structural frame, for elevators and escalators, and for other major equipment items. Maintaining the construction schedule continued to be the controlling factor. To overcome progressive slippage on the schedule, Powers proposed to buy out all subcontracts during the summer as rapidly as plans and specifications became available. The Philharmonic subcommittee agreed, accepting the financial risk of an indefinite final cost.

A continuous effort to control costs did not prevent one increase after another during the summer of 1960. A serious error in a subcontractor's budget estimate for the cost of travertine was discovered when bids, ranging from 50 percent to 70 percent above the budget estimate, were submitted and rejected. The negotiations for the travertine contract involved more than price and budgetary problems. Travertine is available only from the ancient quarries outside of Rome. When it became known in the trade that Lincoln Center was to be built with this imported material, the Indiana Limestone Institute and the Building Stone Institute launched a campaign involving members of Congress, to bring pressure to use Indiana limestone. On the second invitation for bids, the contractors were asked to submit an alternate price for limestone. The architects continued to advocate travertine, although a modest saving seemed possible by using the alternate. One supplier then submitted a travertine proposal based on having the cutting and finishing of the marble done in Italy, and his price was competitive with the limestone bids. But this possibility provoked threats of a strike and picketing on the job if the cutting and finishing of the material were not done by American workmen. The final outcome was a new proposal only 25 percent above the budget and providing for the finished marble work to be done in domestic shops. On this basis the Building Committee confirmed the plan for the use of travertine.

Another cost increase of $74,000 was encountered when the quantities of steel reinforcing bars required in the concrete work for lower parts of the building proved to be substantially more than had been estimated by the engineers. These and other unavoidable increases in cost had reached a total of about $800,000 above the last authorized budget by September 1960. Moreover, in an effort to keep on schedule for opening in the late fall of 1961, an unbudgeted expenditure for overtime labor was anticipated at the end of construction. Fortuitously, an answer came from a development outside of Lincoln Center. The "Save Carnegie Hall" movement had succeeded, and the Philharmonic could remain at Carnegie one more year. It was decided to postpone the opening until 1962.

The more reasonable schedule removed the time pressure in reaching construction and financial decisions, but a number of small changes related to the comfort of the public added to costs. For example, drinking fountains had been planned only in the restrooms. The customs of audiences clearly indicated their expectation of drinking fountains in the general public areas. The architect was directed to make provision for them. The preliminary plan had not provided a marquee to give a sheltered entrance from the Broadway-Columbus Avenue frontage. None of the architects liked marquees. But the constituent managements did not share the architects' confidence in the use of the longer underground routes. Finally, the issue was resolved by an owner's directive to design marquees.

The heart of the building was the auditorium itself. Its basic design had been largely determined before ground breaking and remained substantially unchanged. The dominant acoustical feature was a system of 106 sound-reflecting "clouds" suspended from the ceiling over both the stage and the audience areas. They were so constructed that the precise angle of suspension could be adjusted after musical testing. Clouds hanging over the orchestra were attached to a large movable frame that could be raised or lowered to create different projection and reverberant effects for different types of music. The highest position was for use when the organ, located at the back of the stage, was to be played.

In the fall of 1960 after attending the opening of the O'Keefe Center in Toronto, Abramovitz felt that the interior appearance of Philharmonic Hall would suffer by comparison. Representatives of the Philharmonic-Symphony Society, who had also attended the Toronto opening, concurred. Abramovitz proposed wood paneling on the auditorium walls at an added cost of $125,000 to $150,000. The question remained unsettled until February 23, 1961, when the Building Committee gave a negative answer, because, by that date, the cumulative budget overage for Philharmonic Hall had risen to $2.2 million.

Notwithstanding the prolonged period of design and increased costs, the actual construction of Philharmonic Hall proceeded with remarkable smoothness. During the winter of 1959 and through 1960, the structural shell gradually rose and the columnar rhythm of the building took shape. By June 14, 1961, the structure was topped out.

Photo by Bob Serating

Philharmonic Hall under construction. Garage and plaza in foreground, (May 1961).

Nearly a year later, when the canvas cover that had sheathed it during the winter was removed, a nearly completed building was revealed.

Because of the innovative features in the acoustical design of the hall, Leo Beranek, the adviser, had requested a period for testing and "tuning" the hall well in advance of opening; a "tuning week" was scheduled for May 1962. While much of the hall interior was still unfinished, all of its acoustical elements were in place. But the Philharmonic did not want an actual audience to be present for the acoustical testing. As a substitute, the acousticians used "instant people," sheets of fiberglass in all the seats to simulate the acoustical presence of people. Interspersed among the instant people were a number of dummy heads with electronic ears. A listening panel included William Schuman and the conductors Eric Leinsdorf and Leopold Stokowski.

On May 28, the Philharmonic players assembled for the first time on their new stage. Their musical director, Leonard Bernstein, was ill. After the opening shot from a 12-gauge cannon, to test reverberation, an assistant conductor, Seiji Ozawa, mounted the podium, raised his baton, and signaled the first musical sounds within the first building of Lincoln Center. During the tuning week, the orchestra played each day; different positions on stage were tried; the overhead canopy of clouds was adjusted; the sound reflective and absorptive surfaces were tested. Measurements and records were assembled.

Reactions to tuning week recognized problems that needed correction, but most of the experts believed that, basically, the hall had fine acoustical properties. Two weeks later Beranek presented the results of his analysis of the problems and his recommendations to the Building Committee. Additional clouds and panels between many of the clouds were recommended; sound-absorbing materials were needed on rear walls to eliminate an echo; shaped sound reflectors were needed behind the stage screen. These changes were estimated to cost $250,000, and the only available funds were in the contingency reserve which had already dropped to a perilously low point. The committee weighed the risks of mediocre acoustics in this building against the financial problem and agreed to proceed with all the recommended changes. The acoustical changes produced dust and noise that prevented completion of the organ. Delays imposed on many finishing trades by the acoustical changes and by a strike in the aluminum industry resulted in a rush of work just before opening that called for $300,000 in overtime wages.

With two weeks remaining until opening, Young assured the board that the public areas of the hall would be finished and ready. The backstage area would be usable but without its final coat of paint and other finishing touches; Philharmonic Society offices would not yet be completed. All remaining work could be done gradually after opening without the necessity for overtime charges. But the pressure of those last two weeks caused out-of-sequence operations and last-minute changes. The result was a further expenditure of $175,000. After the opening the directors considered these extra costs as an investment that paid off in the success of the opening of Lincoln Center.

METROPOLITAN OPERA HOUSE

The Metropolitan Opera House was to be not only the largest, but also the dominant, architectural feature of the center. Chronologically, Philharmonic Hall had to be built first, but the three-year period of its construction was, for the opera house, a time of continuing design. By the time of ground breaking, Wallace K. Harrison, the Metropolitan architect for over a quarter of a century, had ready a concept for the outer shell of the building involving a feature that was to survive to the final design: the facade of five great arches from which barrel vaults spanned the auditorium. In this first design, the roofline behind the proscenium became a huge curving surface, enclosing the higher levels of the stagehouse and swooping upward to become the eastern face of an office building tower. This design was dramatic—and controversial. Harrison himself was not satisfied with it, and shortly after ground breaking, he withdrew it and worked on alternatives in more rectilinear forms.

Through that summer and early autumn, Harrison developed his design, retaining the five front arches, but enclosing them in a level roof line that was carried back in a horizontal surface to cover both the auditorium and the stagehouse. The arch treatment of the facade was carried around both sides of the building, and at the western end, the office tower was designed as a simple high-rise structure which would also accommodate all of the opera shops, rehearsal spaces, and the central cooling tower.

With the recommendation of the panel of architects and of the Building Committee, this design went to the full board of Lincoln Center on November 9, 1959. C. D. Jackson, representing both the Building Committee and the New House Committee of the Metropolitan, endorsed the plan. "It has style and excitement and creates the atmosphere of a great temple. Its massive columns and arches establishes its own virility." The board approved the design, as did the Opera board. A crucial architectural matter seemed settled. But such was not the case, for subsequent detailed planning and major cost considerations required many further changes.

Detailed interior planning occurred during the next two months, with much attention given to the auditorium. On January 26, Harrison presented plans providing a seating capacity of 3642 plus provision for 260 standees. A primary objective was to provide a maximum number of seats with clear sight lines to the entire stage. But the Metropolitan insisted on boxes along the sides of the auditorium, and a full stage view is not possible from all side-box seats. The final design kept the number of partial-view seats significantly smaller than in the old house. Harrison's design also achieved another feature desired by the Metropolitan: sight lines from every seat in the house to permit a view of the conductor.

Devereaux Josephs and his opera subcommittee were most concerned at that time with cost estimates. Harrison's plans were developed far enough for the joint venture contractors to give a rough estimate of $32 million, one-third above the official budget and about 10 percent over the more realistic figure unofficially accepted by the Committee on Financial Policy. In spite of the budget overage, Josephs and his committee felt the only wise course was to authorize development of final plans within a $32 million budget ceiling. Any other course would have meant scrapping the entire scheme and beginning anew or eliminating facilities considered by the Opera to be essential. However, more detailed plans brought further cost escalation—this time by $4 million. Harrison then cut out considerable space by lowering the level of the roof and leaving the stagehouse as a projection. He rearranged some rehearsal rooms and opera office spaces. In October, detailed estimates totaled $34 million. In the judgment of the architect and of the Opera subcommittee, the revisions in the opera design had reached a point of diminishing returns, and no further major economies were to be found. While this budget would have to be considered in the revision of planning then underway by the Financial Policy Committee, the board was asked to give its approval to the design so that there would be no delay in proceeding with working drawings. Already, so much time had passed that a 1963 opening had become impossible, and there was a new pressure to open in the spring of 1964, in conjunction with the opening of the World's Fair. The board gave the approval requested.

While Harrison worked with his engineers to convert his preliminary design into detailed drawings, he made many further changes. But, as his plans were refined, Harrison grew more concerned about budgetary matters. In April, 1961, he told the Building Committee that he feared another cost overrun and advocated a contingency reserve of as much as $3 to $4 million.

Shocking news, worse than Harrison had feared, came from the contractors in May. The estimate was $11 million over the budget. The magnitude of the overrun was so great that no minor cuts could approach the budget. The estimate for stage equipment had doubled from $2.5 million to $5 million. The largest overages were in structural estimates, as illustrated by those for the office tower. As designed, it would cost $49 per square foot, whereas the economic breakeven point for such rental space was $30 per square foot.

In response to this problem, Josephs gave Harrison ten weeks to recommend what he considered the best opera house that could be built for $34 million. This directive gave him a free hand, if necessary without regard for the wishes of the Opera management, to make such cost and design revisions for both exterior and interior considered necessary to meet the budget.

Harrison immediately sought the advice of two other Lincoln Center architects, Belluschi and Bunshaft, and also of Donald Oenslager. They concluded that nearly one-third of the cubage would have to be cut. The office tower had to go, and Harrison went to work on a more compact arrangement of the opera shops and rehearsal spaces. He met his redesign deadline, and, on June 30, he presented a revised scheme that reduced the size of the whole building from 14.5 million cubic feet to 11 million. Deep and costly excavation had been avoided by changing the stage elevators from electric to hydraulic, the rear stage had been eliminated, and the entire backstage area greatly reduced in size. Bing and Krawitz insisted that the rear stage was essential and that other backstage spaces were cramped and would have to be substantially enlarged to accommodate the necessary dressing rooms, set storage, and other facilities.

It was evident that some compromises would have to be made, but there was no time for further redesign before reaching a decision to proceed with the building. The time pressure came from the agreement with the governor to complete Lincoln Center in time for the World's Fair.[3] Delays caused by the opera redesign had already made a 1964 opening impossible, and subsequent discussions with the governor had changed the commitment for a functioning opera house to one of a completed exterior on the plaza facade by the opening date of the fair. Construction had to begin promptly to meet even this limited objective. An additional pressure for immediate action was the expectation of a rise in the price of steel at an early date.

To meet this situation, Josephs requested authorization from the board for the Building Committee to order excavation and purchase of steel for an opera house costing no more than $35 million, to be built in accord with such design as would later be approved by the Opera subcommittee. Although Bliss warned that, in a number of respects, the interior plans were unacceptable to the Opera and that solutions for some problems would involve expenditure beyond the $35 million limit, the board accepted those risks and authorized the immediate construction commitments.

During the next month with Krawitz' help, Harrison made further changes in the plans that met the approval of the opera people except for an unresolved problem concerning the nature and cost of stage equipment. With an allowance of $3.5 million for this item, the total estimate for the opera house was $37.4 million. Through other budgetary adjustments related to the cooling tower, the Building Committee had found ways to augment the previous $35 million budget ceiling by $1.35 million. Thus the plans as developed were within approximately $1 million of the budget authorizations.

In September, Josephs urged the board to proceed on the plans thus prepared and to defer action on the $1 million deficit to a later date. At the end of a long and thoughtful debate, the board approved Josephs' recommendation, and excavation for the opera building was started in October, 1961.

Harrison was not yet satisfied with his exterior design, which had become less grand during reductions in the size of the building. He revised it once more, using a system of vertical, travertine-covered fins on all four sides. The Opera board was not pleased with this plaza facade, and Harrison did not push for its approval. He returned to his earlier plan of five arches for the facade, but kept the system of vertical fins on the sides and rear of the building. This new concept was unanimously approved by the Lincoln Center board on December 11, 1961 and somewhat later by the Metropolitan board. This became the exterior design of the opera house as actually built.

Responsibility for construction of the opera house was given to the Fuller Construction Company. Its chairman, Lou Crandall gave it his personal attention, and his involvement was a key factor to its success throughout the building period. He and Harrison had been an effective team in the building of the United Nations headquarters, and the same relationship served Lincoln Center in the building of the opera house.

Crandall negotiated with his subcontractors throughout the summer of 1962 in an attempt to get firm bids within the previous budget authorization of $37.4 million. His most serious problem occurred in the category of stage equipment, for which an allowance of $3.5 million had been provided. Bids from several European manufacturers ranged between $6 and $9 million, including electric stage elevators, which the opera management again insisted upon. No American firm would bid on the entire stage equipment contract because of the specification for electric stage elevators. Eventually, one American firm submitted a proposal at approximately $4 million, but with a requirement that the stage elevators be hydraulic. The opera withdrew its insistence on electric elevators, and the contract was awarded to the American firm.

When the Building Committee met on September 5, 1962, Crandall reported success in all his subcontract negotiations. He had, at that time, firm estimates for three-fourths of the trades involved in the construction, and barring unforeseen difficulties on the remaining trades, it appeared that the opera house could be built within its budget. This note of encouragement added to the sense of accomplishment that was surrounding the approaching opening of Lincoln Center's first building.

NEW YORK STATE THEATER

At the start of Lincoln Center construction in 1959, the theater for the dance (later named New York State Theater) had a lower priority in both schedule and financial provision than was accorded the homes for the Metropolitan, the Philharmonic, and Juilliard. With later developments, the State Theater became the second of the center's buildings to be completed and was opened in 1964. As early as October, 1957, Philip Johnson had been asked to undertake preliminary studies for the design of a dance theater. He worked with Lincoln Kirstein and George Balanchine, whose company, the New York City Ballet, most likely would become the resident company. The major space requirements were quickly established, and Johnson moved to design the interior of the house. In certain details, such as a special stage floor built with springs, their requirements were complex. But their needs for stage mechanisms and equipment were simple by comparison with the elaborate technology considered necessary in a modern opera house. Their new house had to be adequate, musically, for an orchestra in the pit, and the architect was asked to bring the back of the house closer to the stage than a traditional horseshoe plan permitted. Seating arrangements should provide a large number of seats with downward sight lines, desirable for watching ballet. The democratic tradition of their City Center home carried over in a specification that there should be no boxes. Kirstein and Balanchine had a clear conception of the atmosphere they wanted for the audience areas for the theater, based on their European background and experience with traditional opera houses as the customary setting for ballet. Balanchine particularly wanted to stress a festive atmosphere with a commodious promenading area and a grand staircase, "where beautiful women could be seen to advantage."

Johnson agreed with their goals. He was, at that time, involved in the restoration and refurbishing of the old Academy of Music in Philadelphia. This beautiful and beloved home of the Philadelphia Orchestra embodies the characteristics of many European opera houses, and Johnson's respect for its virtues had grown with his work on the project. For the Dance Theater in Lincoln Center, he accepted the challenge of treating these traditional concepts in simple, contemporary terms. The elliptical shape of the auditorium with its rings of balconies was worked out very early, and an exterior concept, pictured in the renderings used in 1960 to support the request for state financing was suggestive of the building as actually built.

Because of the uncertainties concerning the financial provision for this building and its constituent tenant, design work was temporarily halted shortly after ground breaking. In the fall of 1960, the plan for $15 million in state funds as a part of the state's participation in the World's Fair was under serious consideration. Since this financial plan required that the State Theater be completed and ready for use when the Fair opened in April, 1964, architectural planning was resumed in September, with a schedule for completion of the preliminary design by March 1, 1961, and for a start of construction in early 1962.

The preliminary design that existed at the resumption of planning was submitted to the joint venture contractors for a rough cost estimate. With a volume of 5.7 million cubic feet, their estimate came in at nearly $20 million. This was $2.85 million more than the state and city financial plan called for, but at this early stage of design, Johnson was hopeful he could bring the cost down to the budget. As finally established in June, 1961, the budget for the State Theater was $18,225,000 plus an additional reserve of $875, 000 for contingencies during construction.

Spofford appointed a building subcommittee for the theater with Father McGinley and Young representing Lincoln Center. Although the City Center was not officially a constituent, its board members, Kirstein, Morton Baum, and Joseph B. Martinson were named as members.

During the committee's first reviews of Johnson's design proposals, agreement was reached that seating on the orchestral level would follow the continental plan—without aisles but with rows of seats spaced sufficiently far apart for easy entry from the sides of the auditorium. Another feature of the design was an unusually large promenade area suitable for receptions and banquets. This was a facility that Governor Rockefeller and Lt. Governor Wilson had felt would be desirable to accommodate special state functions during the period of the World's Fair.

Johnson and his associate, Richard Foster, met their scheduled deadline for preliminary plans by the end of March. With numerous minor changes they were able to bring the estimated cost within the total of the authorized budget figures. The plans were approved on June 9 by the Building Committee.

The contract with the State of New York called for one more step of official approval of plans by a committee composed of the Lt. Governor, the state commissioner for general services and the president of Lincoln Center. A week later, Young, the acting president of Lincoln Center, took the large roll of blueprints to Lt. Governor Wilson's small New York City office on 55th Street. There, in an act as amusing as it was official, the plans were spread out on the floor, and the Lt. Governor, the commissioner, General Courtland Van Schuyler, and Young crawled about initialing each one of nearly 100 drawings. Public announcement of the plans for the New York State Theater was made at the end of June 1961. Johnson and his engineers moved immediately into the preparation of working drawings. In order to gain a head start on construction, the Building Committee decided to let a contract for excavation and for an advance purchase of steel. Excavation was started on September 11 under a contract that was awarded at a savings of $90,000 below the budget.

During the winter of 1961 and 1962 the excavation was finished, and the working drawings for the complete building were prepared and coordinated. By April 1962, the cost estimate, based on the complete plans and specifications, had risen to $20,470,000, exceeding the authorized budget by $1.37 million. To save time, without waiting for changes to be drawn up, the basis for building the State Theater was changed to a cost-plus-fixed-fee contract. This allowed prompt subcontract awards and permitted continuous construction progress.

Within two months the revised estimated cost had been reduced to a figure within $100,000 of the approved budget, and actual construction work was ahead of schedule.

The design for the New York State Theater had been prepared, with much less revision and redesign than had marked the early stages of both the concert hall and the opera house. This was partly a difference in the approach and working methods of the architects involved, and partly a result of a much simpler organization on the client side of the relationship. Since there was not yet an official constituent for the building, the architect had relatively more control.

There were fewer people for him to deal with and fewer divergent points of view to reconcile. Furthermore, by comparison with the complexity of the opera, Johnson was dealing with a much simpler building.

Finally, on budgetary control, there was less revision and cutting because, when serious architectural planning for the State Theater was begun in the fall of 1960, the budget provisions for all buildings had become more realistic in relation to the size of structures required.

THEATER AND LIBRARY BUILDING

The architects Eero Saarinen and Gordon Bunshaft were chosen to design the repertory theater and the library, originally expected to be separate buildings. Saarinen and his collaborating theater designer Jo Meilziner, held many conferences with Robert Whitehead and Elia Kazan regarding the nature of the theater desired. It was to be a break with Broadway tradition, to have great flexibility, to create intimacy between audience and actor. Since it was to serve a repertory company, its stage design and equipment should foster economy in operation. Their concept of flexibility permitted a thrust stage and a proscenium arrangement, both within a framework of limitations imposed by the sightlines from the sides of the audience area. Whitehead and Kazan recognized that this proscenium concept would require sets especially designed to fit the triangle of sightlines. They regarded this unique concept as an asset, but in later years this limitation was viewed critically by others using the theater. In addition to the main theater and its backstage facilities, there was to be a very small studio theater.

For a full understanding of the functional needs of the library and museum Bunshaft conferred with Edward Freehafer, the library director, and with his staff. The library required special features for each of the three collections of music, dance, and drama. Facilities were to include a library of recorded sound, a children's library, exhibition spaces to handle the museum program, and a small auditorium for lectures.

Neither architect had gone far in translating the functional needs into architectural concepts when each became dissatisfied with his assigned plot. As already described, Saarinen and Bunshaft proposed to solve their problems by designing a single building. Their proposal won the support of all the other architects, and Bunshaft and Saarinen joined forces to work out the exterior together (although each was to be in full charge of all interior planning for his own client). Since there would have to be a single construction contract, one architectural firm had to be responsible for producing the working drawings, and the Saarinen firm was chosen to perform that task. It was an unusual arrangement between the two firms and between two strong-willed design architects.

The exterior design concept emerged rapidly, largely reflecting Bunshaft's ideas. A simple glass front enclosed the theater lobby, with the major part of the library housed in a windowless cantilevered overhang above the theater. The library was given two entrances, one on the plaza and another on Amsterdam Avenue at the western end of the building. This exterior design went through minor refinements and changes, but the structure was built in general conformity with this early design.

The first rough estimate for the library and museum part of the structure, made in November, 1959, was $9 million, versus a budgetary provision of $6 million. This 50 percent overage could not be reduced by any combination of minor changes. Only by a significant elimination of space could the cost estimate be brought within the budget. With the concurrence of the library officials, large parts of museum space were deleted from the plan.

Saarinen's first preliminary cost estimate for the theater, submitted on August 4, 1960, was $8.396 million. The budget provided $7.5 million. This relatively small overage required no major space cuts, but Saarinen looked for ways to reduce costs of the Studio Theater and of equipment for the main stage. Whitehead insisted on the importance of the studio to his planned program, but he agreed that it could be finished on an austere basis, at a possible saving of $400,000. Main stage equipment costs could be cut by $85,000 through elimination of one of the three stage wagons and by several minor changes.

Three months later, the first rough estimate was made by the joint venture. The theater would cost $10.8 million, 44 percent over the budget, and the library, $7.8 million, 10 percent over its budget. Bunshaft thought a few more revisions were feasible to bring the cost of the library in line. But this time, the theater overage was more serious, and cuts would have to be sought in reduced space, in structural design, and in the mechanized equipment. In two months, by January 11, 1961, changes in these areas made by Saarinen brought the rough estimate down by $3.5 million to a figure within the budget. Engineering development of Saarinen's latest plans was pushed with all possible speed so that more detailed cost estimates could be secured and actual construction could begin.

Up to this point the stage and audience seating arrangements had dominated the attention of both architect and the theater professionals. As the building plans moved toward finality, the public spaces came in for intensive review. There were questions concerning the location of the ticket-taking points, of audience circulation before performances and during intermission, of facilities for the handicapped, of bars and refreshment services. To provide for audience coat checking, Saarinen suggested coin lockers. This experimental ideas was favored by Whitehead and by the theater subcommittee, but it was an innovation for the New York theater building code. For a number of months the City Building Department delayed its decision, but, in the end, the locker scheme won approval, as it also did with audiences, for it eliminates checkroom delays at the end of performances.

By June 1961, the theater was sufficiently developed in both plans and models that Saarinen and Meilziner made a full presentation to the board of the Repertory Theater Association and to the Lincoln Center board, with approval by both. In mid-July 1961 the detailed plans went to the joint venture contractors for their cost estimates, to be submitted within two months.

On September 1, 1961 there occurred a sad and tragic development with the sudden death of Eero Saarinen. His theater design was essentially complete, and at the next board meeting, the directors paid tribute to Saarinen in this memorial:

Mr. Saarinen brought to the planning of the Repertory Theater all of his creative genius. In cooperation with his associates on the project, he completed a theater design of beauty, imaginative dramatic possibilities and practical operating efficiency. It remains for Lincoln Center to build the theater as conceived by Mr. Saarinen, a task to which it is dedicated.

The remaining architectural work became the responsibility of Maurice Allen, Saarinen's associate, and continuing collaboration with Bunshaft was assured by his cooperation and confidence in the arrangement between the two firms.

At a joint meeting of the theater and library subcommittees on September 7, 1961, the joint venture estimates were reviewed. Their figure was $15.4 million for the combined building: $7.225 million for the library, and $8.175 million for the theater. This exceeded the budget by $.9 million, a figure that was manageable from the unallocated contingency fund. Although these figures were still preliminary, they enabled the committee to authorize working drawings, and excavation was started in November 1961. But drawings for full construction were delayed when the Repertory Theater Association asked for space for their offices within the theater building. (They had planned earlier to rent space in the opera office tower; when the tower was eliminated, the Repertory had to make new plans for their offices.) While fulfilling this request would not alter the basic design for the theater and library building, it delayed the working drawings for subcontractor bids another three months.

Finally, on May 23, 1962, the joint venture submitted their upset price for the theater and library building. It was 30 percent above their own estimate of only nine months earlier. Moreover, the joint venture had also revised their construction schedule from 20 to 26 months, thus making it impossible to open at the start of the World's Fair. Numerous explanations were offered for this staggering escalation in cost and time. Subcontractors had seemed reluctant to submit competitive bids because of a rush to get other buildings under contract before a change in the zoning law became effective. A major labor shortage was developing from the large amount of construction related to the fair. But none of these explanations eased the acute financial problem or the time pressures.

Lincoln Center rejected the joint venture bid, directed the architects to take two months for a careful plan review with the constituents to eliminate all unnecessary elements, and proposed to invite open competitive bids in which the joint venture contractors might compete with others. The leaders of the joint venture asked that they be permitted to work with the architects and subcontractors to find possibilities for cost reduction and then submit a revised bid before Lincoln Center invited competition. The directors agreed to honor their request, but the dissolution of the joint venture occurred before their revised bid was due. The Turner Construction Company became the general contractor for the theater and library, as well as for the State Theater. The process of architectural revision under Bunshaft's leadership and a fresh approach to construction economies by Turner worked well. In September 1962 a new bid, within Lincoln Center's budgeted figure, was submitted by Turner and promptly accepted by the Building Committee.

JUILLIARD

The Juilliard building is the most complex structure in Lincoln Center and was the last to be built. Its complexity arises both from functional needs and engineering necessities. From its earliest planning the school had a large number of disparate requirements. In addition to classrooms, library, and student lounge, regular facilities for any educational institution, there had to be sound-proof practice rooms and individual teaching studios. Large workshop studios with high ceilings were required for opera, dance, and drama coaching; dance studios needed specially sprung floors. A large orchestra rehearsal room was needed that would be acoustically adequate. Provision had to be made for three pipe organs. Performance halls were needed for individual recitals, for orchestra concerts, for opera, dance, and theater productions. Shops were required for scene building and costume preparation. Student housing was desired. In addition, the Lincoln Center Chamber Music hall, originally planned for location in the Philharmonic building, was shifted in 1959 to Juilliard. For a time, spaces for a large public restaurant, for commercial stores and banks, and for Lincoln Center offices were considered.

Pietro Belluschi, chosen as Juilliard architect in 1958, was required to consider in his planning the inclusion of one after another of these diverse elements. He also had to plan for security and control of access to various parts of the building. Sound insulation and isolation of many spaces in the building were paramount; within each performance area, acoustical properties were as important as in major theaters and halls of the center. He also had to design a building that would relate to the rest of Lincoln Center in external appearance and in height and mass.

The approved site plan for the center placed Juilliard on the half-block addition to the north of the original Lincoln Center site. Budgetary provision totaled $10 million: $6.5 million for the school, $1 million for the chamber music hall, and a plan for self-liquidating borrowing of $2.5 million for student housing. On June 4, 1959, the joint venture estimated $18.15 million as the cost to build according to Belluschi's preliminary scheme. This was so far beyond the budget that the Building Committee directed examination of program requirements, space reductions, and deferral or elimination of some spaces.

By mid-July, the cost reduction studies had brought the estimate down to $14.265 million, still nearly 50 percent over budget. Significant economies would be possible only through elimination of the facilities for either drama or dance training. A cut of such drastic nature was not acceptable to Lincoln Center directors, and, in spite of the unsolved financial problem, they directed a continuation of planning to house Juilliard's training programs in dance and drama as well as in music. A month later the prospect of $9 million from the

Hubbard Trust gave significant encouragement for the Juilliard Building.[4]

Engineering developments during the winter greatly increased space requirements for mechanical equipment, and a new cost estimate in April 1960, was $23 million. No technical or qualitative economies could reduce the estimate to a manageable figure. As a result, Belluschi completely revised the layout for the major elements in the building. By eliminating a service road between 65th and 66th Streets, he was able to propose a lower and longer building, with the Juilliard Theater and the Chamber Music Hall placed side by side rather than one over the other as in his earlier design. Substantial cost savings were achieved, and his rough estimate, based on the new arrangement, was $18 million.

Concurrently, the Lincoln Center capital budget was completely revised on a more realistic basis. On May 23, 1960, when the board increased the campaign goal from $75 to $102 million, the budgetary provision for the Juilliard complex was increased to $17.4 million.

Belluschi's new layout seemed to be near enough to the budget limitation that the Building Committee authorized preparation of a preliminary design as a basis for a more accurate cost estimate. Again, the building grew in size during the design process. By February 3, 1961, the Building Committee was shown a scheme for the Juilliard complex that was 15 feet higher than it had been in the proposal eight months before, and the rough estimate of cost had risen to $19 million.

During these months of design and redesign of the Juilliard building, Belluschi was also working as architect for the city Board of Education on the design for its new LaGuardia High School of Performing Arts that was to be located on the adjoining plot of land at the west end of the Juilliard block. After trying many different schemes, Belluschi reported to his two clients that the program requirements for the two schools were very difficult to accommodate on the single block of real estate. Young suggested that, to solve the dilemma, an alternative location might be found for the high school and that Lincoln Center might buy the western end of the block. He explored such possibilities with city officials, and Milton Mollen, then chairman of the Committee on Slum Clearance, opened an opportunity to place the performing arts high school in a pending redevelopment project just west of Lincoln Center. Mollen took the lead in working out this project, but his progress was slow, for he had problems to solve with numerous other city agencies.

Because the enlargement of the Juilliard site would permit significant improvements in the building, Lincoln Center and Juilliard were prepared to wait. Juilliard planning was stopped until there could be certainty about the site for its building. When Philharmonic Hall was opened, there was still no final solution. But there was optimism, later justified, that the site would eventually be enlarged and that planning for Juilliard could then be resumed.

Photo by Bob Serating

Philharmonic Hall—after completion of the plaza.

CHAPTER 12

The Opening of Philharmonic Hall
September 23, 1962

The official opening of Philharmonic Hall was to celebrate the beginning of Lincoln Center and the opening of its first building. A gala inaugural concert was planned for nine o'clock on the evening of Sunday, September 23, 1962. It was the first in an opening week series of festival concerts to exemplify the variety of musical services the hall was expected to provide.

Since the new hall was to be the home of the Philharmonic orchestra, its musical director, Leonard Bernstein, chose the opening night program. For subsequent events in opening week, Lincoln Center carried program as well as financial responsibility. Reginald Allen had been successful in securing the commitment of both the Boston and Philadelphia orchestras to use Philharmonic Hall for their New York series, and both were eager to participate in the opening week. After Schuman became president, he took a personal interest in the artistic planning for opening week and added the Cleveland orchestra and other distinguished concert performers to the opening programs.

The entire opening week was to be conducted as a benefit for Lincoln Center to cover heavy expenses for pre-opening staffing and training, costs of building operation during the opening week, and promotional costs of the concerts. A graduated scale of benefit prices was worked out and a series of inexpensive and free concerts was added to make the opening week events available to as many people, especially students, as possible. Many artists contributed their services, and the benefit ticket sales produced $426,000 which, supplemented by television fees, adequately covered all opening expenses of the hall.

Careful attention was given to the lists of special invited guests for opening night. The cooperation of government—city, state, and federal—was recognized by invitations to a number of their highest officials. The artistic purposes of the center were reflected in invitations to a roster of distinguished creative and performing artists in the fields of dance and drama as well as music. Leaders of other cultural institutions in New York and across the country were invited.

Two nights before its formal opening, the inanimate pile of marble and glass that was Philharmonic Hall came suddenly to life. The occasion was the arrival on Friday evening, September 21, of the first audience to come to a performance in the new center. Throngs of people were converging on Philharmonic Hall. Eyes were focused on the building, aglow with light and with promise of something special about to happen.

That "something" was the workmen's rehearsal by the Philharmonic Orchestra and its guest artists and choruses in preparation for the official opening of the hall two nights later. Bernstein needed an audience for his dress rehearsals to resemble as closely as possible the acoustical conditions of opening night. The leadership of Lincoln Center and the Philharmonic Society matched that need with their desire to express thanks to the host of workmen who had built the new hall. With the cooperation of contractors, architects, and engineers, invitations were issued to all who had had a part in creating this first unit of the center. Each worker was offered a pair of tickets to this first dress rehearsal. With their wives and friends, they filled the hall. Rockefeller greeted them and expressed Lincoln Center's appreciation for their vital part in the creation of the building. Then Bernstein proceeded with his concert.

The *Herald Tribune*, in an editorial, compared the workmen's rehearsal with the medieval practice to include artisans and laborers, who had worked on a cathedral, in its first services of thanksgiving and said:

Essentially, Lincoln Center is being built for, as well as by, the plumbers, pipefitters, electricians, stenographers, housewives, students, businessmen, doctors, lawyers and indian chiefs, if any, of the world—in a word, for everybody. And to have the first sounds played by an orchestra within its walls fall upon the ears of those directly concerned with its construction makes for poetic, not to mention, musical, justice.[1]

On the morning of the inaugural concert, the hall was full of last-minute activity in preparation for the evening celebration. Carpet was still being laid in the cafe and eight seamstresses were on the floor sewing. Powers and Young, accompanied by construction supervisors and public relations representatives, walked through every part of the building in exactly the paths to be taken that night by important members of the audience. The proper functioning of each door was checked; the planned positions of security guards was reviewed; instructions were issued for any needed last-minute finishing touches; controls were reviewed in order to be sure that the right people would be in the right place at the right time for each event scheduled.

Traffic congestion for the arriving audience was unavoidable. Construction work in other parts of Lincoln Center blocked several roadways that would eventually afford free access to Philharmonic Hall. The garage was not yet open. Only one lane of traffic was possible on 62nd and 65th Streets. However, the city traffic department and the police cooperated to handle the opening night crowd.

Early in the evening a red carpet was rolled out from the Plaza entrance through the portico down to the curbline. A crowd of friendly and curious onlookers assembled behind the barriers. The audience began to arrive early. All were in full evening dress and walked in through a blaze of light for television and press cameras. The *Journal American* began its opening-day news story with the assertion that "the most glamorous premiere in the city's history will be staged tonight . . . ."[2]

At the approach of nine o'clock, Mayor Wagner, escorted by Arthur Houghton, took his seat in the center loge section; Governor Rockefeller, escorted by William Schuman, entered the first terrace VIP area to the right. Mrs. John F. Kennedy and John Rockefeller arrived at the Hall together, and Rockefeller escorted the First Lady from her car through the building to the VIP area on the left. Bernstein came to the podium and raised his baton for the National Anthem. John Rockefeller then came on stage for his brief words of welcome. He expressed the significance of the moment when he said,

Tonight we move out of the world of planning into the world of performance. Now, and in the years ahead, only the artist and his

Rendering by Mutin 1959/Photo courtesy of Lincoln Center for the Performing Arts, Inc.

Longitudinal Section. Philharmonic Hall.

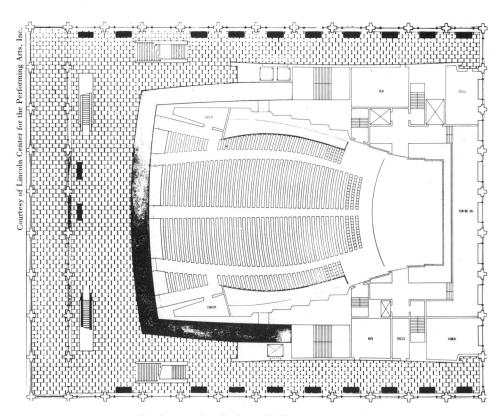

Courtesy of Lincoln Center for the Performing Arts, Inc.

Orchestra level plan. Philharmonic Hall.

Philharmonic Hall on opening night.

art can fulfill the aspirations of the planners and exalt the labors of the builders.

His concluding words were, "We now turn to one of the world's great orchestras to dedicate this hall to music."

For the television audience a succession of special events was arranged during the intermission. In the foyers the governor and the mayor were interviewed; there were numerous shots of the new Hall and its gala audience with commentary by Alistair Cooke; Aline Saarinen (widow of Eero Saarinen) gave an architectural critique. The intermission highlight centered on Mrs. Kennedy and Bernstein in the Green Room. At the end of the program, the audience rose in a prolonged ovation. This celebration atmosphere was continued by serving champagne in the foyers to the entire audience. In addition to the more than 3000 people in Philharmonic Hall that night, the opening was witnessed by an estimated 26 million television viewers throughout the United States. It was, probably, the largest audience, up to that time, to attend a single concert.[3]

The crucial question on the mind of everyone was, "How does the hall sound?" In Schonberg's review the next day he commented, "This was one occasion when the music was far less important than the sound. The major over-riding question in most minds pertained to the quality of sound of the new hall." His impression was that the sound was "inconsistent." In the orchestra "the sound was clear, a little dry, with not much reverberation and a decided lack of bass." But in the top terrace "the tonal characteristics are altogether different. Here bass can definitely be heard ... so full in sound that it almost appears amplified and too live. It is exciting, though, and in climactic movements of the 'Gloria' the effect lifts one off his seat." He concluded optimistically that "some work still remains in tuning Philharmonic Hall. There is no reason why this cannot be done." Referring to the "clouds," he observed that "so far the acousticians have not found the correct settings to send uniform tone throughout the house." Schonberg's initial conclusion: "On the basis of present accomplishment, Philharmonic Hall should turn out to be a fine theater in the modern style; not a mellow house, but a clear, uncolored, vigorous one, in which each strand of musical material will be easily followed."[4]

The acoustical questions did not preclude praise for the hall. The *New York Daily News* termed it "a concert-goer's dream—fabulously handsome, wonderfully comfortable, and with seemingly miles of space for promenading on the perimeter of the music hall itself. It

Ralph Morse, LIFE Magazine, © Time Inc.

Mrs. John F. Kennedy, John D. Rockefeller 3rd, and Leonard Bernstein.

should enrich the life of anybody who goes there."[5] Ada Louise Huxtable in the *New York Times* said, "If the building is serenely handsome by day, it takes on remarkable beauty by night."[6] Saul Levinson in the *World Telegram* said, "Aglow with the spirit of Beethoven and Mahler, Philharmonic Hall, the city's dazzling new cultural pearl, took its place today as one of the illustrious concert halls of the world."[7] John Chapman in the *Daily News:* "It was a beautiful, exciting, memorable evening ... When Leonard Bernstein

Mr. and Mrs. Charles M. Spofford and Gen. and Mrs. Maxwell D. Taylor.

gave the downbeat . . . a profound emotion must have seized the most distinguished audience this great city has seen in decades." [8]

For those with responsibility for Lincoln Center, the essential meaning of the opening was expressed in a statement signed jointly by Lincoln Center's chairman and president, Rockefeller and Schuman, and published in the Opening Week Souvenir Program. It said in part:

> The enormously complex task of bringing Lincoln Center to the point of fruition has been the self-imposed responsibility of devoted men and women from all segments of our society. Lincoln Center exists because leaders in the arts, education, business, labor, the professions, philanthropy, and government believe that the arts are a true measure of a civilization. And Lincoln Center is rising because Americans believe deeply enough in the importance of the arts to give generously of their time and resources to create it. Lincoln Center is many things, but before all others it is a living monument to the will of free men acting together on the basis of their own initiative and idealism.

PART IV

To the Opening of the Opera
1962–1966

Photo by Bob Serating

CHAPTER 13

Building Progress
1962–1966

In the decade required for the construction of Lincoln Center, the opening of Philharmonic Hall was a highpoint of accomplishment and spurred on the much larger building task ahead. Construction continued on the New York State Theater, and excavating proceeded for the opera house and the theater and library building. Much detailed planning for the opera remained to be done by Wallace Harrison and his engineers before its design could be considered final; for Juilliard, Belluschi's planning was still tentative pending the resolution of efforts to enlarge the Juilliard site.

Completion of the first building presented an opportunity to assess the procedures of cost control and to profit by the experience. Therefore, following the opening, Young, who was then executive vice president and Building Committee chairman, met with the architect, contractor, and engineers to develop procedures for the remaining projects. Two areas of construction management were tagged for improvement: job scheduling and cost control involving claims from the subcontractors for extra work and changes. In addition, it was determined that Lincoln Center had to make sure that those who were to use a building were much more accurate in their review of plans and final approvals prior to construction.

Young issued a directive to all architects, general contractors, and subcontractors to accept no orders for changes except from an official representative of the owner, Lincoln Center. All change requests were to be channeled through Powers, who was given authority to approve most items. Major changes must be referred to Morse for review. Lincoln Center established a tough policy to reject all changes except those based on a structural or engineering necessity or on compelling reasons affecting the functional use of the building. The budgeting procedure for each building was tightened to provide a contingency reserve that could be released only by the Building Committee or its subcommittee. An engineer was chosen for each building to follow every detail throughout its construction period. Much had been learned from the construction of Philharmonic Hall that could be applied in the subsequent building program.

PHILHARMONIC HALL

The immediate task following the opening of Philharmonic Hall was to complete the building. A large amount of plaster and paint work was unfinished in the backstage area and in the office spaces for the Philharmonic Society. In the auditorium itself, numerous minor matters had to be corrected or completed, and the air conditioning system had to be balanced, a process expected to take months. A full schedule of concert usage with accompanying blocks of rehearsal time severely limited the hours when much of the work could be done. It was not until January 1963 that the building could be called "finished," and the Philharmonic Society move into its new offices.

New and unexpected problems developed as the hall was used. During a rehearsal of the Cleveland orchestra, one of the heavy metal light "cans" in the ceiling crashed to the floor of the stage, narrowly missing an orchestra player and his instrument. Conductor George Szell, with an expletive, gave the offending light fixture a resounding kick, and the episode added to his mounting dislike for the new hall. Musical sounds had produced vibration that caused a holding ring to give way and let the fixture drop. Each light can in the entire hall had to be equipped with a safety chain.

In the auditorium, lighting was found to be uneven for program reading, and in some places the air conditioning was causing uncomfortable drafts notwithstanding the efforts to balance the system. A more serious problem was that sudden changes in temperature on stage were putting the musician's instruments out of tune. There were complaints about the cafe, its location, its appearance, service, and prices.

But these and similar troubles were trivialities compared to the acoustical problem of the hall. It took only a few concerts to conclude that the major problems were a lack of low-frequency sounds, a shrill or strident quality to the high-frequency sounds, and difficulty experienced by members of the orchestra in hearing themselves and each other. Trained listeners sensed a lack of reverberation, and in some places in the hall, faint echos could be heard.

The first step in the search for solutions was to consult Dr. Leo Beranek, the acoustical adviser to Abramovitz in the design of the hall. In December he proposed changes in the position of many of his clouds and carpet on a rear wall to deal with a continuing echo. The estimated cost was $60,000 to $75,000. Before decisions were reached on corrective actions, Schuman recommended an independent study by a panel of experts. After consulting other conductors, four acousticians with records of success in design or alteration of other halls were retained. [1] In April 1963 this panel recommended more extensive changes, and the estimated cost was $350,000. Although the budgeted reserve for acoustical adjustments was only $100,000, the board recognized that corrective measures had to be taken and authorized the full expenditure.

The principal conclusion of the panel was that the stepped design of the clouds and of the side walls was a basic cause of the cancellation of low-frequency tones. They recommended a cure in two phases of construction alterations. Phase I would deal with the acoustical clouds. Over the stage they were to be raised and their angles changed; all spaces between the clouds were to be filled in with heavy plywood. Over the audience, the clouds were to be raised and relocated into a continuous sweeping curve; about 80 percent of the space between clouds was to be filled in. A reporter expressed the change in meterorological terms: "The 'cloud' cover will be transformed from scattered to an almost total overcast." [2] Phase II would alter the vertical sidewalls near the stage to eliminate their stepped design and to make their surfaces convex. By mid-June, detailed plans for the changes had increased costs to $405,000, but the work was done as planned during the summer. After Phase I there were improvements, but the faint echo had become louder, and in Phase II additional changes were made on the back wall and in the contour of the faces of the rear terraces to eliminate the echo.

When concerts were resumed in October 1963, the initial verdict seemed favorable. Miles Kastendieck in the *Journal American* states:

> What a relief!
>
> The year of hazing Philharmonic Hall is over. With the acoustical adjustments made during the summer, the sound of the hall has gained immeasurably. The time has come to drop the everlasting haggling over acoustics, to enjoy the hall in its proper perspective, and to appreciate it for the wonderful place it is to hear music. [3]

But the dissatisfactions continued. The musicians could not hear themselves and did not sense a close relationship to the audience. The audience still did not feel surrounded by reverberent sound. The most biting public comment came from George Szell:

> Let me give you a little simile. Imagine a woman, lame, a hunchback, crosseyed and with two warts. They've removed the warts . . . [4]

During the winter of 1963 and 1964, Amyas Ames, president of the Philharmonic Society, took the lead in searching for solutions to the acoustical problem. He reported that, among the acoustical consultants, Heinrich Keilholz had won the confidence of the conductors and the orchestra players. Abramovitz was willing to work with Keilholz and was in accord with his approach. On April 7 the building Committee agreed to retain Keilholz jointly with the Philharmonic-Society.

Keilholz' recommendations dealt entirely with the stage. His plan was to enclose the organ loft at the rear of the stage with a system of wooden louvers to form an irregular wall surface, replace the scrim on the stage sides with wood panels, change the height and angle of the overhead clouds, and close spaces between the clouds and the side walls. The Executive Committee authorized an expenditure, outside the capital budget, of $250,000. At the same time they considered the unsolved problems of air conditioning. After 18 months of balancing attempts, the musicians still complained of sudden temperature changes that affected the tuning of their instruments. There were even charges that, in a few instances, instruments had cracked. Independent engineers were retained to develop corrective plans to solve this problem concurrently with the next round of acoustical work.

These alterations, which became known as "Acoustics, Phase III," were scheduled in a three-week period at the end of summer. The work was slowed by a strike of sheet-metal workers, and Keilholz changed his design for the organ louvers while they were being fabricated. These delays extended the job beyond the scheduled period and required overtime work after midnight during the two weeks of the Film Festival. The costs were increased further. However, Phase III was accomplished by the time concerts were resumed in late September at a total of $375,000.

After the first concert, once again the initial critical judgment was encouraging. Alan Rich in the *Herald Tribune* said, "The happy news this morning . . . is that Philharmonic Hall finally sounds like a concert hall." [5] Harold Schonberg in the *New York Times* reported the longer reverberation time of the hall and said:

> There is no doubt that in many respects Philharmonic Hall has a smoother sound . . . . But all is not yet perfect . . . the echo still persists. [6]

Several conductors were generous in their praise. Eric Leinsdorf wrote to Schuman that "it has been an eminently successful effort and both performers and public are in your debt." Eugene Ormandy wrote "Philharmonic Hall now not only looks like a concert hall; it sounds like one."

As the winter blew colder, the warmth of the initial reception chilled. Orchestra players continued to complain. Keilholz recommended other changes that he felt certain would improve the hall still more. He proposed to place curving wood reflecting panels on the auditorium side walls, to remove the carpet and heavy upholstered seats in the auditorium and replace them with seats having a wooden back and cushioned with only a thin layer of padding. The incidental result was a smaller seat that could permit seating capacity to be increased by 210. On May 4, 1965, Ames brought Keilholz' plans to the Executive Committee and proposed that these changes be financed through a self-liquidating loan by applying half the income from the additional seats to the debt service. No additional money would be needed from contributors.

The plan was approved, and both the Boston and Philadelphia orchestras were persuaded to join the Philharmonic in pledging half the new seat revenue to the service of the debt. The eventual cost was a half million dollars.

This fourth round of acoustical changes produced more pronounced changes in the appearance of the hall. The new walls with their large S-shaped protruding panels were in light-colored acacia wood, and the seats were a deep mulberry color. The judgment on the acoustics was favorable but hardly enthusiastic. Eric Salzman wrote:

The acoustics? Ah, yes. Have they beat that rap at last? Have they patched up the Great Acoustical Dud? A provisional answer: quite a bit.[7]

The *New Yorker* admitted "At least, the sound is mellower and not as harshly brilliant as it was and this is all to the good." This damning with faint praise continued to plague Philharmonic Hall, and the saga of its acoustical problems was not over. Nothing more was done to the hall at this time.

NEW YORK STATE THEATER

When Philharmonic Hall was opened on September 23, 1962, the New York State Theater, across the plaza, was only 20 percent completed. However, exactly 19 months later, on April 23, 1964, Lincoln Center was obliged to open the State Theater. This was not just a target completion date; it was a contractual commitment with the state of New York. To fulfill the terms of the appropriation of $15 million by the legislature, the State Theater had to be ready to function as the performing arts arm of the Fair from its opening day. Fortunately, the architectural and engineering plans and specifications were far more complete than had been the case when Philharmonic Hall was begun. Lincoln Center was better organized to reach prompt construction decisions. The cumbersome general-contractor arrangement with the joint venture had been replaced by the simpler and more direct contract with the Turner Construction Company. By the end of 1963 the structural frame for the State Theater was essentially complete.

At this same time planning for the use of the theater was underway. Balanchine participated in detailed reviews of the stage facilities and made urgent requests for changes, for it developed that he had difficulty in reading blueprints and visualizing completed spaces from plans. Only when he could stand on the stage did the plans assume reality for him.

Balanchine looked at the orchestra pit and decided it was much too small. Johnson had not realized that the ballet planned to use a larger orchestra in the new house. Although the pit was fixed in structural concrete, the wall was demolished and rebuilt, sacrificing the front row of orchestra seats. Balanchine was equally insistent that the steel light towers on either side of the stage would block the normal points of entry for his dancers. They were removed and a hanging light bridge was installed.

New York State Theater under construction—January 1963.

A third change was related to the color of the stage and rehearsal room floors. Johnson had chosen a maroon-colored linoleum to harmonize with the color scheme of his theater. When the theater lighting experts saw it, they realized at once that it would reflect its color onto the dancers and their costumes; it was replaced by a light grey linoleum that would be neutral in its light reflections, and the maroon floor covering was salvaged and used in other backstage areas.

The technical reviews also led to a change in Johnson's plan for the main stage curtain. He wanted a house curtain that could be seen and enjoyed as the audience entered the theater. For this purpose, in order that the rigging for the curtain not penetrate the fire wall, he had designed a narrow concrete slot above the proscenium arch into which it would be raised. This ingenious arrangement would permit the house curtain to hang in front of the fire curtain rather than behind it as is customary in theater design. The house curtain was to be a metallic structure on a light steel frame with brilliant spiral elements that would rotate with air currents and produce a glittering effect over the curtain's surface. It was an innovative and spectacular architec-

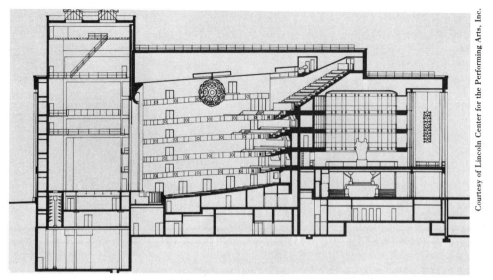

Longitudinal Section. New York State Theater.

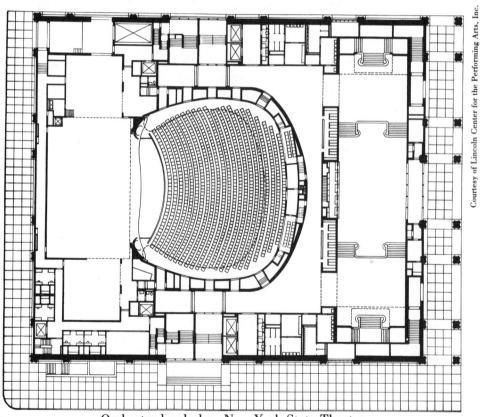

Orchestra level plan. New York State Theater.

tural concept, but it had two functional flaws. There was no way for the fixed metal frame to be parted to permit curtain calls, and in its raised position, the portion remaining visible below the top of the proscenium was certain to catch light rays from the main spotlights focused on the stage. The resulting glitter would be distracting to the audience. Johnson abandoned his original idea and substituted a conventional gold cloth curtain.

As the building neared completion, the companies scheduled to use the theater were checking every detail for their new productions. When the Music Theater technicians reviewed the facilities, they objected to the size of the orchestra pit that had been enlarged to meet the demands of the ballet and was now much larger than wanted for musical shows. Richard Rodgers urged a flexible system that could accommodate two additional front rows of seats to bring the audience closer to the stage. The architect developed a set of removable platforms on which the added rows of seats could be placed.

Despite these changes, Young was able to assure the board in January 1964, that the State Theater would be ready for its official opening on April 23. A number of pre-opening events were planned for this second building of Lincoln Center. There were tours of the theater for all the volunteers in the campagin and in the constituent organizations. A special occasion for city officials was arranged to inaugurate the Lincoln Center fountain. For several months the fountain had been concealed beneath a bright green and white tent which had permitted work on its complex piping and electrical system to continue in all kinds of weather. When, in the first week of April, the tent was taken down and the construction fences removed, the whole

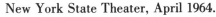

New York State Theater, April 1964.

Photo by Bob Serating

plaza was at last opened out with the fountain as its centerpiece. A group of city officials, led by Paul Screvane, president of the Council, conducted a brief ceremony on April 6. At dusk, short speeches were made; the donor of the fountain, Charles Revson, was honored; a button was pressed, the dancing waters rose and fell, and all was recorded by the press and TV cameras. The assembled city officials then toured the State Theater, which their government had helped to finance and would own after the Fair. The first audience, the work-men who had built the theater, assembled on April 18th for a full dress rehearsal of the New York City Ballet.

Because the New York State Theater had been largely financed by the state, the planning for its official opening was done in collabora-tion with the State Commission on the World's Fair and its chairman, Lt. Governor Malcolm Wilson. It was agreed that the entire opening night audience would have to be an invited group and include top officials, not only from the state government, but also from the city and federal levels. All members of the state legislature were invited, as were all members of the State Commission on the World's Fair. The Fair corporation was represented by its officers and entire board of directors. The board members and staff of all the Lincoln Center constituents and a large number of performing and creative artists were invited. The protocol problems of seating were gigantic.

On the evening of April 23, the opening hour was heralded by a fanfare from the portico of the theater. For entertainment, the inau-gural program provided a scene from "Carousel," presented by the Music Theater and two ballets, "Allegro Brillante" and "Stars and Stripes," by the New York City Ballet. Between the performances, several short speeches were made, and Governor Rockefeller con-cluded the ceremony with a special recognition of Philip Johnson, the architect, and with praise to the legislators: "It takes courage to vote for culture when you are in public life." After the program, the audience was invited to a tour of the building and to a reception in the Grand Promenade, hosted by the governor.

"Theater Opens—A Vista of Elegance," was the *World Telegram* headline the next morning. Its lead story began, "Mark up the New York State Theater as another triumph of private and public team-work." [8]

The *New York Times* reported that "the overwhelming consensus among first nighters was that the town had a new hit." Architectural critic, Ada Louise Huxtable, wrote:

Lincoln Center's democratic theater has been designed by an architectural aristocrat . . . . [The Promenade] promises to be one

Opening night telecast: Richard Rodgers, Robert Trout (CBS), Philip Johnson, Lincoln Kirstein, George Balanchine, Jacques d'Amboise.

of the most impressive public spaces New York has ever seen. Like the rest of the theater, the Promenade is sumptuous, elegant, sophisticated, and sensuously beautiful.[9]

The *Journal American* called it "the finest theater in the world today."[10]
Irving Kolodin wrote in the *Saturday Review*,

The theater itself is the happiest kind of alliance of the elegant and the utilitarian. . . . The areas around it [the auditorium] are spacious beyond any prior possibility in a New York theater where square feet and round dollars locked in mortal combat. Only in a structure incorporated, as this one is, in a gradiose plan of civic development could the heartless realities of economics be vanquished on behalf of a Promenade even larger than the famous foyer of the Paris Opera, and as true to the artistic spirit of today as that one was to the time of its origins.[11]

The acoustics of the New York State Theater were, understandably, a subject of concern. Fortunately, Jay Harrison could write in *Musical America*,

> Then there is the matter of acoustics—and here for the first time there is cause of joy at Lincoln Center. They are, to put it in brief, first rate. They are neither blatant nor remote; they are dead center correct.[12]

Other comments also were favorable, though some were expressed with reserve. Herbert Kupferberg in the *Herald Tribune* reported:

> The acoustics of the new house seemed excellent . . . . A rich and clear sound throughout the house except for a muffling beneath the overhang at the rear of the orchestra.[13]

These reactions were, of course, based primarily on the use of the theater for ballet. Johnson and his advisers had designed it, as requested, to be a musical house, and it had a reverberation time of 1.7 seconds. For the spoken word and vocal music an amplification system had been installed.

The initial air of calm satisfaction over acoustics was shaken in May 1964 when the Royal Shakespeare Company opened its engagement with "King Lear." They had refused to use amplification or to have a preview performance although advised by Lincoln Center to do so. As a result, the opening night audience had great difficulty in understanding the actors. In later performances the accomplished British actors were able to adjust to the problem by slowing their pace to meet the longer reverberation time in the house. Nevertheless, the director of the company, Peter Brook, made an angry public outburst that revived the public's preoccupation with acoustics. In July, when the Music Theater opened with its revival of *The King and I*, full use was made of the built-in sound system, and Howard Taubman, in his *New York Times* review said:

The Grand Promenade.

New York State Theater with New York City Ballet on stage.

You will have no trouble in hearing and relishing the music—and the amplification system is no more obtrusive than loudspeakers anywhere. As for the spoken dialogue, I had no trouble in two different parts of the house. [14]

One question remained—how well would the State Theater serve opera without use of its sound system? The New York City Opera opened on February 22, 1966, and, on the worrisome subject of acoustics, Schonberg concluded that "the sound was much better than anyone had dared hope it would be." [15]

Allen Rich, in the *Herald Tribune*, was stronger in his praise.

It seemed to these ears that these [acoustical] problems have so far been solved very well indeed ... the sound in the First Ring was excellent ... if things continue this well, Mr. Rudel can concentrate on the music from now on. [16]

In the four years of this time period, the New York State Theater was built on schedule and within 1 percent of its authorized budget. It served, as planned, for the two years of the Lincoln Center World's Fair Festival. It became home for the resident companies of the New York City Ballet, the New York City Opera and the Music Theater of Lincoln Center, and its acoustical properties were judged to be good.

THE THEATER AND LIBRARY BUILDING

The financial plan for city capital funds for the Library was approved by the Board of Estimate on September 25, 1962, completing the final legal step for construction of the combined theater and library building. By December, the Building Committee received the encouraging report that the general contractor had awarded half of the subcontracts at a saving of approximately $250,000 under the guaranteed maximum price for the combined building, and that the foundation walls were being constructed.

Problems soon arose in connection with the contract for theater stage equipment. There was an allowance of $528,000 for all of the specified equipment, including the complex mechanism for converting the theater from thrust to proscenium stage. But the best bid received was 40 percent over this amount. Then an English company submitted a proposal for stage equipment at only $34,000 over the allowance. Although their bid involved a few changes and eliminations, these were acceptable to Whitehead and Kazan, and the bid was approved.

During the summer of 1964, a strike in England affected their production schedule and delivery dates in New York. Soon additional uncertainties arose over a threatened longshoreman's strike in New York harbor which would delay even further the delivery of the British stage equipment. This new risk made it unwise to attempt a spring opening of the Vivian Beaumont, and the opening date was moved ahead to the fall of 1965.

Meanwhile, management and financial crises in the Repertory Theater had resulted in a change of professional leadership from Whitehead and Kazan to Herbert Blau and Jules Irving. They made their own detailed review of the equipment, rigging, lighting, and mechanical devices then being installed and concluded that many additional items would be needed for a fully functioning theater, at a cost of $125,000. Lincoln Center accepted the additional cost as its obligation.

When the installation of the theater equipment was finally completed in the fall of 1965, Blau and Irving moved the rehearsals of their opening play to the Beaumont stage. Immediately they encountered serious problems in the system of stage lighting. This system was automated and designed to reduce to a minimum the number of stagehands and electricians required. It included 565 individual spotlights and 180 dimmer circuits, controlled by a memory system utilizing computer punch cards and designed to recall exactly the lighting required by each light cue in a show. It was a new system and used technology that had not had previous theater application.

The malfunctions in the lighting system were many and serious for the preparation of the opening show. Part of the problem was the unfamiliarity of the stage crew with the new sophisticated equipment, but the computer system and the electronic controls were, in operation, causing erratic and disrupting lighting changes. The stage technicians made use of the manual fall-back provisions for meeting emergencies, but the manual system was inconvenient and inefficient compared to a conventional light board. Young called in the designers of the system and the contractors who had installed the equipment. They made corrections and assigned their most competent technicians to work with the stage crew during opening week and to cope with any emergency situation. The opening night came off without a serious error in the lighting system.

The contractors continued to work out the problems and to eliminate the bugs in the system. The electrical system was put through a shakedown period and was made reliable, by general standards for

computer and electronic operations. But it never became fully satisfactory in its theater application and was eventually replaced with a
conventional lighting control system.

The first audience in the Beaumont, following the Lincoln Center
custom, was composed of the workmen involved in the design and
construction of the building. They were invited to a dress rehearsal of
"Danton's Death," held on the evening of October 9. A dedication
ceremony to mark the formal opening of the Vivian Beaumont Theater
was conducted in late afternoon on October 14, 1965 before an invited
audience. Rockefeller's remarks paid tribute to those who had made
this theater a reality—to Saarinen and Mielziner for their design, to
Whitehead and Kazan for their concept of both the building and a
performing company, and to Mrs Allen:

> Our fullest tribute is due to the generous lady to whose memory
> this theater is dedicated... Vivian Beaumont Allen was not only
> one of the largest individual contributors to Lincoln Center—she
> was one of the first. Her meaningful and far-sighted gift inspired
> and lifted the spirits of those of us committed to the concept of
> a fine center in the heart of Manhattan for the presentation of the
> best in all the performing arts.
>
> In the search for wide public support, gifts given early buy more
> than bricks and mortar: they buy hope. Mrs. Allen's gift gave us
> hope.

After a week of preview performances, the Repertory Theater
Company opened on October 20, with a benefit gala, and, the next
evening, they held their "first night" for the critics and for their first
subscription audience.

Once again, in the Lincoln Center succession of openings, the
press paid generous attention. The *World Telegram and Sun* stated:

> The Vivian Beaumont Theater in Lincoln Center has a stage area
> nearly four times larger than any other legitimate theater in New
> York, yet a probably unmatched intimacy out front between
> people and player.[17]

The *Daily News* commented:

> The intimacy of the house is exceptional; one can see everything
> from anywhere—and hear well, too. The lighting of the stage is
> superb but unobtrusive.[18]

Photo: Susanne Faulkner Stevens

Vivian Beaumont Theater.

Interior of Theater.

Larry Morris/THE NEW YORK TIMES

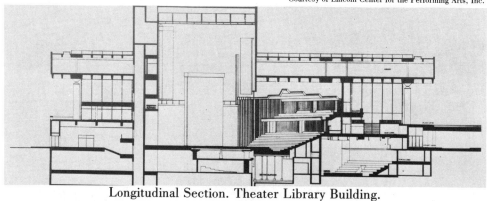

Longitudinal Section. Theater Library Building.

Plan at orchestra level. Theater Library Building.

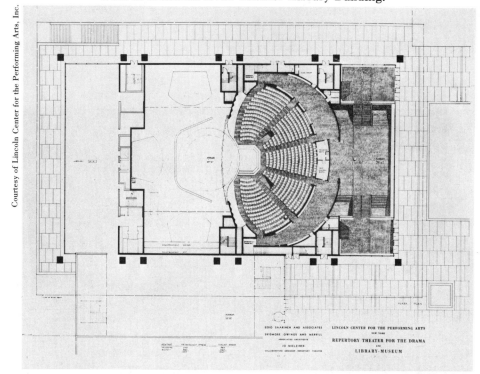

The library and museum building was substantially finished early in 1965. The New York Public Library delayed its move until the city acted on its request for an appropriation of operating funds. This matter was finally resolved at City Hall in May, and the Library then began the gradual move of their large collections. Because of the crowded conditions of these departments at the main library building, quantities of these reference materials had long been in storage. It took time for proper organization and shelving of such material for ready reference use.

The ceremonial opening of the Library-Museum of the Performing Arts was held on the morning of November 30, 1965 in the Beaumont Theater before an audience drawn from the creative side of music, dance, and drama. Rockefeller made a brief talk expressing thanks to the architect, Gordon Bunshaft, and to others who had had significant roles in the concept, design, finance, and construction of the building. Gilbert Chapman, president of the New York Public Library, and Edward G. Frehafer, the director of the Library, pointed toward the uses, both for the general public and for scholars, which would be possible in the new library home. Schuman then officially turned over the building to Mayor Robert F. Wagner, who accepted it on behalf of the city.

METROPOLITAN OPERA HOUSE

The summer of 1962 had seen a period of inactivity in the actual excavation and physical preparation for building the opera house. The massive hole for the opera substructure had partially filled from summer rains, and the resulting pond, visible from the terraces in

Entrance to Library—Museum. Calder's "Le Guichet" in foreground.

Photo: Susanne Faulkner Stevens

Philharmonic Hall, was dubbed "Lake Bing." Immediately after the opening of Philharmonic Hall, Devereux Josephs called weekly meetings of the Opera subcommittee to expedite the completion of planning and begin construction. By this time the budget for the opera house was $37.4 million. Based on a number of subcontract bids, the general contractor was optimistic that it could be built for that amount. However, the Metropolitan representatives came to the first subcommittee meeting with a list of extras that they considered essential for full operation, including the restoration of some features of the stage lifts that had been deleted in an earlier economy move, a cyclorama, an allowance for the main curtain, and bells in the organ. The cost of these extras was estimated at $1.38 million. Action was deferred, awaiting more definitive information on all construction costs.

Josephs placed priority on maintaining a building schedule to meet Lincoln Center's commitments with the governor and the World's Fair for a completed facade in 1964 and a finished building in 1965. In order to avoid any delay, the committee authorized resumption of excavation work, so that digging and blasting to the prescribed foundation levels would be completed and ready for concrete pouring by the first of the year. Immediately there was a need to provide space for storage of materials adjacent to the opera site, since its only street access was at its west end. With the help of Moses, Crandall negotiated an arrangement with the city Parks Department to use space in Damrosch Park, south of the opera and above the Lincoln Center garage. It was necessary to shore up the garage roof to support the heavy weight of the steel beams and other materials and to reimburse the Parks Department for the extra cost of surface construction and landscaping. In order to proceed at once with the opera construction, Lincoln Center had to accept these charges.

It was soon evident that in other ways the battle of the budget for building the opera house was by no means over. The original allowance for finishing the interior of the auditorium proved inadequate in Harrison's planning. The budget for design and engineering on the entire building was nearly used up at this early stage and would have to be increased to see the building finished. A revised budget, reflecting all these increases, came to $42.7 million, an overage of $5.3 million. Josephs brought this new need to the Building Committee on November 14, 1962, and Morse urged prompt acceptance of the higher budget and approval of the pending subcontracts. He warned that several subcontractors had indicated they wanted to be released from their bids; delay was certain to bring still higher prices. Like it or not, these higher costs were necessary to build an adequate functioning opera house, and the $42.7 million budget was authorized.

Meanwhile, Harrison had been concentrating on his architectural design for the auditorium. The Metropolitan New House Committee reacted with enthusiasm when he presented it to them; they were relieved that the ceiling plan avoided the use of hanging acoustical clouds. The box faces and undersides had become important, sound-reflecting elements. The architect, contractor, and technical personnel of the opera resolved innumerable other details during the first half of 1963, but there were delays in approvals of plans by the city Building Department. There was also the somber cloud of a threatened citywide strike of construction workers. Actual construction had fallen behind schedule, and in spite of the strongest effort and cooperation from all concerned, by July it was clear that the 1965 completion date could not be achieved. The Metropolitan decided to remain in its old house for one more year and to open in the fall of 1966 in Lincoln Center. Building completion was scheduled for the end of 1965 to give ample time for the opera to make its complicated move into the new building.

Troublesome problems soon arose in cost control. Conditions encountered in actual job progress were adding to costs. For example, charges for excavation (to reach rock of proper density to bear the tremendous weight) rose by $250,000. Even greater cost increases were coming in the course of translating approved design into working drawings, especially as a result of requests for changes and additions from engineers and consultants. In November 1963, several organizational changes were made to impose new measures of control. In Harrison's office, direction and control of his consultants was strengthened. In Lincoln Center's construction management, Carl Morse was designated "Owner's Representative" for all construction, with Stanton and Young as advisers. The building subcommittees were discontinued.

In the early part of 1964, as Harrison worked to complete the decorative details for the auditorium, he was caught between a desire from the opera leadership for a traditional and rather ornate effect and a directive from Lincoln Center for a simpler, more contemporary treatment. With counsel from Stanton, Harrison reached a solution acceptable to both points of view. On February 28, 1964, the Building Committee, augmented by five officers and directors of the Metropolitan, approved Harrison's design, and the house was built in accord with that plan.

Harrison then turned his attention to the front of the house. He designed a long sweeping curve for the grand staircase. This immediately became a construction challenge. Crandall eventually found craftsmen expert at boat building to make the concrete forms required. The nature and quality of finishes in these public spaces became a subject of debate in October. The budget would permit only exposed concrete; Harrison recommended a combination of marble, gold leaf, bronze, and other quality surfaces. Bliss, Crandall, and Morse strongly urged approval of the more elegant finishes in spite of $600,000 in additional cost. Josephs reasoned that this entrance area must be finished in a manner that the public would regard as appropriate for an opera house and for the central building in Lincoln Center. His view prevailed with the Executive Committee, and an expenditure of $500,000 beyond the budget was authorized.

Some months earlier Harrison had commissioned Dr. Hans Harald Rath, the head of the Vienna firm of J & J Lobmeyr, to submit designs for crystal chandeliers and for small fixtures throughout the public areas. Rockefeller negotiated with Austrian Chancellor, Alfons Gorbach, suggesting that the Austrian Government make a gift of the light fixtures to Lincoln Center, and in due time the Bundestag approved the gift. Dr. Rath's designs featured a number of innovative crystal sunbursts. In the auditorium, several large ones of varying sizes would be in fixed ceiling positions, with a semicircle of smaller sunbursts hung near the fronts of the boxes and equipped with winches to raise them out of the range of audience sightlines as the house lights were dimmed for the start of a performance. Dr. Rath also planned an arrangement of suspended crystal sunbursts to hang in the foyer and be visible from the plaza through the glass of the facade.

While these financial, organizational, and design matters were dominating the attention of Lincoln Center's top leadership, the actual building of the opera house was moving steadily ahead. This was the period of structural steel erection for the stage and backstage complex, and on January 20, 1964, the structure reached its highest level; Rudolph Bing and opera stars Leontyne Price and Robert Merrill signed their names on the topmost steel beam before it was hoisted into place. By April 23, 1964, the opening date of the New York State Theater, the five arches forming the front of the opera house were in place and visible, and the cooling tower on the west end of the opera was in operation.

During the summer of 1964, the configuration of the auditorium gradually took shape. In a forest of scaffolding, concrete was poured for one after another tier of boxes and balconies. Then the pouring began for the great barrel vaults forming the structural roof, starting at the east facade and gradually moving toward the supporting structural beams above the proscenium. In a series of movements of the huge inverted semi-cylindrical forms, one after another of the seg-

Opera House as seen from stage—May 1964

ments of the roof structure became reinforced concrete. Finally, on October 8, 1964, the final pour was celebrated.

Major building construction was accomplished by the end of 1965. Finishing work continued in some parts of the building after that date, and in the spring of 1966 the Metropolitan's scenery and costume shops and their personnel gradually moved into their new quarters. During this last year of opera construction the cost control system kept further changes to a minimum, but it could not prevent some cost escalation. By the time of building completion, the total cost of the opera house had risen to $46.877 million.

As completion of the Metropolitan drew near, questions of acoustics were foremost on the minds of management and artists. Their questions could be resolved only by an actual test, with singers on stage, an orchestra in the pit, and an audience in the house. On the afternoon of April 11, 1966, a performance of Puccini's "Girl of the Golden West," previously scheduled for a full student audience in the old house was shifted to the new one. At the first intermission, Young met Bing and Harrison as they came out into the foyer. Each was beaming and wore a look of enormous relief on his face. Acoustically, the opera house had passed muster. Word of mouth about the sound in the new house was favorable from that day forward.

Rehearsals for the opening season of the Metropolitan began on June 15. This early start permitted the opera staff and their technicians to learn to use their new and complex environment and gave time for a shakedown in the functioning of the sophisticated equipment. Most of these technical systems worked well during the preopening rehearsals, but there were two exceptions. A serious failure occurred in the turntable during a dress rehearsal of "Antony and Cleopatra," the opera scheduled for opening night. This production called for a sphinx to turn several times. During the rehearsal, the supporting structure of the turntable floor buckled and made the entire mechanism inoperative. A quick investigation turned up a series of facts. Five years before, the technical staff of the Metropolitan had specified a weight limit of 10,000 pounds, and the turntable had been engineered and built to sustain that weight. During the rehearsal, in addition to the weight of the sphinx, a cast of over 300 had been crowded on to it, a total weight of at least 40,000 pounds. Simple repair was not possible, nor would it solve the problem of the initial error in the weight specifications. Eventually the Metropolitan built a new turntable at its own expense. For the opening production, they mounted the sphinx on casters, and nine stagehands inside rotated it manually. In rehearsal, their feet slipped on the new floor, so nine pairs of sneakers were ordered posthaste by the Met.

The second equipment breakdown occurred in the hoisting mechanism for the small sunburst light fixtures which were operated on a system of synchronized electric winches. During a dress rehearsal, the motor on one of the hoists jammed, stopped the whole mechanism, and left all the fixtures in the line of sight from the balcony. Overnight the contractors released the jammed motor, but they had no explanations for its failure, nor could they guarantee that it would not happen again. Bing would not risk a possible failure that was peripheral to his operatic production and ordered that the light fixtures be kept in their ceiling positions. After hundreds of round-trips for the fixtures during several weeks of work between midnight and dawn, one motor shaft was discovered to be out of alignment. That motor was replaced, and Bing permitted their regular use.

A full decade had passed in the creation of the new Metropolitan Opera House. Wallace Harrison took his nebulous plans of 1956 through innumerable revisions, refinements, and enlargements. The financial requirements went up again and again and again; new budgets and new goals were set, and the money was raised. The building was under construction for four and one-half years, but, finally, in September, 1966, the new home for the Metropolitan Opera stood ready to receive its audiences.

JUILLIARD

In 1962, only the new home for the Juilliard School was not yet under construction. Preliminary architectural planning had been suspended pending the outcome of negotiations with the city to purchase the west end of the Juilliard block. This area, then occupied by the obsolete High School of Commerce, was designated by the city for its new LaGuardia High School of Music and Art. For this site to become available for Lincoln Center, a larger alternate site had to be found for the new high school. The Lincoln-Amsterdam Urban Renewal Project west of Lincoln Center was in the planning stage, and sufficient land could be made available there.

As the next step to advance this plan, Milton Mollen, Chairman of the City Housing and Redevelopment Board, asked Lincoln Center in October, 1962 to make a written offer to purchase the old Commerce high school at a price equal to its appraised reuse value, or the net cost to the city of acquiring the alternate site under the urban renewal procedures, whichever was higher. The probable price would be $1.2 million, a sum which real estate advisers considered fair. Funds for such a purchase were assured from Rockefeller's pledge to the

Special Gifts Fund, outside the campaign goal. (See Chapter 10, p. 138.)

The board authorized purchase of the High School of Commerce site on the basis suggested, but at a maximum price of $1.2 million. The city officials rejected this offer, maintaining that the Board of Estimate would never approve it with the stipulation of a maximum price. After nearly six months of stalemate over this issue, it became clear that the political realities in the situation made the city's position immovable. The Lincoln Center board agreed in May 1963 to buy the property without the protection of the maximum price. Within a month, the city accepted Lincoln Center's new offer.

However, this city action did not make the enlarged Juilliard site immediately available. Since the old High School of Commerce was then in use for 3000 students, the Board of Education could not close it until another new high school on the west side of Manhattan would be opened in 1965. This imposed a delay of at least two years before construction of Juilliard could begin. Notwithstanding this delay, the solution of the site enlargement problem permitted resumption in 1963 of preliminary planning. Belluschi maintained continuous consultation with Peter Mennin, president of the school, and Philip Hart, his staff associate. The general layout, when adjusted to the enlarged site, brought marked improvements in the functional efficiency of the building and achieved the architectural objective of a longer, lower building that bore a better relationship to the rest of the center. But detailed planning also enlarged the total volume. In working out definite plans for the use of its multipurpose theater, the school increased its audience capacity from 600 to 1000; clarification of the functional uses of the 15 studios for opera, dance, and drama training resulted in larger floor areas and higher ceilings than earlier plans had provided. A further increase in cubage came from the specifications of Heinrich Keilholz, the German acoustical consultant. For adequate reverberation in the chamber music hall, the Juilliard Theater, and the orchestra rehearsal hall, he called for greater ceiling height. To achieve a low noise level throughout the school, he specified a low velocity air flow in the ventilation system. This required supply and exhaust ducts to be larger than in a normal building, thus adding to the total cubic volume.

The cumulative effect of these changes was such that, on March 3, 1964, Belluschi warned the Building Committee that the increase in building size would increase costs well beyond the authorized budget of $17.2 million. Throughout the summer and fall of 1964, in numerous planning and review sessions with Mennin and Hart, Belluschi tried to reduce the building size, but without significant effect.

However, his plans became sufficiently detailed that more definite estimates could be made by Morse and the general contractor. When their figures were assembled, the estimate exceeded the construction budget by $8 million, or nearly 50 percent. Morse had a list of possible reductions in construction costs, but his most optimistic forecast would require a budget increase of $4 to $5 million if the building were to be undertaken as planned. The only way to bring the cost of the building down to the budget level would be through elimination of some activity of the school and of its related building space. From the standpoint of Juilliard, the drama or dance divisions were the only possibilities that could, if required, be eliminated. But both divisions had been included in the educational plan at the initiative of Lincoln Center to assure that the school would offer professional training in all the performing arts. No one favored elimination of either division.

The Building Committee concluded that the only sound course of action was to proceed with the plans at hand, to utilize as many of the cost reductions suggested by Morse as possible, and to recommend to the board an increase in the Juilliard budget of $4 million. This was authorized, recognizing that it would have to be raised beyond the campaign goal.

The schedule for start of construction in 1965 was again threatened by a Board of Education decision to delay the closing of the High School of Commerce because of a continuing city-wide shortage of high school classrooms. Since the school was housed in two buildings, the Board proposed in February, 1965 to close Commerce High in two stages: in June they would vacate the older of the two Commerce buildings, adjacent to the Juilliard site; but they would continue to use the other Commerce building as a high school annex for at least three more years.[19] This plot added to the Juilliard site was large enough to accommodate Belluschi's design for the building, and Lincoln Center agreed to purchase it.

These decisions settled the timing of the start of Juilliard construction. They also set in motion a long chain of legal steps with the city. The High School of Commerce site was treated as an amendment to the Lincoln Square Urban Renewal Project, and a year later received final approval. Excavation for Juilliard began in April 1965 on the Broadway end of the block; the old high school was demolished in the summer; foundations and basement wall construction followed during the fall and early winter.

Concurrently with these first stages of construction, the general contractor, in close consultation with Morse, was negotiating the numerous subcontracts for the superstructure and finishing of the building. In some trades, Morse's optimism for savings was justified, but in others substantial savings proved to be impossible. The most serious problem developed with respect to the structural steel contract. The quantity required had nearly doubled from the estimated 3800 tons to an actual 6800. A searching inquiry disclosed that, although a major error had been made earlier by the engineers in calculating the tonnage requirements, no claim for damages could be sustained. Another cause for the increase was the heavy concrete specified by Keilholz to create thick walls and floors for sound isolation of studios and practice rooms, many of which were located above the theater and chamber music hall. Thus the ceiling beams had become enormous girders to bridge the wide spaces and bear the weight above. This greater complexity of structural design accounted for nearly one-third of the increase of $1.6 million in the steel bids.

The net result from all the subcontract negotiations was a need for $3.14 million more than the budget provided. This set of disturbing facts and the resulting cost escalation occurred immediately after the adoption in December, 1965 of a new capital budget for completion of the center, a plan that had presumably covered all needed cost increases.[20] It was an extraordinarily difficult time to seek another budget increase. But the complex problems were presented in full to combined Executive and Building Committee meetings, and on March 31, 1966, the directors accepted the fact that these costs could not be avoided. As a result of this action, the budget authorized for the Juilliard building became $24.34 million.

Concurrently, in March 1966, the schedule for Juilliard construction was reviewed. A 1967 opening could not be achieved, and efforts were now focused on completion in 1968. But during the summer of 1966, more construction delays were encountered. A strike of hoisting engineers seriously interfered with the progress of steel erection. Schuman accepted 1969 as the date for the opening of the chamber music hall, and Mennin adjusted his plans for the later opening of the Juilliard School.

During these four years since the opening of Philharmonic Hall, the Juilliard site had been enlarged in prolonged, complex, but successful negotiations with the city. Planning for the Juilliard School had gone through numerous revisions. As with the opera building, costs had risen and budgets increased. Construction of Juilliard was underway. When the Opera was opened, progress in construction was on schedule for completion in 1969.

CHAPTER 14

Visual Arts in Lincoln Center
1960–1970

In the early days of planning Lincoln Center, the architects and directors regarded the arts of sculpture and painting as important features of the environment they were creating. Works by eminent artists were sought and commissioned. The directors, in their first financial planning, considered a specific provision for the visual arts in the capital budget. A consensus emerged that special gifts of art or of funds designated for the purchase or commissioning of art would be welcomed, but no specific amount would be budgeted.

Aesthetic decisions regarding selection or acceptance of art works required some screening process, and in April 1960, Arthur Houghton agreed to draw together a small group for this purpose. A year later, the board created a Committee on Arts and Acquisitions; Frank Stanton, who was elected a director at the end of 1960, was named chairman with two distinguished museum directors chosen as members: René d'Harnoncourt from the Museum of Modern Art and Andrew Ritchie from the Yale University Art Gallery. This Art Committee, working with each architect concerned, functioned quietly and effectively throughout the building period of Lincoln Center.

The first major work of art was commissioned for the Grand Prome-

nade in Philharmonic Hall through a special gift from the Ittleson
Family Foundation. In his concept for the Grand Promenade, Max
Abramovitz, the Philharmonic architect, wanted a sculpture "that
would float in space and relate in a contemporary manner to the
interior of the foyer just as the magnificent crystal chandeliers of a
former day took command of their space." He recommended Richard
Lippold as the artist he felt could best create a sculpture that would
satisfactorily meet these desires. Lippold designed a construction
composed of two mirror images extending the full length of the
Promenade area. He named the work "Orpheus and Apollo"; 190
strips of highly polished Muntz metal, a copper alloy, are suspended
by steel wires from the ceiling. At the opening of the hall in September 1962, the sculpture was only partially installed, but it was
soon completed and dedicated on December 19. The huge sculpture,
which is visible from the Broadway frontage as well as from within the
Promenade area, immediately became a subject of great public interest. The *New York Times* reported:

> "Orpheus and Apollo" can be looked at in two ways. As a decor-
> ative object sparkling and reflecting rays of light, it catches and
> holds the eye. More importantly, its geometric irregularity
> animates the whole vast interior space cradling it and relieves the
> severely plain and unadorned character of the architecture.
>
> The very fact that it appears to float obedient to none but aes-
> thetic laws provides a welcome contrast to the inevitably calcu-
> lated practicality of the building.[1]

Soon after the installation, admiring the sculpture from the escalator directly beneath it, Young realized that one metal plate had been
hung by a single wire, while all others had two. The matching second
half also had one plate with a single wire. Lippold had designed his
work to provide for movement from air currents on these two single-
wired plates. The strength of the wire and its "fatigue factor" from
slight twisting movements were questioned, and no guarantee could
be given that the wire would not break. The knifelike plate suspended
by a single wire directly above each escalator was a risk that could not
be tolerated, and the artist was persuaded to install a second wire.
    Also in Philharmonic Hall, a bronze sculptural work by Antoine
Bourdelle, a "Tragic Mask of Beethoven," was given by Mr. Albert J.
Dreitzer and installed at the south end of the Grand Promenade. A set
of four panels of Steuben glass, with figures representative of the arts
of symphony, opera, ballet, and drama, etched by Don Wier, was

Photo by Bob Serating

"Orpheus and Appollo" by Richard Lippald, hangs in the Grand Promenade of Philharmonic Hall.

given by Arthur Houghton and displayed in the Green Room. Soon after the hall opened, a bronze of the head of Gustav Mahler, done by Auguste Rodin in 1901, was received as a gift from Mr. and Mrs. Erich Cohn. It can be found on the west side of the Promenade level.

A bust of the composer Antonin Dvorak by Ian Mestrovic was presented in 1963 to the New York Philharmonic-Symphony Society by the Czechoslovak National Council of America and placed in the penthouse garden terrace outside the Society's board room at the north end of Philharmonic Hall.

A gift of funds for art, designated for Philharmonic Hall came late in 1962 from David Rockefeller. From these funds, two contemporary sculptures were commissioned. The first one, "Archangel," by Seymour Lipton, was unveiled on February 18, 1964. It is a large, abstract construction of Monel metal and bronze and is situated at the east end of the entrance foyer where it is also visible from the outside of the building. The artist said of his work:

> I thought the spot needed something voluptuous, baroque. Also, I wanted to make an affirmation of life, its positive forces, an argument against death. I wanted to say that man can survive.

He also said that he wanted an effect of "crashing through." As he worked on the piece, he found the conclusion of Handel's "Messiah" was most in his mind. He described the finished work as "a sort of Hallelujah sculpture."[2] The second sculpture, commissioned for the west end of the entrance foyer, is a dark bronze work by Dimitri Hadzi, titled "K458–The Hunt." When it was unveiled on October 27, 1964, the artist related the name of the piece to his fondness for Mozart's string quartet, identified by that number. "The quartet is gay and lively, and I think my piece is, too."

In the New York State Theater, Philip Johnson wanted to counter the highly rectilinear nature of the Grand Promenade with two very large pieces of sculpture in curvilinear forms. He wanted them to be in a polished, white marble, for, with high-powered spot lights focused on them, they were to serve as one of the major sources of reflected light in the room. So strongly did he feel that the room needed this feature that he decided to contribute the two pieces of sculpture to Lincoln Center as his personal gift. Johnson chose two pairs of female figures, done by Elie Nadelman in the 1940s. He felt these were exactly right in their forms, but much too small in scale for the enormous room. His solution was to commission copies, enlarged to twice their original size, to be carved by Italian artisans in Carrara

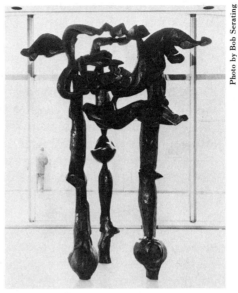

"Archangel" by Seymour Lipton.   "K458—The Hunt" by Dimitri Hadzi.

marble from the same quarry that had been used by Michaelangelo. The sculptural figures arrived in November 1963 and became the most controversial feature of the building; feelings about them were strong, both pro and con as works of art, as enlargements from the artist's originals, and as appropriate to their setting. No one seemed neutral or disinterested in them. An article in the *New Yorker* described them:

> . . . holding down the floor . . . are two monumental sculptures, each a pair of nude or nearly nude women, made of Carrara marble so highly polished that it resembles yogurt. I am not sure that they are great sculpture, but they are at least very good substitutes for it, having substantial mass and weight, and reminding one that one is in a place where human beings are still important, namely a theater.[3]

One critic characterized the figures as "monstrous" and "absolutely pneumatic," but John Canaday, art critic of the *New York Times*, placed his seal of approval on them:

> . . . the sculpture in the New York State Theater is bang-up. . . [the Elie Nadelman enlargements] are the most satisfying orna-

ments serving a comparable function since Carpeaux's sculptures on the facade of the Paris Opera nearly 100 years ago.

These paired female figures have a combination of high style, sly levity and swelling monumentality that unifies them with the scale and elegance of the architecture and, at the same time, involves them in a kind of amorous badinage with its angularities. In this perfect marriage between sculpture and architecture, either would miss the other in separation. But the sculpture is the dependent partner. As pure sculpture, these superb confections are not much more than deft and devilishly clever, but as architectural adjuncts they are brought to fulfillment.[4]

While the New York State Theater was under construction, Johnson also proposed the purchase of several sculptures by Reuben Nakian, Edward Higgins, and Lee Bontecou, and a painting by Jasper Johns for the entrance foyers of the theater. Approval was given by the Art Committee and by the Lists for financing from their gift. Two bronze sculptural works were made available by Mrs. John D. Rockefeller 3rd for the New York State Theater. She placed the "Birth of the Muses" by Jacques Lipschitz on indefinite loan to Lincoln Center and made a gift of the "Grande Martirio Sanguinante" by Francesco Somaini. These two sculptures can be seen at the ends of the side corridors that provide access to the theater's orchestra level.

The largest single gift for the visual arts at Lincoln Center came in 1961 as a part of a grant of $1 million from the Albert A. List Foundation. Half of the grant was designated for purchase of works of sculpture or painting and $100,000 was set aside to commission art posters, a special interest of Mrs. List. (The balance of the grant was for construction of the opera house, recognized by naming the chorus rehearsal room "List Hall.") Under the poster program leading American artists have designed posters for the celebration of the opening of each building and of each festival series of artistic presentations. The first marked the opening of Philharmonic Hall and was created by Ben Shahn. Other commissions were awarded to a number of contemporary artists, including Robert Indiana, Ellsworth Kelly, Frank Stella, and Andy Warhol.

In November 1961, the Art Committee met with the architects to consider possibilities for placing a major sculptural work in the reflecting pool of the North Plaza. Their overwhelming first choice was the British sculptor, Henry Moore. Already recognized as one of the

Photo: Susanne Faulkner Stevens

"Two Female Figures" by Elie Nadelman.

Photo by Bob Serating

"Birth of the Muses" by Jacques Lipschitz.

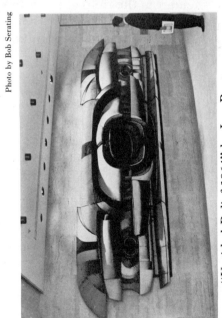

Photo by Bob Serating

"Untitled Relief 1964" by Lee Bontecou.

greats among living sculptors, Moore was in great demand. Stanton knew him well, told him of this choice, and persuaded him to visit the Lincoln Center site in March 1962 when he was in New York. Moore was impressed with the immensity of the space and was especially intrigued with the large reflecting pool as a setting for sculpture. He left New York uncommitted, but on March 12, 1962, he wrote Stanton from his home in England saying:

> I am beginning to collect my thoughts about the Lincoln Centre. I was very impressed by the whole scheme, and by being able to grasp by visiting the site, what a grand vision it has behind it. I am sure it is going to be a most marvelous achievement and the more I think of it, the more I would like to take part in it.

He also wrote Rockefeller in the same vein, concluding, "I have decided I would like to take part in it."

Moore's acceptance of the challenge of Lincoln Center meant a great deal to all associated with the project. In responding to his letter, Rockefeller wrote him:

> Your interest in and increasing enthusiasm for Lincoln Center is tremendously gratifying to all of us here. We are pleased not only in terms of the particular piece of sculpture about which we have been talking with you but because it means much to us that a leader in the field of the arts such as yourself should be so moved and stirred by our project. As you can imagine, we have had many ups and downs in relation to the Center and as a result sometimes we are more conscious of the difficulties and the problems than the promise and the excitement.

The Lists were party to the progress in the negotiations with Moore and agreed that the purchase of the sculpture should be made from their gift. Gordon Bunshaft and Stanton saw Moore frequently during the next two years as his ideas for the sculpture were taking form, and by the summer of 1964, he had completed his modeling of the Lincoln Center Reclining Figure. Several of the architects, members of the Art Committee, and Young had seen the finished plaster model and reported enthusiastically on its suitability for the Lincoln Center setting. Casting in bronze was begun in Berlin with completion scheduled for the next spring. During this period frequent correspondence between the architects, Moore, and the foundry clarified information about weights, anchorage, water level, wind resistance, lighting, and other technical details needed to prepare the site for the installation of the finished sculpture in the summer of 1965.

By Ben Shahn.

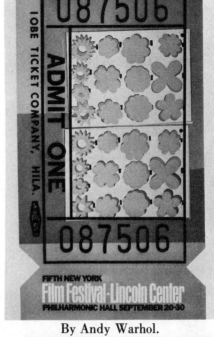

By Andy Warhol.

By Robert Indiana.

By Marc Chagall.

Posters sponsored by List Poster Program

Henry Moore considers Lincoln Center as a site for sculpture (Frank Stanton and Edgar B. Young at left).

Mr. and Mrs. Howard Lipman, collectors and patrons of contemporary arts, admired the work of Alexander Calder and offered to give one of his large stabiles. The Lipmans said they " . . . had chosen Lincoln Center because they considered it the proper setting for the works of outstanding American artists of our time. And we think of Calder as one of America's outstanding artists." The Art Committee welcomed the possibility of acquiring a Calder. The artist had a large stabile, already completed, that seemed right for a position in the North Plaza near the entrance to the Library and Museum. Bunshaft, the architect of this building, was eager to have a Calder work there, and he urged approval of this particular stabile, entitled "Le Guichet," or the ticket seller's window.

Since this location was on public property, owned by the City of New York and under the jurisdiction of the Parks Department, the proposed work of art would have to be approved by the Commissioner of Parks, Newbold Morris, and then by the Municipal Art Commission. The same approvals were needed for the Henry Moore sculpture, since its location was also in a city-owned area of the center. Because of the eminence of both artists in the contemporary art world, prompt approval was expected with appreciation for the addition of two such distinguished works to the cityscape. But such was not the answer.

Young took up the question of the Calder and the Moore with Parks Commissioner Morris, gave him photographs of the two works which Lincoln Center proposed to place on indefinite loan to the city, and asked him to forward the proposal to the Municipal Art Commission. Morris demurred on the Moore, but replied on March 24, 1965, with reference to the Calder work:

> I regret I cannot approve it. . . . My duty is to stick to certain standards, which may be based in part upon my own taste, and to resist the use of park property for artistic experiments. Unlike private art collections, works of art cannot easily be removed or replaced once they are accepted by the City; many of these become outdated with the passing of time. Furthermore, we must select objects of art which will be most rewarding for the most people. . .
>
> The word "stabile" is new in my vocabulary, but I guess it means a piece of immovable metal or concrete, which is not art. Whether this is art or not, it does not appeal to me for installation in a *park* area.

Lincoln Center officers began immediately to resolve the problem through other city officials, and by April 5th the conflict had reached the press. The members of the Municipal Art Commission were brought to Lincoln Center to look personally at the proposed sites and were supplied full information on both pieces. On June 1, Morris wrote that, under orders from the Mayor, both works were being submitted to the Art Commission. But he remained personally opposed to them, regretting that he "was instrumental in contributing two horrors to what is otherwise such a perfect area for the performing arts." The Art Commission deferred action at its June meeting because only seven of their 12 members were present. A month later, by a narrow margin of five to four, the Commission approved the placement of both the Moore and the Calder on city property in Lincoln Center.

The two bronze pieces of the Moore figure arrived in New York in

Henry Moore at work on model.

August 1965. Moore, with his founder, Hermann Noack, were on hand to oversee the installation and to give the bronze its final finish. A trial positioning was required to determine the precise orientation in the reflecting pool and its relationship to the water level. The artist and the architects decided to raise the figure by eight inches, and Noack fabricated the extensions on the site. The two castings were then hoisted into place and anchored by concrete poured into the bases.

The official presentation of the Moore figure occurred in a simple ceremony on September 21, 1965, attended by many distinguished persons in the art world as well as by city officials and Lincoln Center leaders. Stanton spoke of Moore and of his artistry. Schuman officially presented the work on permanent loan to the City of New York, and in accepting it, Mayor Wagner awarded Moore the city's Handel Medallion for Cultural Achievement. The Lists were honored for their generous contribution. At the conclusion of the ceremony, New-

Installation.

bold Morris came to Young and said simply, "Ed, I was wrong. It really is beautiful."

On the day of dedication of the Moore, the *New York Post* lead editorial was headlined "Unconventional Victory."

> Commissioning of the Moore sculpture is welcome evidence of the center's determination to encourage audacity and originality as well as excellence.

In a conversation with Moore soon after the official presentation, Young asked him what he hoped people would see in his "Lincoln Center Reclining Figure." His reply, from a tape of the conversation, was, in part:

> This sculpture is really a mixture of two things .... Rather than just making a sculpture of rocks or making a sculpture of a

Photo: Susanne Faulkner Stevens

"Lincoln Center Reclining Figure" by Henry Moore.

Photo by Bob Serating

Alexander Calder at the
installation of "Le Guichet."

human figure . . . in this "Reclining Figure" and in the others of
mine you find not only a human outline, but also references to
landscape or rocks.

The human figure is, for me, the basis of sculpture, of all our
sense of form. If we weren't six feet high on the average, if we
didn't stand upright, if we were like animals that walked on all
fours, our sense of balance—all our architecture—would be different. Everything would be different if we weren't human
beings—if we weren't the shape that we are. So, in my opinion,
one can never get away from the human form. Even if one thinks
one is being abstract, that is really based on our sense of proportion, based on our own bodies. I have never thought that I was
aiming at pure abstraction, disconnected entirely from life.

The Calder stabile, "Le Guichet," was installed in the plaza approach to the Library & Museum entrance, and the artist personally
supervised the assembly of the large painted steel plates.
On November 15, 1965, in a presentation ceremony, the artist

and the donors of the work, Howard Lipman and his wife, Jean, editor of "Art in America," were honored. The occasion had its humorous side, with the final round in the "fight" with Newbold Morris. When Calder was introduced, as the *Times* reported,

> He stepped up to the speaker's platform, clasped his hands overhead in greeting, then pointed to Mr. Morris and said 'In this corner, embattled Newbold Morris!' The crowd roared. Mr. Morris was unruffled. 'It was only a technical knockout,' he said to Mr. Schuman as they left the platform.[5]

Mr. and Mrs. Lipman continued their interest in Lincoln Center as a setting for contemporary art. Later they presented a sculptural abstraction by David Smith, entitled "Zig IV." This work is located in the plaza level foyer of the Vivian Beaumont Theater.

The Metropolitan Opera Association owned a large collection of portraits and sculpture of present and former opera singers, and the foyers on the concourse level of the new house provided a suitable location for most of these works. The Metropolitan had its own Art Committee, and an agreement was reached with Lincoln Center that the Opera's Committee would have exclusive jurisdiction over all works of art in the auditorium and in spaces in the building designed for the sole use of the Metropolitan, but that new art works proposed for the public foyers and the exterior of the building would be reviewed by the art committees of both.

The first art object contributed for the new Opera House was a bronze sculpture "Kneeling Woman" by Aristide Maillol, a gift from A. Conger Goodyear. The piece was installed in the foyer area of the Dress Circle. Another bronze "Kneeling Woman" by the German sculptor, Wilhelm Lembruck, was contributed to commemorate the gift of $2.5 million from the Federal Republic of Germany toward the cost of the stage facilities in the Metropolitan. The donors of this sculpture were Gert von Gontard and the Myron and Anabel Taylor Foundation. The piece is located at the top of the grand staircase.

On the Grand Tier level, Harrison had designed two concave marble walls as background for sculptural works. In addition, two very large bare walls facing the front made a setting for huge paintings or murals. A gift from the Henry L. and Grace Doherty Charitable Foundation was used to purchase two sculptures of standing figures by Maillol for placement on pedestals against the high curved marble walls. One is "Summer," cast in 1910; the other is "Venus Without Arms," created in 1920.

"Die Kniende" (Kneeling Woman) by Wilhelm Lehmbruck.

Mark Chagall with "Le Triomphe de la Musique."

Also from this gift, the Metropolitan commissioned Marc Chagall to do the two huge paintings that cover the two front walls. These paintings are also visible from the plaza through the glass facade of the five arches and make a striking and colorful addition to the front of the Opera. Herman Krawitz, Assistant Manager of the Metropolitan, who maintained close contact with Chagall throughout the artist's creation of this pair of paintings, has described them:

Chagall chose a vivid red as the dominant hue to celebrate "Le Triomphe de la Musique" on the south side. Ballerinas, singers, and musicians intermingle with images of St. Patrick's Cathedral, Rockefeller Center and the New York skyline, as Chagall pays homage to American, French, and Russian music through jazz, folk and opera references. Humorous and affectionate accents are interposed by Rudolf Bing's appearance in gypsy costume (the central figure in a group of three on the left), by portraits of the Chagalls and of Maya Plisetskaya of the Bolshoi Ballet, who posed for this likeness.

In the predominantly yellow painting on the north "Les Sources de la Musique," cornerstone concerns of Chagall regarding love, hope and peace are pervasive themes, through the tree of life

Photo by John Young

"Three X Three Interplay" by Yaacov Agam.

(floating on the Hudson against the Manhattan skyline), through the lyre shared by a combined King David and Orpheus, through nods to Beethoven's FIDELIO, Mozart's MAGIC FLUTE, Bach, Wagner and Verdi.[6]

Four works of sculpture were given to the Juilliard complex. Miss Tully gave a bronze cast of Bourdelle's "Beethoven a la Colonne" (1901), for the foyer of Alice Tully Hall. A Louise Nevelson work, "Nightsphere-Light, 1969," an intricate construction of wood, painted black, was another gift from Mr. and Mrs. Howard Lipman. It covers the entire end wall of the Juilliard Theater lobby. A large untitled abstraction in black Swedish granite, sculptured by the Japanese artist, Masayuki Nagare, commands the landing of the main staircase. This work was given by John D. Rockefeller 3rd to commemorate the contribution of $1 million made to Lincoln Center by the Keidanren, the Japan Federation of Economic Organizations. In 1970, Mr. and Mrs. George Jaffin, on behalf of the American-Israel Cultural Foundation, donated to the School a work by Israeli artist, Yaacov Agam, titled "Three x Three Interplay." This sculpture, located on Juilliard's terrace above the entrance to Alice Tully Hall, consists of three tall zig-zag columns of polished stainless steel.

Through the generosity of donors with special interest in the visual arts, Lincoln Center has become the architectural setting for a number of works by artists of world renown. These sculptures and paintings add significantly to the public enjoyment of the center.

CHAPTER 15

Completion Requirements and Campaign
1962–1966

The capital budget for the entire Lincoln Center project, as adopted in May 1960, was $142 million. Four-fifths of this was assured by September, 1962. The $40 million expected from city, state, and federal sources was committed, and of the $102 million required from private contributors, $76.5 million had been raised.

A "Completion Campaign" had been launched in May 1962, and the summer effort had brought in $3.1 million. In the weeks following the Philharmonic Hall opening, over $1 million came through repeat grants from the John A. Hartford and the James Foundations and the Carnegie Corporation. By December, three new patrons had been added to the roster through pledges for $100,000 or more each.

Unexpected encouragement came from two legacies. A bequest of $1 million to Lincoln Center was included in the will of Hazel Hopkins Ford, a person who was unknown to anyone raising funds for Lincoln Center. Vivian Beaumont Allen, who died on October 10, 1962, left one-half of her residuary estate to the Vivian Beaumont Allen Foundation with an expression of her wish that the Trustees give special consideration to the needs of the Beaumont Theater.

The most significant prospects in the Completion Campaign were the Ford and Rockefeller Foundations. Close contact was maintained with the officers of both foundations who indicated their growing doubt that Lincoln Center could be built and placed in full operation within the budget limits of its announced goal. The officers of Lincoln Center had already recognized that escalation in building costs called for adjustments in the financial plan and that there were other inevitable expenses that would have to be met. The foundation concern gave added pressure to conduct a thorough financial review.

This financial analysis of needs and of plans to meet them was presented in January 1963 in a report, "Requirements for Completion." The increased cost of construction to carry out approved building plans amounted to $10.6 million. In addition, other nonconstruction needs were faced realistically and were included in the projection of the total required to complete the center and to bring it fully into operation: $5.5 million to cover costs of administration, fund raising, and building maintenance during the period of construction and $2.5 million to establish a New Projects Underwriting Fund. (See Chapter 16, p. 229.) The total of these items added $18.6 million to the previous goal of $102 million (as established in 1960) for a new campaign goal of $120.6 million.

This addition to the campaign goal, added to the $24.8 million still needed to meet the former goal created a staggering gap of over $43 million. The report indicated the amounts needed from each category of donor.

	Figures in Millions	
	Already Raised	Balance Needed
From Individuals	$35.0	$10.0
From Foundations	33.0	27.5
From Business and Labor	6.7	3.4
From Foreign Grants	2.5	2.5
	$77.2	$43.4

Rockefeller wrote Henry Heald, president of the Ford Foundation, transmitting the "Requirements for Completion," and specifically requesting a grant of $12.5 million, a sum equal to their two earlier grants. The foundation officers responded immediately that they were concerned with the future financial viability of the artistic institutions that were to comprise Lincoln Center, and they did not feel they could consider the capital request for the center apart from the needs of the constituents. They urged Lincoln Center to compile a composite report on all Lincoln Center organizations, indicating their needs to see them firmly established in the center. Since total financial independence of the constituents was a firm policy of the center, the Ford Foundation agreed to consider separate requests from each constituent. Meanwhile, a request for another major grant was made to the Rockefeller Foundation.

Each foundation held meetings of their trustees in April, and each acted on the Lincoln Center requests. The Ford Foundation approved a grant of $12.5 million to Lincoln Center, making its total commitment $25 million, the largest single source of support for the Center. Conditions attached to the new grant required matching funds from other sources on the basis of $2.5 to $1, thus providing strong leverage for other gifts. The Rockefeller Foundation made an outright grant of $5 million, bringing the total of its grants up to $15 million. These grants pushed the total raised in the campaign to $101.8 million.

A gap of nearly $19 million remained. The campaign leaders hoped to raise this sum largely from donors capable of making large contributions. This would require the personal attention of the directors and key campaign volunteers, and it was hoped to be of short duration. The campaign staff was reduced, the East Side office was closed, and the small remaining staff was absorbed in the Lincoln Center headquarters nearer the center. While success in meeting this remaining capital need had first priority, planning was beginning for the financial future of operation and programming of Lincoln Center. To assist in this, Edward Gemmell, administrative vice president of Princeton University, was retained as a consultant. In order to clear the decks for the new annual fund raising, Gemmell advocated an even more concentrated effort, by the most effective campaign volunteers and other community leaders, on large and promising prospects. A new Development Committee, replacing the Capital Campaign organization, was approved by the board in June 1963; Clarence Francis remained as chairman. For continuing staff service and professional planning of future fund raising, Gemmell recommended a full-time staff member to supervise the fund-raising staff work and to provide services for the volunteers, and Henry Bessire, also from Princeton, was appointed Executive Director, Development. Bessire later became a vice president of Lincoln Center and served in responsible and constructive staff leadership for the next six years, until Princeton University recalled him to become its vice president for development.

The reorganization of the campaign, the new approach, the impetus for completion expected to follow the two large foundation grants, all failed to develop a new momentum in the money-raising effort. By the end of 1963, barely $2 million more had been added. At this low point in the campaign. Rockefeller was deeply concerned over the slow progress and particularly disturbed by the lack of constituent cooperation and participation. He called a special meeting of constituent representatives that resulted in the enlistment of a number of trustees of the Metropolitan, the Philharmonic, and other constituents who were prominent corporate executives. Their presence among the campaign volunteers added strength to the second round of appeals, and it was in the area of banks and corporations that the stalemate in the completion drive began to break.

The strongest impetus to all phases of the completion campaign came from a challenge made personally by Rockefeller. When he met with the new Development Committee in February 1964, $16 million was still needed to reach the capital completion goal. Rockefeller offered to be responsible for obtaining contributions to match all that others in the campaign organization might secure. He was willing, alone, to accept an $8 million goal; the campaign group accepted his challenge.

Immediately, the pace of the campaign increased, and the successful opening of the New York State Theater in April, with its favorable nationwide publicity, served as another stimulus. Large repeat pledges were made by the Bell Telephone System, Chase Manhattan Bank, and First National City Bank, and four of the directors became patrons. Three gifts of $1 million each came from the Federation of Economic Organizations in Japan, the Louis Calder Foundation, and the James Foundation. The Metropolitan Opera mounted its own drive among opera subscribers especially for patrons of Lincoln Center and donors of seat endowments.

During the year 1965, the succession of major contributions continued. Miss Alice Tully added substantially to her gift designated for the Chamber Music Hall. Mr. and Mrs. Van Allen Clark gave $1,169,000 to the Fund for Education. This was the first of several gifts from the Clarks and their foundation to provide the main financial backing for the Lincoln Center Student Program. In fulfillment of the hope Mrs. Allen had expressed in her will, a grant of $1.5 million came from the Vivian B. Allen Foundation. Major designated pledges of $1 million each came from C. Michael Paul for the recital hall in Juilliard, and from Shelby Collum Davis for the museum features of the Library and Museum. The campaign goal was reached by November 1965, but no public announcement was made, for the campaign was rolling with momentum and every dollar that could be raised as an overrun was needed to meet still more capital needs already authorized.

The board meeting held on December 13, 1965 was not just an

end-of-the-year roundup. When Clarence Francis gave his report as campaign chairman, it marked the successful end of a decade of fiscal planning and capital fund raising. The total raised in the campaign was $122.1 million, $1.5 million over the goal, and more "in the pipeline." The directors and the campaign volunteers had more than met Rockefeller's challenge; his own efforts had more than matched their results. At this time Francis felt he had accomplished the task he had been asked to do, and his long desire to step down from the campaign chairmanship could be fulfilled, although he agreed to remain on the board.

Hoyt Ammidon, chairman of the United States Trust Company, had agreed to head a new continuing program to raise annual operating support. Board chairman and official representative of the Music Theater, he was already an active director of Lincoln Center; he was elected a member of the Executive Committee to succeed Francis.

But the clean break from capital fund raising was not immediately possible, in spite of the success in more than reaching the campaign goal. Delays in building completion and higher construction costs were bringing new capital needs. Therefore, a three-year plan for transition to full-scale, recurring, annual campaigns had been worked out by Ammidon, Schuman, and Bessire, in consultation with Gemmell. Ammidon presented this plan immediately following Francis' report of the capital campaign success. The plan outlined all of Lincoln Center's financial needs anticipated during the next three years, drawing a sharp distinction between those that were an extension of the capital goal, related to the creation and establishment of the center, and those that were related to its continuing educational and artistic programs. The magnitude of these ongoing needs and the plan to deal with them is described in Chapter 21, p. 291, since those facts bear directly on the operating and financial developments at that later period in Lincoln Center's history. The items in the extended capital category totaled $10.4 million, including construction overages, an unallocated contingency for the remaining construction period, and estimates for building operating needs pending completion of the center. Toward this need, the campaign overrun (then estimated to produce $3.5 million) was available. A capital budget revision would allocate $4.3 million in unrestricted pledges previously assigned to complete the Fund for Education and the New Projects Underwriting Fund. The justification for this diversion of program funds to capital needs was the expectation of success in replenishing those funds through annual campaigns. The balance of $2.6 million in extended capital needs was to be raised through a quiet, unpublicized solicitation of memorial gifts and bequests.

The board approved these recommendations, but Rockefeller was concerned over the risk that the third point in the plan, the continuing capital fund raising, would interfere with the appeals for current operating support. In a confidential letter to Spofford, dated December 16, 1965, he pledged to give $2.5 million, the approximate amount needed to close this final gap. His purpose in making the pledge at this time was

> . . . to support those on whom the future financial burden of Lincoln Center will rest so that they can start their efforts with a virtually clean slate and without a burden carried over from the Center's initial capital needs.

At the same time Rockefeller also pledged an additional $2.5 million for the Special Gift Fund, outside the capital campaign goal. It was his hope

> . . . that this contribution, and whatever might accrue to it through prudent investment, will be held in reserve as a last resource to be called upon by vote of the Board, to be used only to meet the most important and pressing needs of the Center—needs for which no other funds are available or can be found.

So concerned was Rockefeller that his two pledges, for a total of $5 million, not reduce the remaining momentum in the capital campaign nor deter the efforts and success of the new drive, for operating funds that he asked Spofford to limit knowledge of his pledge to Lincoln Center's top leadership. To the Board, Rockefeller's pledge was reported as coming from an anonymous source.

————————————————————————————

Public announcement that Lincoln Center had reached and surpassed its campaign objective was made on January 31, 1966. By this time the total raised had gone $4.7 million beyond the goal, for a total of $125.3 million, the largest amount ever raised for artistic purposes. The importance of large gifts was indicated by the fact that 20 contributors accounted for $91 million, or 72 percent of the total. On the other hand, the widespread appeal of the center was evidenced by 8707 gifts in amounts less than $1000 that had been received for a total of $.5 million. Grants from 160 foundations made up half of the total; $50.1 million came from individuals, including 106 patrons and 2558 seat endowment gifts; $10.1 million was contributed by 377 corporations, a breakthrough in corporate philanthropy. In addition to these funds from the private sector, governmental funds of $40.1 million brought the project total, at this date, to $165.4 million.

The happy state of affairs expressed in the public announcement was short lived. Despite a firm intention to reject any further capital overruns, early in 1966 Lincoln Center was once again confronted with new and unavoidable capital needs related to the Juilliard building and to the opera house that added $3.6 million to the cumulative capital overages, as already described (Chapter 13, p. 202).

These emerging capital needs did not dampen the aura of success surrounding the capital fund achievement, nor interfere with the dinner, scheduled for April 20, 1966, to mark the first ten years of the development of the center and to celebrate the completion of the campaign. This event brought together the entire Lincoln Center family—the board members and professional staffs of all the constituents and of Lincoln Center, the volunteer leaders in the campaign, the principal donors, and the chief public officials involved. Including their spouses, a company of nearly 500 assembled at the Plaza Hotel. It was an occasion to express thanks and to look ahead to the future. Clarence Francis was especially honored for his sustained and effective campaign leadership. Schuman presented his vision of the program potential of Lincoln Center. The high point of the evening was a surprise expression by Spofford, on behalf of all of the constituent officers and directors, of appreciation and recognition of the leadership of John Rockefeller, to take the permanent form of a bronze plaque in the North Plaza.

CHAPTER 16

Programs Begin
1962–1966

"The validity of our efforts will be determined by the use we make of the several stages and many classrooms of Lincoln Center." These words of John Rockefeller at the opening of Philharmonic Hall affirmed the belief of the founders and accepted the warning from the critics that buildings alone mean nothing in the realm of the performing arts. To the job of creating the center was added the task of making it work. In no way did the opening mark completion—only one of the several stages was in use, and the many classrooms would not be available for several years; millions of dollars had yet to be raised, and Philharmonic Hall represented less than one-sixth of the planned construction. But a significant turning point had been reached.

William Schuman, Lincoln Center's new president, had been chosen to lead in artistic and educational directions. This was his strength; his enthusiasm and vision of the potentialities ahead were boundless. At Schuman's request, Edgar Young, executive vice president, continued to direct the construction and physical operation of the center and to work with Francis, Rockefeller, and Spofford in financial planning to meet the capital needs of the center. In a corporate sense, Schuman was chief executive officer, responsible to the chairman for management in all respects. Young, as executive vice president, was administratively responsible to Schuman; as Building Committee chairman, he was responsible to the chairman and the board.

The artistic programs for all of the center were to be based on the performances of the constituent companies. They had first claim on the use of their halls. The program responsibility of Lincoln Center, Inc. was to supplement and complement these artistic offerings either by booking outside attractions or by direct presentation of artists and performing companies. Lincoln Center had total responsibility for filling the free time in Philharmonic Hall under the terms of the part-time lease to the Philharmonic orchestra. Also in the New York State Theater, program responsibility for the World's Fair years of 1964 and 1965 rested entirely on Lincoln Center. But later, the year-round leases of the opera house, the Beaumont and the State theaters to the constituents were expected to place primary responsibility for filling free time on them, in consultation with Lincoln Center.

In developing Lincoln Center's programs, Schuman's interest centered on those that Lincoln Center, as an impressario, would itself present. It would make its own arrangements and contracts with artists, take the financial risks involved, and receive credit for bringing them to the public. Early in his program planning, Schuman asked for a revolving fund that could be drawn on to underwrite his proposals. He explained that Lincoln Center has many opportunities and obligations to increase performing activities within its halls and to make available presentations from the world's artistic output. The center must, therefore, have at its disposal a fund for the initial expenses of new programs and to meet possible losses. The resources of the fund were to be called upon not only to launch specific projects undertaken by the center itself, but also to assist new constituent organizations and all of the constituents in areas of activity new to them. The New Projects Underwriting Fund, with an immediate campaign goal of $2.5 million, was approved on January 14, 1963.

The first help to a constituent for a new activity was a grant of $75,000 to the Philharmonic to aid in their planning for the first series of Promenades, concerts of lighter music in a relaxed atmosphere, for the spring of 1963. Lincoln Center had built into the new hall the flexibility to turn the orchestra level into a series of terraces for tables and chairs.

The winter schedule for Philharmonic Hall began with the Philharmonic subscription season of 24 weeks, with four concerts each week, using about 40 percent of the time available during the entire year. The advance booking commitments that Reginald Allen had succeeded in making prior to Schuman's presidency already filled

a considerable number of the open dates. The Boston and Philadelphia orchestras were firmly on schedule for their New York series,
as were a number of major solo artists. For that first winter, Schuman
developed an "Introduction to Lincoln Center" series for young
people at popularly priced Saturday matinees. The series offered a
sampling of the various performing arts that would eventually be
available in all the halls of the center. Efforts were continued to fill
the remaining free time in the winter season by booking other artists
and attractions.

But filling the hall in the summer was a different matter, for that
was a period traditionally slow in artistic activity in New York.
Concert managers were reluctant to risk commitments for summer
appearances by their artists. Schuman felt that Lincoln Center must
itself present concerts to test the assumption that, with its air conditioned halls, a year-round audience could be found for serious music.
He initiated a concert series called "August Fanfare," which was well
attended and proved at once the existence of a summer audience.
Losses on the series were $19,500, but these concerts had paid
$20,436 in rental fees for the use of the hall. Since an empty hall
involves certain fixed charges, Lincoln Center had to raise money to
meet a deficit, whether for a program presented or for a hall not used.
But the former added musical services to the public; the latter was a
dead loss.

Plans for a Film Festival were developing, and Schuman announced, on December 10, 1962, a two-week festival to be held in
September of the next year. This series, presented by Lincoln Center,
Inc., established the art of film as an accepted part of the
center's artistic territory and brought large and new audiences to
the center. Financially, this first Film Festival incurred a deficit of
approximately $20,000, but it paid for its period of hall usage an
offsetting $15,000 in rental fees. Renewal of Film Festival plans for
1964 was worked out in association with the British Film Institute and
the Museum of Modern Art. In each succeeding year, the New York
Film Festival has achieved greater recognition and become an anticipated event, outstanding of its kind in the United States. But with the
elaboration of each festival, its budget also grew, and the modest
initial deficit rose to nearly $170,000 by 1965. The New Projects
Underwriting Fund was called upon to provide these increasing
amounts.

The summers of 1964 and 1965 were to be filled with programs of
the World's Fair Festival. Reginald Allen had initiated plans for that
period, but at the end of 1962, Allen accepted the invitation of the

Metropolitan Opera to return to the post of assistant to the president of the Association. World's Fair planning was continued by Allen's assistant, Richard P. Leach. A year later the programming staff was further strengthened by the appointment of Schuyler Chapin, who came to Lincoln Center from wide experience in the classical recording industry and in concert management. His contacts with artists and artist managers were worldwide. Chapin's title became Vice President for Programming at the end of 1963.

The most urgent World's Fair Festival planning was related to the New York State Theater. In December 1962 Lincoln Center extended an official invitation to the New York City Ballet to appear at the State Theater for 20 weeks in each of the two years. The precise financial terms became the subject of prolonged negotiations. Morris and Baum were striving to minimize City Center's risks; Rockefeller, Schuman, and Young were searching for a basis that Lincoln Center could afford and that would be consistent with policies and terms for other Lincoln Center halls. Not until April 1, 1963 was there acceptance of Lincoln Center's final proposal: the ballet would receive the first $65,000 of each week's box office receipts (from a possible gross of $89,000 at capacity) and, in addition, the ballet would have a grant of $200,000 from the Fund for Education and Artistic Advancement to underwrite expenses of new productions and to augment student admissions.

Schuman wanted to fill the second largest blocks of time in the State Theater with a music theater. He and Richard Rodgers worked out the plan for such an organization, and the Music Theater of Lincoln Center fulfilled this role in the World's Fair festival. (See Chapter 17, p. 241.)

To supplement the seasons of ballet and music theater, bookings were made for such distinguished overseas groups as the Royal Shakespeare Company and the Bayanihan Dance Company from the Philippines. These and other overseas bookings required no financial subsidies; on Schuman's recommendation, the board rescinded the $250,000 underwriting previously authorized for that purpose and made a $30,000 appropriation for advertising and promotion of the World's Fair Festival.

More ambitious program planning was undertaken by Schuman in 1965 for a series of summer festivals after the Fair, starting with "Festival '67." With the major performance halls of Lincoln Center due to be open by the summer of 1967, it was possible to plan for a month-long festival of all the performing arts. To encourage all constituents to participate, Schuman recommended that Lincoln Center guarantee each against financial loss. He also planned to augment the presentations of the local companies with appearances by distinguished foreign groups such as the Hamburg Opera. Schuman estimated that with full houses the festival might break even; if audiences were at 75 percent of capacity, there might be a deficit of $353,000. A maximum loss of that amount was underwritten from the New Projects Fund.

The center's educational program began two years before its first building was completed. Educational leaders on the board, especially Stoddard and McGinley, sensed an opportunity for the center to enable more young people to experience the arts of live performance, and the Lincoln Center Student Program was started as the first activity of Lincoln Center, Inc., apart from construction. Unlike the Juilliard School, whose educational focus is on the professional training of young artists, the Student Program is an effort to provide opportunities for large numbers of young people to be exposed to the enjoyment of all the performing arts. The program undertook to do this on a two-way street—it took the arts and artists from Lincoln Center into the schools, and it brought students to performances at Lincoln Center.

The Metropolitan and the Philharmonic had, for a number of years, sponsored special matinees for high school students from the New York area. In 1960 and 1961, Lincoln Center made modest grants to both and to the Juilliard School to aid in preparation of special programs for young people. The Opera developed the Metropolitan Opera Studio and took abridged versions of opera into the schools. These studio productions were simple, sung in English with piano accompaniment. They used a few props, beautiful costumes, but almost no scenery. For the opera, the Studio provided valuable training opportunities for young and promising singers. For the young people in the schools, it opened up a new world of live, exciting music.

The Philharmonic Orchestra developed a new series of afternoon student performances, which began in Carnegie Hall and continued in Philharmonic Hall. Juilliard offered the schools a wide range of solo and group performances by their most talented young artists. These youthful performers immediately established a warm rapport with their young audiences. The performing experience became important in their training, and the modest fees paid by the schools for their services were welcome.

The dean of Juilliard, Mark Schubart, who was already involved in the Student Program, was chosen by Schuman to direct the Student Program, beginning in January, 1963. A year later, he was appointed vice president for education.

By the end of the third year, the Student Program was reaching about 150,000 young people annually in 150 schools in New York City and its suburbs. An appropriation of $210,000 from the Fund for Education continued the program for another year. Planning for a three-year period through 1967 was authorized, providing a basis for substantial expansion of the program. There were negotiations with Dr. James E. Allen, Commissioner of Education for the State of New York, and with Dr. Bernard E. Donovan, New York City School Superintendent. Both school jurisdictions endorsed the program and authorized local schools to include, in their official budgets, items to cover the artist fees for performances in the schools. Previously, school funds for such purposes came only from limited local funds or auxiliary sources such as parent-teacher associations.

This official endorsement and public financial support led to a rapid expansion in the entire Student Program. By 1966, it was reaching over 400,000 students annually through more than 350 performances in 250 schools in Metropolitan New York and in upstate communities. Financially, the cost of the program rose in proportion to its size, but the level of Lincoln Center expenditure remained stable at about $250,000 annually. The difference, three times the annual Lincoln Center amount, was met by the funds from the participating schools.

A program of Lincoln Center Student Awards was inaugurated in 1965. Financed by a special gift from Mrs. Enid A. Haupt, editor and publisher of *Seventeen* magazine, these awards brought 1000 students, chosen each year by school principals, to a series of regular adult performances by each of the Lincoln Center performing companies. Attendance provided an in-depth experience in the appreciation of the performing arts to these highly motivated young people, and it became a distinct honor in a local school for a student to receive an award. They were continued through 1970.

Much of the success of the Student Program in the schools came through Lincoln Center's efforts to help teachers prepare their students to appreciate performances. Curriculum materials and teaching guides were prepared; institutes and convocations were held at Lincoln Center to interest and train teachers and school administrators.

The principle of drawing upon and subsidizing the constituents for the artistic content of the Student Program was an important key to its success. Lincoln Center, acting as catalyst and coordinator, strengthened the constituents and encouraged something new and larger than they as individual organizations could do. To foster the cooperative atmosphere surrounding the Student Program the

Photo © Lawrence Fried

Together with chamber music.

Photo by A. V. Sobolewski

A dance specialist meets a class.

Photo: Susanne Faulkner Stevens

Metropolitan Opera Studio at a high school.

Photo © Martha Swope

Students set up stage for a
repertory theater performance.

Photo: Susanne Faulkner Stevens

Juilliard Drama Division performs for students.

Lincoln Center student program.

Photo: Susanne Faulkner Stevens

A set designer meets a 7th grade class.

Lincoln Center Council on Educational Programs was established in October 1964. Under the chairmanship of Schubart, this council drew together for consideration of policy and program the key staff members and volunteers engaged in student activities in all the constituents. The original participation by the Metropolitan, the Philharmonic, and Juilliard was gradually enlarged to include the New York City Ballet and Opera, the Repertory Theater, and eventually the Chamber Music Society and the Film Society of Lincoln Center.

The art of choral music had not been given specific recognition in planning Lincoln Center, but the reservoir of choral works and the development of fine singing groups throughout the world made an international choral festival an attractive possibility for sponsorship. With an initial stimulus from Spofford, plans were made for a week of festival singing at Lincoln Center, and in October, 1964, the board authorized the use of $100,000 from the Fund for Education for such a festival. During the next 12 months, an associate of Schubart, James Bjorge, travelled nationwide and worldwide and assembled 20 university choral groups from the United States and 16 from overseas. Robert Shaw was retained as musical director of the festival and as conductor of the combined choral groups.

The Choral Festival opened in Philharmonic Hall on September 22, 1965 with a gala performance that began and ended with the united voices of 850 choristers. In a week of concerts, each group displayed its specialties, often in native costume. The choruses from overseas were formed into several touring groups that reached 63 campuses and were feted and praised throughout their tours. The success of this first International Choral Festival led to its repetition three years later.

As one after another building was completed and placed in use, the task of making the physical environment of the center work to the satisfaction of both artists and audience assumed increasing importance. It was a job of maintenance and operation of the buildings and grounds of the center. In addition it involved skills, trades and unions peculiar to theater operation: stagehands and front of the house staff such as ticket takers, ushers, rest room attendants, and box office treasurers.

Responsibility for these varied functions is not uniform throughout the center, for it is affected by the different forms of building leases. Since the Philharmonic is a part-time tenant, Lincoln Center, Inc. operates the concert hall. During the period of the World's Fair, it managed the New York State Theater, but, in 1966, City Center assumed full operating responsibility. The Vivian Beaumont Theater, the Metropolitan Opera House, and the Juilliard School Building are each operated by the constituent tenant. But the central mechanical plant, which serves all buildings for air conditioning and heating, is the direct responsibility of Lincoln Center, Inc. The public areas of the center, including not only the plazas and parks, but also the lower concourse roadways, pedestrian passages, and the garage, are owned by the City of New York and administered by its Park Department.

These various leasing, ownership, and operational arrangements created a complex and confused situation with numerous points where friction and frustration were frequent and where cooperation was needed in their management. But from the standpoint of the people who use the center, there is no complexity or confusion; whenever anything, anywhere, goes wrong, Lincoln Center, Inc. is assumed to be responsible, and complaints are directed to its management. Therefore it has become necessary for Lincoln Center to be vigilant throughout the complex and to anticipate and assist in solving any problem. Young rode herd in the area of building operation. The engineering aspects were initially organized under Powers, who selected and supervised the chief engineer in the central mechanical plant and in the two buildings directly operated by Lincoln Center. Each of these buildings was, in turn, staffed with its own operating engineers, mechanics, and electricians on shifts around the clock. Allen, executive director for operations, established staffs for operating the stage and front-of-the-house with a house manager in charge in each building.

In the summer of 1964, new problems arose when the garage was opened. Although it was under the jurisdiction of the Parks Department, it was actually operated by a concessionaire. Almost immediately problems of health, safety, and convenience for the public arose. There were complaints concerning gargage ventilation, especially evident as the garage emptied after performances when traffic congestion on the surrounding streets impeded the flow of exiting cars. The city Traffic Department and the Police Department agreed to change some traffic patterns to improve the flow. Inspection and tests by state health and safety authorities indicated that the ventilation system was adequate, but that the concessionaire had not been using it fully. Also, there were a number of incidents in the garage, as well as in the public areas of the center, that called for greater security protection. Efforts to arrange additional city police protection were only partially successful, and in 1966 Lincoln Center established its own security force, staffed largely with retired police officers.

A growing restiveness developed among directors over the costs of building operations. In the case of Philharmonic Hall, by the end of its third year, its accumulated deficit had climbed to $567,000.

Young, with the help of Amyas Ames, president of the Philharmonic, enlarged the responsibility of the hall manager, effected economies in staffing patterns and in contracts for services. More bookings were secured. The trend of deficits was reversed, but the operating loss was not eliminated. Late in 1965, Schuman retained the consulting services of Victor Borella, the retired president of Rockefeller Center, Inc. His experience there enabled him to bring numerous suggestions for efficiency and improved public service into the management of Lincoln Center. A Committee on General Services was established with representatives from the constituents, to formulate policies for maintenance and operation.

A fresh approach to the relationship between Lincoln Center and the city Department of Parks became possible with the inauguration, on January 1, 1966, of Mayor John V. Lindsay. The new Mayor and his new Commissioner of Parks and Recreation, Thomas P. F. Hoving, became ex-officio Directors of Lincoln Center. A significant change in arrangements was negotiated under which Lincoln Center undertook direct management of the cleaning and maintenance of the public areas under contract with the Parks Department.

During these four years of evolving opertions, the top leadership of Lincoln Center was continued with very little change. Rockefeller remained as chairman, with Houghton, Josephs, and Spofford as vice chairmen and Schuman as president. The Executive Committee exercised increasing control over policy and fiscal matters, and Spofford remained its chairman.

Among the directors, death took its toll. Irving Olds died on March 4, 1963, after a long illness. C. D. Jackson died on September 18, 1964. Each of these men had played a significant part in the origin and early development of the center. To succeed Jackson on the Lincoln Center board, the Metropolitan designated its chairman, Lauder Greenway, who had been active in the Lincoln Center campaign from its start.

Arthur Houghton retired from the chairmanship of the Philharmonic in October 1963. David Keiser, who had been its president, succeeded him, and Amyas Ames was elected Philharmonic president. Houghton remained on the Lincoln Center board as a public director and as vice chairman until February 28, 1965, when he resigned to take on the responsibility of president of the Metropolitan Museum of Art. Keiser and Ames became the two representatives of the Philharmonic. In business, Ames was a senior partner in the investment firm of Kidder, Peabody & Co. He quickly became one of the leading directors of Lincoln Center.

In 1966 the board was gradually enlarged. On Ammidon's recommendation, J. Howard Rambin and Lawrence A. Wein were elected directors. Rambin served only a short time, but Wein became an increasingly active member of the board, serving as a member of the Executive and Education Committees and later as vice chairman of the board. Professionally, Wein is an attorney; he is a well-known real estate investor and a recognized leader in numerous philanthropic causes.

Young remained in the post of executive vice president through 1965. He had been an associate of John D. Rockefeller, 3rd for many years, had worked with him on Lincoln Center matters from its origin, and had been on a full-time loan to Lincoln Center since the emergency in 1961, when he was named Acting President. Throughout his service as an executive officer of Lincoln Center, it was understood that eventually he would return to the Rockefeller office. At the end of 1965, Rockefeller asked him to resume, on a full-time basis, his former associate position. In addition to his need to have Young back at his own office, Rockefeller felt the time had come for Schuman to assume complete executive responsibility for all facets of Lincoln Center. He was particularly concerned that Schuman carry the full responsibility for the financial planning for the future. Young remained on the board and, at Schuman's request, continued as chairman of the Building Committee to assure continuity in the completion of the building program.

Between 1962 and 1966, as Lincoln Center became operational, it had developed in three major ways. It had become an entrepreneur for a growing number and variety of quality artistic presentations to supplement the programs of the constituent institutions. It had developed an educational program in the performing arts that was making a significant impact on young people. It had accepted a primary role in making Lincoln Center, as a place, work so that both artists and the public could feel comfortable, secure, and pleased to be there.

CHAPTER 17

Vexations of Federation
1962–1966

Throughout the four years between 1962 and 1966, a persistent effort was made to complete the federation of artistic and educational institutions. By 1962 agreements had been reached with the Philharmonic-Symphony Society, the Metropolitan Opera Association, and the Juilliard School; The New York Public Library was effectively, though not contractually, in the project; The Repertory Theater was proceeding under its own leadership and was assumed to be more independent than later facts would substantiate. This infant institution would require more nursing. Of the six constituents in the original plan, only the one for residence in the New York State Theater was not yet resolved, although it was assumed that City Center would come in as sponsor of both the New York City Ballet and the New York City Opera. Both City Center and Lincoln Center had a rough road ahead before agreements would be reached.

Lincoln Center started as a concept of six federated institutions, each at home in a building designed especially for it. This organizational concept was not a limiting one; the founders thought of the center as an evolving federation with flexibility to grow. In a territorial sense, the center was limited by its site. But there might be room within the buildings to incorporate additional artistic or educational institutions.

William Schuman brought to Lincoln Center ideas for new constituents, particularly for chamber music, modern dance, and music theater. A hall suitable for chamber music concerts had been included in the first architectural plans, and financial provision was assured in 1958 when Miss Alice Tully made her first pledge toward the cost of such a hall. In early planning, its location had been moved from Philharmonic Hall to the Juilliard complex, where it was eventually built.

Several distinguished chamber music groups performed in New York, but none functioned in an institutional framework. It soon became clear to Schuman that if an organization were to be developed in this field, it would have to be initiated by Lincoln Center. Although delays in the construction timetable for the Juilliard building kept postponing availability of the chamber music hall, discussions of the long-range objective of such an institution were held with interested people, particularly with Miss Tully and Frank Taplin, chairman of the Marlboro Arts Festival.

By the spring of 1966, Miss Tully's interest had grown, and she had increased her pledge toward the cost of the hall. She agreed to drop her anonymity and to allow the hall to bear her name. Schuman's discussions with her and with others encouraged the formation of a chamber music organization. Charles Wadsworth, an American pianist and artistic director for chamber music at the Festival of Two Worlds at Spoleto, was engaged to work up detailed plans for a chamber music performing group. In close collaboration with Schuman, he developed specific plans and budgets for a series of chamber music concerts to be presented by Lincoln Center.

Schuman's efforts to bring modern dance into Lincoln Center first began in 1963. He had many friends in this field through his contacts as an educator and a composer. Each of the modern dance companies then in existence was attached to a highly individualistic choreographer. None had a strong institutional framework with an active board of trustees and fund-raising capability, and there was, on all sides, a reluctance to collaborate in the formation of a joint institutional umbrella. However, in response to Schuman's urging, several of the choreographers and their companies combined for appearances in March 1965 in an American Dance Theater program as a part of the World's Fair Festival at the State Theater and $70,000 from the New Projects Underwriting Fund subsidized the event. Schuman continued to work with this group and hoped to build it into a constituent. He could give moral support and advice only; no financial commitment was authorized by Lincoln Center. By this time the directors had become wary of risk-taking in the development of new organizations. To Schuman's keen regret, his hope for a modern dance constituent was never realized.

In the artistic field of music theater, much more rapid progress was achieved. Schuman felt that music theater was an indigenous American art form deserving recognition. He had many talks with Richard Rodgers that were directed toward formation of a constituent to present revivals of musical shows and opportunities for new works. Their specific plan was to start with a summer program to present two six-week runs of musical revivals, then to develop a resident company in the State Theater. Some, though not all, of their shows would be chosen from the long list of successes created by Rodgers and his librettists, Moss Hart and Oscar Hammerstein. Rodgers and his group of associates provided all the professional and technical leadership required, but an institutional framework of lay leadership would be necessary for organizational continuity, for nonprofit status, and for fund raising. However, both Rodgers and Schuman were optimistic that the musical revivals could be staged on a break-even basis; if successful, touring schedules might be worked out on a profitable basis. Hence the financial need was expected to be much less than that of constituents sponsoring other arts.

In January 1963, Hoyt Ammidon, chairman of the board of the United States Trust Company, agreed to become chairman of the new organization, and a small group, largely of businessmen, agreed to be directors. They were incorporated as the Music Theater of Lincoln Center, approved as an official constituent, and Ammidon was elected a Lincoln Center director. Rodgers became a member of the Lincoln Center Council. On June 20, 1963, a loan of $65,000 from the New Projects Underwriting Fund was approved to aid the Music Theater in its initial financing and to enable it to sign artist contracts for its 1964 season. For the official opening of the New York State Theater on April 23, 1964, the Music Theater, as well as the New York City Ballet took part in the program, representing the anticipated resident performing companies.

No understanding had yet been reached concerning the institutional status of the Ballet and City Center. Immediately after the theater opening, Schuman advised City Center that Lincoln Center stood by its former invitation to become a constituent, and once again, negotiations were opened.

Young conferred several times with Morton Baum and reduced the number of unresolved issues but reached no final agreement. The basic problem, control of the free time in the theater, remained. City Center wanted complete control of their new home, similar to that they had enjoyed for years in the lease of their 55th Street theater. Lincoln Center was offering a lease on the pattern of that of the Philharmonic for 30 weeks each year, with priority on choice of time, and was preserving a season of 12 weeks in each year for the Music Theater as well as scattered periods, totaling 10 weeks, for booking outside attractions, largely from overseas.

The negotiations dragged on with minor concessions from both sides, but with no resolution of the issue over control of free time in the house. Baum was adamant in his insistence on a year-round lease; Lincoln Center held firm to its need to be able to book the free time in the house. Differences were exacerbated by press accounts frequently expressing half-truths or exaggerated positions. While negotiators on both sides tried to maintain an official silence, there were leaks and a few angry outbursts.

The public financing of the building had been accomplished on the premise that the theater would become the home for City Center as an integral part of Lincoln Center. After six months of frustrating effort by the two organizations to find a basis for compromise, both state and city administrations were eager to see the conflict settled. At the end of 1964, leaders of the opposing centers were brought together with the governor and the mayor, who exerted further pressure for compromise.

The officers of Lincoln Center reexamined the issues involved in the booking of free time in the State Theater. Except for the obligation to preserve time for the new Music Theater constituent, booking any remaining time could be handled under a lease, comparable to that already negotiated with the Metropolitan Opera, that would give year-round operational responsibility and control of the theater to City Center, with a guarantee of at least 12 summer weeks for Music Theater and a provision for consultation with Lincoln Center in arranging any outside bookings. While Baum wanted absolute control of the theater, with no involvement of Lincoln Center, this compromise was one he could live with. By January 11, 1965 a general understanding on these terms was reached. Lincoln Center director, Father McGinley, agreed to work out remaining contractual details. He was able to enter this emotion-charged situation as a new, calm voice, unhampered by prior negotiating difficulties. On April 12, 1965, final agreement was accomplished, and City Center became, at last, an official constituent of Lincoln Center, and its ballet and opera companies became resident performing companies in the State Theater. City Center's representatives, Mrs. Lytle Hull and Morton Baum, were elected directors of Lincoln Center, and George Balanchine and Julius Rudel became members of the Lincoln Center Council.

The Repertory Theater of Lincoln Center had been established as an independent corporation before the Philharmonic Hall opening under the professional leadership of Robert Whitehead and Elia Kazan and the board leadership of George Woods. Unavoidable delays in starting construction of the Vivian Beaumont Theater deferred their opening until 1965. Since their agreements with artists were based on a 1963 opening, these delays presented serious problems. Whitehead's strong desire and the Repertory board decision was to adhere to that original timetable for the company, with the consequent need to find another theater for their first two years of operation.

Kazan and Whitehead wanted a theater similar in architectural concept to their permanent home. They developed an idea for a temporary building, on a minimal basis, that would duplicate the thrust stage and the semi-circular arena seating planned for the Vivian Beaumont. There was no available space for a temporary theater on the Lincoln Center site; however, Dr. George Stoddard, a director of both Lincoln Center and the Repertory Theater and also the chancellor of New York University, found a site on land owned by NYU near Washington Square.

George Woods, the Repertory chairman, found these ambitious plans financially disturbing and reported his concern to the Lincoln Center Executive Committee on January 30, 1963. Lincoln Center took a firm position that it could not help in financing such a building; the Repertory Theater organization would have to take full responsibility.

Whitehead sought financial help from ANTA and its chairman, Robert Dowling, and his negotiation with ANTA and with NYU moved ahead rapidly. Woods continued to be concerned about the financial viability of the project. By mid-February 1963, he told the Lincoln Center Executive Committee that he had lost confidence in Whitehead. However, Whitehead's plan seemed sound to both ANTA and New York University and was approved by a majority of the Repertory board. By July, formal contracts covered the capital financing of the temporary structure and the lease of the site. By September, construction of the steel and sheet-metal building was underway. Whitehead and Kazan were moving ahead in the training of their acting company with the aid of the grant of $500,000 from the Fund for Education and Artistic Advancement; the Miller play, "After the Fall," was in rehearsal.

The press build-up for the Repertory Theater company brought an advance sale of 65 percent of the number of seats available in their first season. But in spite of this record, as the opening date of January 13, 1964 approached, the new organization was in a deep cash-flow crisis. The $500,000 from the Education Fund had all been spent, and on December 23, 1963, Woods appealed to Lincoln Center for further assistance. The Repertory Theater was granted a loan of $100,000 from the New Projects Underwriting Fund.

The opening night of Miller's play, "After The Fall," brought mixed critical response, but favorable audience reaction assured a strong box office sale throughout its scheduled run. The first season of the new Repertory Theater continued with presentations of Eugene O'Neill's "Marco's Millions," and a new play by S. N. Behrman. But the new organization came through its first year with only moderate success. The inital surge of subscription sales, a total of 47,000 for the entire first season, dropped to 19,000 for the second. New contributing sources were hard to find, and the Repertory Theater ended its first year with a deficit of $350,000. There was no prospect of early repayment of the $100,000 loan from Lincoln Center.

In August 1964, George Woods, asked to be relieved of his responsibility as Repertory president, now that it had been established and had completed its first year of operation. A month later Robert L. Hoguet, Jr., agreed to serve.

Hoguet was senior trust officer of the First National City Bank. He appreciated good theater and was willing to work for its establishment on a sound institutional basis. He was already well informed about Lincoln Center, for his wife had for years been a leading member of the board of the Philharmonic and was one of the key volunteers in the Lincoln Center Campaign. On October 19, 1964, Hoguet was elected a director of Lincoln Center, representing the theater constituent; Woods became chairman of the Repertory Theater board and remained a public director of Lincoln Center.

In late 1964 there was, behind the scenes among several members of the Repertory board, a growing discontent with the leadership of Whitehead and Kazan. Woods' earlier worry about financial control had not been dispelled, and the mounting deficit aggravated his loss of confidence. Kazan had, in their second year of operation, practically withdrawn from administration though he remained active in directing the company. The opening play in 1964 was a Kazan-directed revival of the classic, "The Changeling," and was assaulted by the critics as a disaster. It was withdrawn before the end of its scheduled run and was followed by the more successful "Incident at Vichy" by Arthur Miller.

Hoguet felt that his first responsibility on becoming president was to work out changes in the management and financial control of the organization. Under the Lincoln Center concept of constituent independence, his problem should have concerned only the Repertory Theater board, and Lincoln Center should not have been involved. However, he sought Schuman's help in finding a new managing director. Subsequent developments led to a violent controversy in the public arena that shook the foundation of federation in the new center. The controversy broke on the front page of the *New York Times* on December 5, 1964, with a headline: "Bing Attack Airs Dispute on Theater of Lincoln Center." Rudolf Bing, General Manager of the Metropolitan Opera charged that the Center was "apparently deteriorating into a free-for-all jungle," and he planned to resign from the Lincoln Center council.

Behind this public charge was Schuman's response to Hoguet's request for help. Schuman had suggested that Herman Krawitz, the assistant manager of the Metropolitan Opera, might be a candidate and had offered to sound out Krawitz' possible interest. There were tragic gaps in communication. Hoguet, anticipating discretion and secrecy in the development of his personnel search, had not yet given Whitehead or Kazan any intimation of an impending change in their status. Neither Anthony Bliss, the Opera President, nor Rudolf Bing, the General Manager had been advised. Schuman talked to Krawitz.

As reported in the press the sequence of unfolding events started on Friday, November 27, when Schuman met Bliss, the Opera president, and told him that he had recommended Krawitz to Hoguet. On the next day Bliss met Hoguet and told him how important Krawitz was to the Metropolitan. Hoguet then met privately with Krawitz. Several days later, according to Bing, Schuman "offered him [Krawitz] undisputed control of the Repertory Theater."

Krawitz was quoted:

I told the Metropolitan management that I was not asking for release. At the same time, the Met informed me it would not give me a release.

Bing's further public comment:

I am deeply disturbed over the matter because I see in the way it's been handled the breakdown of the Lincoln Center concept, that is, a group of constituents, of sister organizations, who, under the umbrella of Lincoln Center, work toward a higher goal of artistic achievement.

If, because of the president of Lincoln Center, it is apparently deteriorating to a free-for-all jungle where constituents can raid each other at will, this does not seem to me to jibe with these lofty ideals.

In the press, Schuman remained silent; Whitehead said he would prefer not to discuss the situation at this time; Kazan could not be reached. For three weeks the story was inflamed and inflated with quotations of charges and countercharges from the people involved. It seemed clear that Whitehead was to go, and so, on December 10, in the *World Telegram*, Kazan stated, "I'm with Bob Whitehead. If he's not there, I'm not there." The acting company was said "to be threatening to walk out in a body if they didn't get Whitehead back, but Whitehead had talked them out of it." Finally, on December 27, a *New York Post* headline read "Storm Over Lincoln Center." It reported a succession of resignations, saying,

> The doors and corridors shudder with the exits of the mighty. Robert Whitehead, Arthur Miller, Elia Kazan, Maureen Stapleton, Joseph Verner Reed.

Reed, a director of the Repertory Theater, compared

> the problems at Lincoln Center with those of this country in its formative stages (and since.) How much federal power shall there be? How much power reserved to the States?

As a result, by the end of 1964, the Repertory Theater was left without professional leadership but with a handsome, new theater nearing completion. Lincoln Center's public image had been badly tarnished. But within Lincoln Center, Schuman's position was secure despite the criticism that had been heaped on him in the press. He gave a full report of what had transpired to the board in December. He emphasized that "all efforts had been made to retain the solidarity of Lincoln Center as an institution," and he defended his public silence as "an effort to avoid reducing the dispute to the personal." Both Schuman and Bliss stressed that the main objective at this time should be to rebuild. At the conclusion of discussion the board expressed complete confidence in Schuman.

Hoguet continued to seek the help of Lincoln Center in finding new leadership for his theater organization. By January 1965 their search resulted in an offer to the team of Herbert Blau and Jules Irving, who were codirectors of the San Francisco Workshop Theater. Stoddard reported this decision to the Lincoln Center Board, describing them as "bright and dedicated young men who have always had to act within reasonable budgets." They were elected members of the Lincoln Center Council, replacing Whitehead and Kazan. (Rudolf Bing, in spite of his angry threat, did not resign from the council.)

While the leadership crisis of the Repertory Theater dominated the headlines, an interim solution for its financial crisis was necessary to its survival. On December 1, 1964, Lincoln Center granted $300,000 on a matching basis. This need was considered to be a "last resort" call on the Rockefeller special gift fund. The cash-flow crisis deepened, and two more times the directors felt they had no alternative to providing help to keep alive the theater organization they had created. After its near collapse, the future began to look brighter with a new team on the job.

Blau and Irving assembled their acting company and by June were starting rehearsals for their opening play, "Danton's Death." The Repertory board developed new plans to raise ongoing financial support; the Guild of the Repertory Theater was established to raise funds, and it planned an elaborate benefit for a preview of the opening play. After the opening night, held on October 21, 1965, Blau gave the Lincoln Center board an enthusiastic report of the new company and theater, which he described as "the most effective theater of its kind in the United States." But despite his initial satisfaction and favorable prospects for their new company, within a year Blau decided to return to academic life. Jules Irving was, however, eager to stay and became sole director of the theater for the next six years. Financial problems continued and Hoguet appealed to Lincoln Center for additional aid; two times a loan of $100,000 was extended.

These four years were a period of growing pains in the center. The members of the new informal federation had to learn how to live together and in a fruitful alliance with Lincoln Center. Lincoln Center, Inc. was itself feeling its way. The crisis over the Repertory Theater's leadership demanded a careful analysis of the nature of the Center's relationships with all its constituents. Under Rockefeller's impetus, there was a firm acknowledgment of the independence of the constituents and a disclaimer of any desire on the part of Lincoln Center to control them.

But the problems of constituent relations were both broader and deeper than revealed in the Repertory situation. Frictions developed with the Metropolitan over summer usage of the new Opera House. Schuman and Chapin were upset by a Met announcement of summer rentals to impressario Sol Hurok without prior consultation with Lincoln Center. Rudolph Bing was upset by repertory choices of the Hamburg Opera, brought to Festival '67 by Lincoln Center, and of the Rome Opera for 1968.

An issue arose with the Philharmonic over the high costs of operating the concert hall. The initial hope for a breakeven basis was not realized, and the Philharmonic was called upon, as provided in the contract, to meet its proportionate share of the deficit. The high operating costs were blamed on an "excessively large and expensive building," and a few felt that such a costly building has been imposed on them by Lincoln Center. A review of the record of the Building Committee showed that, at every step of the way, the Philharmonic leaders had participated in decisions and that the building in all essential features had been designed and built with full agreement by the Philharmonic.

Nevertheless, in May, 1966, Amyas Ames, the president of the Philharmonic, asked for a change in their rental contract. He wanted a fixed charge per concert established that would free the Philharmonic from its deficit obligation. Lincoln Center directors saw immediately that Ames' proposal not only created a financial problem, but that agreement would place Lincoln Center in the position of subsidizing the Philharmonic, a relationship different from that with any other constituent. Not until late in 1966 was agreement reached essentially confirming the principles of the original contract.

The issues raised by the Philharmonic were symptomatic of problems encountered by each constituent after its move into its new home. A period of adjustment to its new environment and to a new financial situation was difficult. In spite of careful planning and continuous participation, the move brought unforeseen problems and frustrations as well as satisfactions.

Another kind of dispute developed with Juilliard, even though its building was not yet completed. Again, the issue was over money, specifically the relationship between a grant of $0.5 million to Lincoln Center from the Carnegie Corporation (designated for Juilliard scholarships) and Lincoln Center's commitment of $2.5 million to support the Juilliard drama training program. Peter Mennin, president of Juilliard, with strong support from his trustees, took the position that the Carnegie grant was separate from, and in addition to, Lincoln Center's obligation. Schuman's position was, on the other hand, that the Carnegie grant should be credited to this obligation. Several attempts at negotiation and amicable settlement failed. In November 1965 the board approved Schuman's position, with the further proviso that accumulated interest earned on the Carnegie grant should also remain with Lincoln Center.

The Juilliard reaction was strong and bitter, and this issue remained a festering sore in the Juilliard relationship. Four years later, the matter was reconsidered and with concurrence of the Carnegie Corporation, mutual agreement was reached. The Carnegie grant was credited to the drama program, but the sizeable interest accumulation belonged to Juilliard rather than to Lincoln Center.

These frictions in the constituent relationships became a subject of deep concern to Rockefeller. He felt they indicated a lack of trust and confidence in Lincoln Center and its officers, and a lack of consensus on where and how Lincoln Center should be moving. During the winter of 1965 and 1966, in a succession of private conferences between Rockefeller, Schuman, Josephs, and Spofford on behalf on Lincoln Center and small groups of constituent officers and trustees, efforts were made to achieve a better understanding of the underlying concept of the center, based on a common set of objectives and a cooperative approach to the solution of mutual problems.

The Plaza on Opening Night.

CHAPTER 18

The Opening of the Metropolitan
Opera House

September 16, 1966

And so, last night, it finally came to pass: the grand, grand
opening of the grand, grand Metropolitan Opera.

It was quite a spectacle, situated on the cosmic scale somewhere
above the primeval atom that caused the original Big Bang, and
somewhere below the creation of the Milky Way. It was a spectacle that connoisseurs will put in their memory box and treasure
forever.[1]

Thus began Harold Schonberg's opening night review in the *New York
Times*. For the Metropolitan Opera, the opening was the fulfillment of
desires for a new home harbored for 58 years; for Lincoln Center, it
was the culmination of a decade of planning and building to foster all
the performing arts and to serve the public. In architectural terms,
the opera house crowned the setting. It completed both Lincoln
Center Plaza and the more cloistered North Plaza. As the largest and
the most costly of the center's buildings, it had received a great
amount of advance attention. Public interest and anticipation was
high.

The opening event was conceived and carried out by the Metro-

251

politan. To open the first season in the new house, Rudolf Bing wanted a new opera and an American one. More than two years in advance, Samuel Barber had been commissioned to compose a new opera for the occasion. He chose for his theme a musical version of Shakespeare's "Antony and Cleopatra," and his librettist and collaborator was Franco Zeffirelli, who was also the designer and director of the production. Bing cast the opera almost entirely with Americans; Leontyne Price and Justino Diaz sang the title roles, and Thomas Schippers conducted.

The one ominous cloud that hung over the opening was a labor dispute between the American Federation of Musicians and the Metropolitan. Prolonged negotiations had reached a climax in the week before opening, and the union had called a strike. The orchestra members agreed to play for the opening night without a contract, but all succeeding performances were affected. Bing postponed the other two premieres scheduled for opening week, and the entire opera season was in jeopardy. The audience came to the opening night not knowing when opera might be performed again in the new house.

The opening night gala was held as a benefit for the Metropolitan Opera. The $400,000 gross was a most welcome addition to their coffers, for they needed every dollar this special event could produce to help meet the high costs of nine new and refurbished productions for this first season in their new home.

In the late afternoon of Friday, September 16, Lincoln Center Plaza was prepared for the evening event. A wide red carpet was rolled from the doors of the Opera House down the steps and across the plaza. Police stanchions separated this walkway for ticket holders from the crowd of over 3000 interested and curious onlookers. Those members of the audience who had made dinner reservations at the two restaurants inside the house began to arrive, in full dress, before six o'clock. Dr. Hans Rath, the Viennese designer of the crystal chandeliers, and his wife arrived in a style unique for New York. When they came out of the Plaza Hotel that evening, no taxis were available. Undaunted, Dr. Rath saw, across the street, the lineup of horse-drawn carriages for tourist rides in Central Park; he hailed one and directed it to Lincoln Center. The carriage pulled up on the roadway at the eastern end of the plaza to the applause of the crowd.

A special dinner party had been arranged in the Metropolitan Board Room for guests of honor. Diplomatic dignitaries arrived, were applauded, photographed, and welcomed by Bing on the plaza at the entrance to the Opera House. Governor Nelson Rockefeller and Mayor John Lindsay with their wives, United Nations Secretary General U Thant and others came at the appointed hour, and the principal guests, the First Lady, Mrs. Lyndon Johnson and guests, President and Mrs.Ferdinand E. Marcos of the Philippines, were escorted into the house by John Rockefeller. The nature of the opening-night audience was described the next day:

> Hundreds of formally dressed tycoons, aristocrats, nabobs, bankers, moguls, diplomats, potentates, fashion plates, grande dames, and other assorted Great Society overachievers. . . the kind of glamour the nation has come to associate with New York on a good day.[2]

As the audience gathered for the performance, they lingered in the foyer, for their first interest was to watch the arrival of others. The vantage points on the grand staircase and along the balconies of the upper tiers filled rapidly. The crush of people became an almost immovable mass until the chimes summoned them to their seats. According to plan, after the playing of the National Anthem, there

Opening Night audience.

Photo by Bob Serating

Photo by Bob Serating

The Opera foyer on opening night

were two brief addresses. John Rockefeller, speaking on behalf of Lincoln Center, officially turned the new Opera House over to the Metropolitan, and Anthony Bliss, president, accepted it for the Opera Association. Then came the world premiere of Barber's new opera. At the end of the second intermission, Bing stepped in front of the golden curtain and, as one reporter put it, gave "the most triumphant third act prelude since 'Lohengrin.'" He announced:

> The dispute with the musicians is settled. The strike is over. The season is secure. The years of frustration, animosity and unpleasantness depart and I welcome this fine orchestra.[3]

The new house clearly competed with the new opera for attention that night. Said the *Times* the next day: "The overwhelming consensus was that the building was a smash hit."[4] On the crucial question of acoustics, Alan Rich reported, in the *World Journal Tribune:*

> . . . it is obvious that everyone's major area of concern, acoustical properties, had ceased to be a concern. The house sounds great.[5]

Harold Schonberg, in the *Times,* was more reserved. Referring to the high promise indicated by the acoustical test of the preceding April, he wrote:

> But last night the Metropolitan Opera seemed more interested in spectacle than in sound. Often the entire stage was used, without a backdrop. As a result, singers found their voices going as far back as forward.[6]

In later usage, the initial favorable impression was fully confirmed. The acoustical success was especially remarkable because of the huge size of the auditorium. With 3800 seats, it has 175 more seats than the old house. By comparison with the great opera houses of Europe, it is gigantic. Paris seats only 2347; London's Covent Garden, 2200; La Scala, in Milan, 2135; and the Vienna Opera only 1620. Moreover, each seat in the Metropolitan takes up more space than does a small crowded seat in the old houses. Wallace Harrison and his acoustical advisors, Wilhelm Jordon of Denmark and Cyril Harris of New York, had accepted the challenge of the large house and had succeeded.

The audience had a greater feeling of closeness to the stage than they had known in the old Metropolitan. Harrison had widened the horseshoe and reduced the curve at its end. This brought hundreds of seats closer to the stage. Gone were the posts that had obstructed vision, as well as a large number of seats with a partial view. The size of the public spaces impressed the first nighters. Promenades and refreshment areas were spacious in contrast to the cramped quarters of the old house. Also, it was a democratic house. Exactly the same comfortable seats and the same upholstery were found in the family circle at the top of the house as in the orchestra level. All levels opened into the same general open foyer space, and the entire audience used the same main entrance. Gone was the segregation of entrances, stairways, and elevators to the higher reaches of the house.

Large as it is, the auditorium of the new house represents less than one-third of the total space in the building, a reversal of the propor-

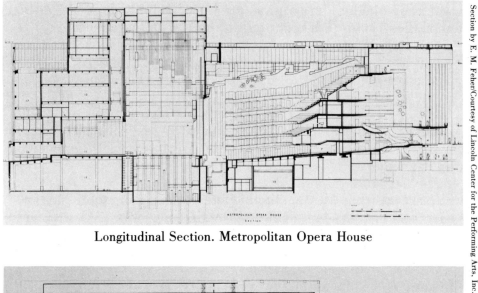

Longitudinal Section. Metropolitan Opera House

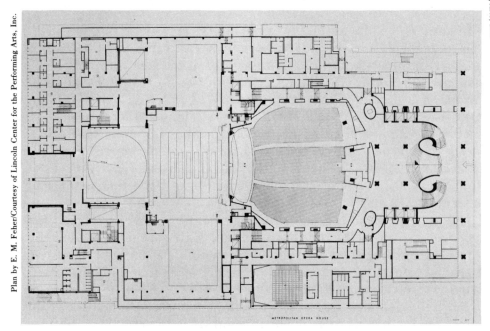

Stage and orchestra level plan. Metropolitan Opera House

tions in the old house. The new proscenium and the visible stage are almost identical in size to the old, but the invisible stage provides three more areas, each duplicating the playing area—one directly behind it and one on each side. Each of these auxiliary stages is equipped with wagons to roll entire sets into place in a matter of seconds. The height of the fly loft over the main stage is 110 feet, the equivalent of an 11-story building. Twenty rehearsal rooms are provided, three of them large enough to duplicate the main stage. The orchestra pit will accommodate 110 players.

The enormous spaces to the sides, above, and below the stage itself contain artist and chorus dressing rooms, storage space for all the productions needed in half of each season, and the shops for making costumes, wigs, and props. The carpentry, metal-working, and paint shops are capable of fabricating complete scenic sets. The paint shop has an open floor area large enough to lay out an entire canvas backdrop, and a vertical paint frame that moves, like an elevator, through a distance equivalent to six floor levels. After the opening, there was near unanimity in the judgment among opera professionals that the facilities, technical and mechanical, in the new house were ideal for opera; at that time they were the largest and the finest anywhere in the world.

In the architectural profession, the judgment of the new house was controversial and often critical. Ada Louise Huxtable, in her review in the *Times*, credited its technical and acoustical excellence and its success in terms of audience circulation, but said:

> Architecturally, however, in the sense of the exhilarating and beautiful synthesis of structure and style that produces the great buildings of our age, it is not a modern opera house at all.

She recognized the problem the architect had encountered in the insistence by the Metropolitan on "the gilded trappings of tradition." She criticized the decorative embellishments of the house as

> . . . a style that is most notable as a curiously unresolved collision of past and present of which the best that can be said is that it is consistently cautious in decor, art and atmosphere. It is a sterile throwback rather than creative 20th century design.[7]

However, Alan Rich, after acknowledging Harrison's obligation "to honor in word and deed the 83 year-old conception of what the Metropolitan Opera House has to be," concluded:

His [Harrison's] whole solution is amazingly shrewd. In outline, even to some extent in decor, the new Met is a traditional house, with all the good and bad implied in that term. Where he has been modern, it has been in areas where it really counts: in the vastly improved production facilities, in other words, and in the use of space outside the auditorium itself. Thus, if you want to

Photo by Bob Serating

The Metropolitan Opera House.

call the new Met an old house, you have every reason to do so; if you want to call it modern, you can't lose there, either.[8]

Architectural Record declared:

> Like opera itself, it [the new Met] is more flamboyant and more colorful than life; an elegant setting of gold leaf, red plush, and crystal; latter-day Baroque architecture for the most Baroque of the arts—grand opera.[9]

In the *Times* the next Sunday, Schonberg summed it all up in an article headlined "After It All Was Over":

> The building itself is going to be disliked in many quarters, praised in a few others. Nobody these days can put up a building that is going to satisfy everybody. . . Nobody is going to like it except the public. . . The new building seems to be disliked in direct ratio to one's sophistication.

> But there are several things that cannot be taken away. The stage

facilities are stupendous, and the auditorium is an acoustical success. Those are two not inconsiderable items in an opera house.[10]

The true significance of the new opera house lay in the philosophy of its design. The first consideration was to provide the best for the production and enjoyment of grand opera. That had not been true of the old house, where the first objective had been to display the members of the audience to each other. This change in emhasis was crucial to the attainment of Lincoln Center's dual objective: to foster the development of the performing arts and to enhance the enjoyment of those arts by a growing, appreciative public.

PART V

Completion
1966–1970

CHAPTER 19

End of Construction
1966–1969

The opening of the Opera House in 1966 marked the end of seven years of intensive architectural planning and construction activity. The primary unfinished task was the building of the Juilliard School, and it would take three more years before this final building in the center could be opened. But immediate pressures arose from the need for follow-up and corrective work in the buildings already finished.

The Metropolitan Opera made full-scale use of its new facilities upon resumption of its season following the opening-night settlement of the musicians' strike. During the first week, a number of relatively minor problems arose and were solved through the ingenuity of the stage crew and the constant availability of the technical personnel of the builders. An air of confidence prevailed as the Opera entered its second week. But in the afternoon preceeding the first subscription performance of the new production of "La Traviata," a crisis occurred with the stage elevators. An anguished call from Krawitz summoned Crandall, Townsend, and Young to an immediate conference in Bing's office. The facts in the situation were quickly established. The entire stage was immobilized because the stage elevators, which had previously been fixed in a stepped arrangement, had jammed and could not be moved. In an attempt to move only one of the locked elevators, the steel bars of the locking mechanism had bent severely and could not be withdrawn. The only way to free the elevators would be to saw through each of the numerous heavy bars. This might be done within the few hours available before the evening performance, and the stage floor could be leveled, but the elevators would be inoperative for the several weeks needed to accomplish complete repairs. This meant that the elevators could not be moved into the multi-level pattern required to accommodate the elaborate third-act set of "La Traviata."

Bing was furious: "We will be the laughing stock in the world of opera." He blamed the manufacturers of the elevators, the general contractor, and Lincoln Center. He threatened cancellation of the "La Traviata" performance and a public denunciation of the "the defective opera house." But calmer counsel prevailed. It was possible to use the first-act set for the third act. In the diminishing hours available, the steel locking bars were cut, the stage floor leveled and the performance went on.

This serious episode and a number of lesser malfunctions created a growing irritation on Bing's part, and he talked freely about the deficiencies of his new opera house. Fearing that Bing's assertions might damage contributor's confidence in Lincoln Center, Young wrote Spofford, then chairman of the Opera Executive Committee:

The Opera has, by its own choice, moved into a totally new and immensely complex technical environment. This is an environment that opens great opportunities never before available. But it is a limited environment. All of the energy and drive and goodwill on the part of the personnel concerned cannot overcome the limitations built into this technical equipment. No artist likes to accept any such limitations; but he exceeds these limitations at his own peril and at the risk of having the machinery break down. . . .

Although Bing's annoyance in the early months of occupancy of the new Opera House was strong, at the end of the season he wrote Rockefeller:

Now that the first season in the new house ends, I would like, if I may, to tell you that in spite of all the immense problems and difficulties of the first year, the new house has been a great source of satisfaction to all of us and to me personally. The beautiful acoustics are of course a matter of record, but altogether the house seems to be settling down and almost everybody—artists and public alike—are happy.

A serious problem of a very different sort occurred on the plaza outside the front of the Opera House immediately following its opening. The situation became known, within Lincoln Center, as the problem of the "fallen women." Repeatedly, as the audience left the opera house, one, and sometimes several people—usually women—tripped or fell on the three low steps leading down to the plaza. On one evening, 19 accidents occurred. Seldom was anyone seriously hurt, but there were sprained ankles and bruises, and an occasional ambulance call. As crowds left the Opera House, their eyes were attracted to the lights of the State Theater and Philharmonic Hall and to the fountain playing, and they seemed to be unaware of the steps.

The situation was complicated because the steps causing the problem were owned, not by Lincoln Center, but by the City of New York. As an immediate warning and deterrent, temporary barricades with flashing yellow lights were erected. For a more permanent solution, Harrison designed metal railings with lights underneath the handrail, directed onto the steps. The design was approved by both Lincoln Center and the Parks Department, but the latter had no financial leeway for such an improvement in its current year's appropriation. After three months of fruitless searching for a quick solution by the city, the Lincoln Center Executive Committee authorized an expenditure of $50,000 for the railings, as a gift to the city. This broke the logjam; the railings were fabricated and installed, and the accidents ceased.

In the State Theater, a floor in a basement rehearsal room cracked and sank unevenly, due to a nearby city water main break that had washed away some of the earth fill. There was a long and inconclusive legal battle over responsibility, and eventually Lincoln Center laid a new floor. The Library & Museum staff discovered that condensation was occurring in cold weather in several bookstack areas housed in the cantilevered overhang. Insulation and humidity control in the ventilation system was improved. In the Vivian Beaumont Theater, corrective work on the automated lightboard, begun when the theater opened, continued for months. Scientists from the Bell Telephone Laboratories were brought in to study its electronic problems. They found nothing faulty in the electronic design, but each one of the hundreds of circuits, involving as many as ten relays, had to be individually checked out and debugged.

The reflecting pool in the North Plaza had been plagued with leaks since it was finished in 1965. It was built by the city as a part of the garage contract, and a series of corrective measures were taken by the city's contractor but were unsuccessful. Lincoln Center's "leaky pool" became a subject of embarrassing press attention. Further-

more, the leaks were disturbing to the center's accounting and construction staff, whose offices were located beneath it. Temporary
drainage devices were installed above the office ceilings, to carry the
water off to collection points or drains. Subsequent efforts at retiling
the bottom, at installation of a new waterproof membrane, at rebuilding the edges and the drainage scuppers, all failed to stop the leaks
entirely. Only when permanent drainage ducts were finally installed
under the pool were ceilings below kept dry.

In Philharmonic Hall, the continuing problem was acoustical.
Amyas Ames, the Philharmonic president, took the lead in the analysis of the problems and recommendations for further action. In
October 1967, he reported a proposal from the German acoustician,
Heinrich Keilholz, for a major alteration involving complete removal
of the acoustical clouds and their replacement by a new ceiling. Other
changes in the decor of the hall were recommended for their psy-
chological effect. Keilholz' proposals would be costly and time-
consuming. Since the hall was already scheduled for heavy use for
Festival '68, the alterations were postponed until the next summer. By
1969 Ames was involved in Lincoln Center's operating financial
crisis, and he persuaded his colleagues on the Philharmonic board
that, since improvement in the hall was fundamentally in their interest, they must accept a major share of the costs. They contributed
$1.2 million, and Lincoln Center $200,000.

A completely new ceiling was installed, beginning rather low at the
back of the stage and rising gradually to the rear of the hall. The
ceiling and the sidewalls were of wood, painted an off-white to contrast with the red of the seats. New inverted crystal bowls in the
ceiling provided illumination. The appearance of the hall had become much more traditional, and members of the audience seemed
pleased.

The acoustical judgment was short of a rave, but generally favorable.

Harold Schonberg, who had been the hall's most severe critic,
reported in the *Times:*

> Apparently the removal of the clouds and the insertion of a solid
> ceiling did the trick for Philharmonic Hall. The bass is not as
> strong as one would like to hear, but otherwise the results are a
> complete success. For the first time, strings have a smooth, silky
> quality. Choirs of the orchestra mesh well, and listening is no
> longer a strain. Most important, the annoying echo has been
> exorcised.[1]

Photo by Sandor Acs

Philharmonic Hall after acoustical alterations in 1969.

Members of the audience seemed content, but conductors and musicians still had problems. The final solution did not come until 1976, when a complete redesign and rebuilding of the inside of the hall was accomplished. (See p. 306.)

Supervision of construction at the staff level was changed at the end of September 1966 when Col. Powers was persuaded by the Kennedy Center to become its Executive Director, Engineering. Col. Clyde F. Townsend, who had been the engineer representing Lincoln Center in building the Opera House, was appointed Director of Construction. The Building Committee continued to give policy guidance and to exercise financial control.

Construction of the Juilliard building had not gone beyond its foundations, footings, and basement walls when the Opera was opened, because a strike of hoisting engineers had delayed the erection of structural steel. By November 1966, when construction was resumed following settlement of the strike, most of the subcontracts had been awarded by the general contractor. But Morse, the owner's representative, and the contractor were still negotiating to achieve reductions in the cost for work on four segments of the building: the movable ceiling in the Juilliard Theater, its stage equipment and lighting, millwork throughout the building, and furnishings.

In order to vary reverberation time of the theater to serve spoken drama as well as vocal and instrumental music, Keilholz specified a movable ceiling to be mounted on four synchronized, motorized jackscrews. The original estimate of the cost was $208,000, and a budget allowance had used that figure. However, in the course of detailed engineering design, the movable structure required to bridge the ceiling and carry the weight proved to be unusually complex, and the estimated cost rose to $590,000, a figure that proved impossible to reduce. Belluschi and Keilholz considered the possible elimination of the movable ceiling, but concluded that this feature was essential.

On the matter of stage lighting and equipment, Juilliard leaders insisted on their educational need for an elaborate automated system. The lighting and stage consultant, Jean Rosenthal, had specified the most advanced theater technology. A difference in judgment arose between Lincoln Center and Juilliard theater technicians over the necessity for so much expensive equipment. Curtis Canfield of the Yale Drama School was called in for advice and he sustained Lincoln Center's proposition that an adequate and effective stage could be provided with fewer electric winches and less lighting equipment. The Executive Committee directed a cut in the cost by $220,000, and left to Juilliard decisions on the precise nature of the cuts.

The issue over the cost of millwork was drawn when the best bid came in at $1.442 million in contrast to a budget allowance of only $553,000. Wood surfaces and millwork in many parts of the building were acoustically necessary or aesthetically important in Belluschi's design. He and the subcontractor worked out simplifications that brought the millwork cost down to $1.118 million, but still an overage of $565,000.

The budget for furnishings, carried at $1.02 million, was a "catchall" that included the three pipe organs required for Juilliard instructional purposes, over 2500 theater seats for the four performance halls in the building, and acres of carpeting, much of it required for acoustical reasons. The largest single category on the furnishings list was

Photo by Bob Serating

The Juilliard Building under construction: September 1967.

for audio equipment, at $370,000, to cover the entire system of re-
cording for student training. After weeks of efforts to trim the total
furnishings requirements, a need for $1,308,000 remained, an over-
run of $288,000.

The cumulative effect of these budgetary decisions, of other increases and decreases in subcontract awards, and a contingency item
of $1 million brought the total budget for the Juilliard complex to $27.5
million, an increase of $3.16 million. This new budget was authorized
on February 20, 1967.

The Juilliard Theater under construction.

While these financial matters dominated discussion in Building Committee meetings, actual construction of the Juilliard building moved steadily ahead after the start of structural steel work. By early summer, 1967, the structural shell was complete, and, on July 31, the erection of the precast panels began to form the outer walls of the building. These were floor-height members, with travertine facing attached at the time of casting. On September 19, 1967 a special tour of the building was arranged for the Lincoln Center directors. The shape and size of all the major elements in the complex were clearly visible: Alice Tully Hall at one end and the Juilliard Theater at the other; the small recital hall and the drama workshop theater; large studio rooms with high ceilings; 85 individual practice rooms; the commodious individual teaching studios and the large library space. This tour of the building did more than any number of verbal reports to convey to the directors the immensity and complexity of this last of the Lincoln Center structures and the justification for its cost.

As the building neared completion, there were unexpected delays in the delivery of items in the stage equipment contract that postponed the finishing of the Juilliard Theater until the end of 1969. Most troubling was a problem with the automated memory system for the lightboard, which was to use advancements in computer technology that had occurred since the ill-fated Vivian Beaumont lightboard. The manufacturer had technical problems in making the new system work reliably, and Lincoln Center cancelled that part of the contract and substituted a conventional ten-scene preset, manually operated lightboard.

Cost control was rigorously enforced by Carl Morse through the three years of Juilliard construction. Nevertheless, after the last budget authorization in February 1967, there were added charges that brought the final building cost to $29.748 million.

Juilliard began to occupy its new home in June 1969. On an evening soon after the move, Mennin, Young, and their wives were walking through the building; Mennin sat down at a piano in one of the practice rooms. The others moved on to another practice room about 50 feet distant and discovered that they could clearly hear Mennin's playing. In spite of Keilholz' extravagantly protective specifications and unusual care during construction, there were definite problems of audibility in a number of places where total sound isolation was required. The sound transmission discovered that evening was carried by a single structural steel beam above this row of rooms. Measures were taken to insulate these ceilings more fully. A thorough check was made of all 85 practice rooms; sound leaks were found in some air conditioning ducts and around perimeter heating pipes running through several rooms. More materials were installed. Additional sound deadening was accomplished by furring out walls with insulation in the air space. All the practice rooms were equipped with heavy, sound-absorbant drapes to help confine the sound within the room, and eventually, the problems of sound transmission were solved.

Registration of students and the start of instruction began in the new Juilliard School in September 1969. *The New York Times*, headlined a story, "Taj Mahal of Music." The concluding paragraph read:

With its move to Lincoln Center, the Juilliard School has become the most impressive conservatory in the entire world, with facilities at its disposal that no other conservatory can begin to approach.[2]

Architectural criticism of this, the last building of Lincoln Center, was favorable. Ada Louise Huxtable wrote:

The style . . . is a kind of restrained establishment modern. It is

The Juilliard School.

Section by E. M. Feher/Courtesy of Lincoln Center for the Performing Arts, Inc.

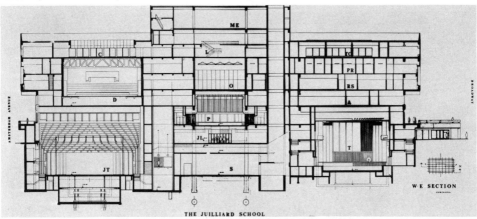

Longitudinal Section. The Juilliard Building.

Plan by E. M. Feher/Courtesy of Lincoln Center for the Performing Arts, Inc.

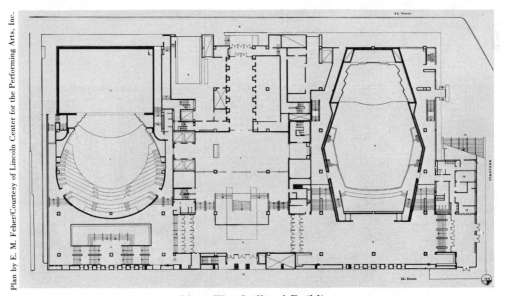

Plan. The Juilliard Building.

not avant-garde, but its refinements and simplicities are timeless. With the Beaumont Theater, Juilliard offers architectural
and aesthetic reality to the cultural confusion of Lincoln Center,
ending 14 years on an upbeat.[3]

Architectural Record gave a fullsome account in pictures and text. Its
opening began:

Contained within the serene, well ordered, simple and rather
innocent facades of the new Juilliard School (the world's first

Interior of Alice Tully Hall.

Miss Alice Tully with John D. Rockefeller 3rd and John W. Mazzola.

conservatory for all the performing arts) is an almost infinite variety of spaces fitted together with a sorcerer's skill in an arrangement as intricate as a Chinese puzzle.[4]

Two special events celebrated the formal opening of the Juilliard complex. Alice Tully Hall was opened on September 11, 1969 with an inaugural concert by the Chamber Music Society of Lincoln Center, the resident constituent in the hall. In brief opening remarks, Rockefeller paid special tribute to Miss Tully, whose generosity had brought the dream of a chamber music hall to reality. Critics, musicians, and audience members were universally pleased with the acoustical results in this hall.

On the afternoon of Sunday, October 26, a special concert marked the formal opening of the Juilliard School, and the completion of Lincoln Center. Concert participants included three distinguished Juilliard alumni: Van Cliburn, Itzhak Perlman, and Shirley Verrett, with the Juilliard orchestra. Leopold Stowkowski conducted the opening of the program, and the concert proceeded under the baton of Jean Morel. A distinguished audience included Mrs. Richard

The Juilliard Theater

Ezra Stoller © ESTO

Peter Mennin, President of the Juilliard School, with John D. Rockefeller 3rd.

Nixon, Mr. and Mrs. David Eisenhower, and Governor and Mrs. Nelson Rockefeller. The network telecast of the concert by CBS, with Leonard Bernstein serving as narrator, reached a nationwide audience estimated at 8.8 million individuals.

In his dedicatory remarks, John Rockefeller recalled the beginning of the building of Lincoln Center ten years before. He spoke of the fulfillment of goals set by the planners:

> . . . that Lincoln Center should include all the performing arts, and that education for the performing arts be a fundamental part of the center. . . .

And so the setting is complete—dedicated to art, to public service and to the training of the young. Now it is the time of the artist and his audience, for only they can make this Center a living testament to the quality of life.

CHAPTER 20

Conclusion of Capital Fund Raising
1966–1969

Although achievement of the Capital Campaign goal was announced early in 1966, the directors knew then that additional funds were required to complete the Juilliard complex and to meet the final costs of the Opera house. These construction overages eventually ran to $6.4 million.

In addition, two categories of nonconstruction needs had to be included in the totals of revised capital goals. During the years of continuing construction, the costs of building operation and of administration were charged to the capital fund accounts. Analysis of the actual and projected expenses for these purposes through the completion of the last building showed that more would be needed than the revision of the capital budget in 1965 had provided. The other addition to the capital requirement was an amount to cover interest charges on borrowed money. Gustave Levy, the treasurer monitored the cash-flow situation very closely, because approximately $10 million of the capital already raised was in the form of pledges payable over as many as five years. Anticipating a cash-flow shortage, a line of credit up to $6.2 million was arranged with banks, using outstanding pledges as security. In response to requests, a number of pledge payments came in more rapidly than scheduled, and borrowing was

277

avoided until February 1968. But at that time, the cash-flow picture ahead and the borrowing requirements indicated that as much as $900,000 would be needed to cover interest payments. By October 1968, these three factors, actual costs of building construction, operational costs, and anticipated interest payments, added $9.8 million to the capital requirement, for a new project total of $178.2 million.

During the time that these needs were accumulating, capital fund raising was conducted in a low-key manner, concentrating on a list of selected donors. Rockefeller felt a personal responsibility to help secure these additional funds, and a new member of the board, Lawrence A. Wein, joined him in this task. With Ammidon, these three had secured, by October 1968, contributions totaling $4.4 million. Two gifts of $1 million each had been received, one anonymously and one from Mrs. DeWitt Wallace. The balance had come largely in new patron gifts. These contributions brought the total committed for the project to $170.2 million, still $8 million short of the recognized need. Ammidon proposed at this time a somewhat wider capital effort focused on Wall Street firms, and a few new patron prospects. By the end of 1968, this drive had brought in $1.4 million and reduced the gap to $6.6 million.

While these developments relating to the capital fund were occurring, a major reorganization and retrenchment in the program and operating side of Lincoln Center was undertaken. (See Chapter 21, p. 296.) Ames had become chairman of the Executive Committee and was exerting strong leadership in the resolution of the center's critical financial problems. He felt, even more strongly than had others before him, that for Lincoln Center to have a viable future, it was imperative to bring an end to capital fund raising. In April, 1969, Ames, Rockefeller, and Young developed a plan to meet most of the remaining capital needs by June 30, the end of the fiscal year.

The first step in the plan was to reduce the capital requirement by eliminating all items not yet committed. A reserve of $500,000, planned to build Lincoln Center offices was the first casualty. A number of smaller items were sacrificed for a total reduction in the capital goal of $2.15 million. The second step was for the center to become its own banker by lending $2.3 million to its capital fund from reserves of that amount in the Special Gift Fund, for which there was no need in the near future. Lincoln Center could afford to forego investment income on that fund in order to pay off that amount of bank loans and substantially reduce the interest obligation. The security for this internal loan was an equivalent amount of campaign pledges, which, when paid, restored the Special Gift reserves. The third step in the plan was to make an outright transfer to the capital fund, without obligation for repayment, of $1.8 million, representing unused and uncommitted portions of Rockefeller's 1965 contribution to the Special Gift Fund. The total of $4.1 million in cash from steps two and three was used to pay off that amount of the bank loans, thus eliminating a substantial part of the budgeted amount for interest.

The board unanimously approved these financial transactions on May 12, 1969, with the net result that the remaining capital gap had been reduced to just over $2.5 million. Wein offered to give personal leadership to the raising of this final amount. Then after the board meeting he conferred with Rockefeller, and they decided to make personal gifts of $1.25 million each. The capital campaign for Lincoln Center was, at long last, brought to an end.

The money had been raised, the center had been built, and the public, especially the donors, were due a report of stewardship. A cumulative 13-year report was prepared by Young in 1970.[1] It summarized the sources of all the funds received by Lincoln Center and the application of those funds between incorporation in 1956 and building completion in 1969. For clarity in public understanding, the data on the Capital Fund and the Special Gifts Fund were consolidated; investment income and activities financed out of income were also included. The result was a capital total of $185.4 million. The highlights of capital received and spent are shown in the accompanying table.

The financial feasibility of Lincoln Center was proven by participation of numerous sources. An important factor was the successful collaboration between private philanthropic and governmental efforts. For each dollar of public funds in the project, four came from the private sector. Gifts from individuals equaled the grants from foundations, each category representing over two-fifths of the total given. Corporations made 7.5 percent of the contributions, and the gifts from foreign governments and groups represented 3.6 percent. The number and size of gifts indicates the importance of large gifts in the total raised.

Analysis of gifts by number and size

Size of gift	Number	Total	
$ 1 +	8,848	$ 500,000	.4%
1,000 +	2,164	3,821,000	2.7%
10,000 +	306	7,700,000	5.4%
100,000 +	163	27,900,000	19.7%
1,000,000 +	24	101,500,000	71.8%
Total	11,505	$141,421,000	100.0%

Statement of sources and application of funds

From June 22, 1956 (date of incorporation) to June 30, 1969

Sources: From private sector			
Contributions (including pledges of $7,927,000) *			$141,421,000
Investment income			
On construction funds		$ 4,834,000	
On Fund for Education and Artistic Advancement		1,389,000	
			6,223,000
Income from additional seats, etc.			605,000
			$148,249,000
From government			
City of New York		14,970,000	
State of New York		15,383,000	
United States Government		6,767,000	
			37,120,000
Total sources			$185,369,000

Applications:			
Physical plant			
Land		8,583,000	
Buildings		151,981,000	
Works of art		892,000	
		$161,456,000	
Fund for Education & Creative Artistic Advancement			
from contributions	$9,182,000		
from investment income	1,389,000		
		$ 10,571,000	
Building operations		$ 2,617,000	
Supporting services			
Management and general administration:			
from contributions	1,728,000		
from investment income	4,210,000		
	$5,938,000		
Fund raising	2,335,000		
Interest on borrowed funds	396,000		
		$ 8,669,000	
Total, applications			$183,313,000

Balance in reserve for:			
Acquisition of land		1,000,000	
Acquisition of works of art		472,000	
Undesignated		584,000	
			2,056,000
			$185,369,000

Including Special Purpose Gift Funds.

In the applications of the \$185.4 million, the investment in the physical plant of Lincoln Center represented 87.1 percent of the total. The funds for educational and artistic purposes received 5.7 percent; building operations and supporting services accounted for 6.1 percent, and 1.1 percent remained in reserves.

Analysis of gifts by source			% of total
Contributions:			
Individuals	\$ 62,712,000		34.0%
Foundations	62,819,000		34.0%
Corporations	10,710,000		5.8%
Foreign government and groups	5,180,000		2.8%
Total contributions:		\$141,421,000	76.6%
Investment income		6,223,000	3.4%
Total		\$147,644,000	80.0%
Government funds:			
City of New York	14,970,000		
State of New York	15,383,000		
U.S. Government	6,767,000		
Total government		\$ 37,120,000	20.0%
Total		\$184,764,000	100.0%

The final building costs were 26 percent above the estimates made in 1960 when building plans were indicative of the structures actually built. The volume of space constructed was 35 million cubic feet, 3 percent more than had been estimated, placing the measure of construction cost escalation at 23 percent. This increase occurred during a period when the index of local major construction costs rose by 38 percent.[2]

CHAPTER 21

Crisis and Resolution
1966–1970

The issues that arose in the period between 1966 and 1970 were not new ones, but were intensified and climactic extensions of problems that had emerged during the four years leading up to the opera opening. These problems related to the role of Lincoln Center, Inc. in sponsoring presentations of artistic programs and to the relationships between the central organization and the constituent institutions. Inexorably linked to these questions of operating policy were the problems of money for continuing and expanding activities. Financial commitments were growing; annual fund-raising results were disappointing.

In the fall of 1966, Schuman and his programming staff completed the plans for Festival '67 and were making preliminary arrangements for Festival '68. Lincoln Center, Inc. promoted, managed, and subsidized these international festivals, as it did its other program presentations, such as the August Mozart series and the Great Performers series. Although there were a number of very practical reasons for Lincoln Center to sponsor these presentations, Schuman's primary motivation for them and for assumption by Lincoln Center of artistic and financial responsibility was his conviction that Lincoln Center's latent potential for leadership in the arts rested on such activities.

But development of Lincoln Center's own program presentations involved additional financial commitments. At the same time, new contributions were lagging behind financial plans and expectations; the level of the operating reserve funds was dropping. This threat to the financial stability of Lincoln Center became a matter of growing concern, especially to Josephs, Rockefeller, Spofford, and Young. They felt that programs must be adjusted or postponed to conform to financial reality. Josephs especially believed that Lincoln Center had advanced too rapidly in its programs and in its commitments as an impressario. He felt it must resist the role of a constituent, lest it become merely another one among the group. He wanted it to remain distinctly different from them and to be their coordinator.

Schuman, on the other hand, articulated a philosophy for the approach he believed should be followed by cultural centers in an address on the subject of "The New Establishment," delivered before the Princeton University Conference on "The Performing Arts: The Economic Problems," held on December 9, 1966. Schuman developed the idea that, in America, the new cultural centers, of which Lincoln Center was the pioneer, represented "the new establishment," a new center of power among performing arts institutions that would bring a greater "participation from a broader representation of community leaders." He then stated "Schuman's Law and Postulates."

Nonprofit institutions in the performing arts compromise their reason for being in direct proportion to the programs and policies which are adopted for fiscal reasons extrinsic to artistic purpose.

His postulates identified tendencies to increase imagination in programming, or, conversely, timidity. Then he asserted:

Earlier I stated that all of us in the performing arts swam in the same sea: the sea of deficit. This sea is obviously a red sea, and only a p-r-o-f-i-t can part it. Now, as deep as that red sea is, I think it should be deeper. Basic to our problem is not that our deficits are too large, but that they are too small.

Before the combined forces of America's trustees and fund-raisers rise to strike me dead, let me explain. When I say that our deficits are too small, it is obvious that I am stating a conviction that the size of our budgets does not permit us to do the job properly. . . . A budgetary deficit which does not provide latitude for experimentation and, indeed, failure is unrealistic and, worse, self-defeating. It denies artists the right to displease, to provoke, to puzzle: basic ingredients all, for artistic health.[1]

After reading Schuman's Princeton address, Rockefeller wrote to him saying he had found one part in it

> ... disturbing, as it seemed to me it is subject to misinterpretation. You emphasized the desirability of larger deficits if art institutions are to attain artistic heights without equally emphasizing that such deficits must be within the bounds of obtainable contributions if the project is to survive. This kind of deficit philosophy can be the downfall of Lincoln Center or any other artistic institution unless as much attention is given to sound financial planning and effective fund-raising as to the creation and development of programs.

Equally disturbing at this time was the slow development of a "creative partnership" in relations between Lincoln Center and the constituents. The attitude of many constituent leaders toward Lincoln Center had become critical rather than cooperative. Some perceived the program development of Lincoln Center, Inc. as both artistic and financial competition, and they resented it.

Father McGinley was elected chairman pro-tem of the Executive Committee early in December 1966, in the absence of Spofford, who had suffered a stroke. At the end of the year, Rockefeller, Schuman, Josephs, and McGinley met to review major issues of concern at that time. From that meeting, a consensus emerged, as expressed in a summary letter from Rockefeller to Schuman. They agreed that:

> The development of imaginative and high quality programs is important ... but [we] have three concerns: (a) the rate of progress, (b) the case as to whether others on the outside might not well carry more of the load ... and (c) the feeling among the constituents that Lincoln Center is a competitor.

> In the last analysis the constituents' success will determine the success of Lincoln Center .... Hence it is ... obviously in our interest to aid and abet them to the extent that we possibly can ... the relationship with the constituents must always be given highest priority.

Rockefeller's letter emphasized the need for living within our means, for financial planning, for setting priorities, and for mutual trust and confidence in all the relations with the constituents. He quoted Josephs' dictum: "Cultural leadership must be earned."

At the beginning of 1967, renewed emphasis was placed on the involvement of constituents in the development of program; the Lincoln Center Council increased its frequency of meetings from quarterly to monthly; the constituents carried a larger role in planning and conducting the Festival '67; steps were taken to move toward constituent institutions for film and for chamber music, so that Lincoln Center's activity in these arts could be terminated.

Since 1964 when the Film Festivals had been authorized, it was expected that this activity would eventually be spun off to independent status. But the film program had remained a department of Lincoln Center. Its annual deficit had grown to $275,000 for 1967 and was therefore a significant item in the financial problems of Lincoln Center. No progress had been made in finding citizen leadership to form a film society. Schuman turned for advice to an old friend, Martin E. Segal, a businessman active in a variety of civic and philanthropic causes in New York City. Throughout his life Segal had had a special interest in film; in the 1930s, as a youth of 19, he had

Edward Hausner/THE NEW YORK TIMES

William Schuman meets with the Lincoln Center Council.—January 1967. From left to right: Edward G. Freehafer, Jules Irving, Peter Mennin, Richard Rodgers, Julius Rudel, Rudolph Bing, Carlos Moseley.

organized the Film Guild of New York, a nonprofit attempt to present unknown and unrecognized films. Segal recommended William F. May, president of American Can Company. He was interested and agreed to serve as chairman of a Lincoln Center Film Committee, with Segal as vice chairman. On January 7, 1967, May was elected a director of Lincoln Center; at a later time, Segal also became a director, and both men have continued to serve Lincoln Center in significant ways beyond their initial involvement with film. A Lincoln Center Film Committee was organized and Schuyler Chapin, Lincoln Center's vice president for programming gave it staff assistance. Throughout 1967 and into 1968 this group was engaged in a fund-raising effort in preparation for an independent Film Society, but the results were slow.

Parallel with these developments for film, Schuman took steps to organize a program for chamber music that would lead to independence. In February, he formed a Lincoln Center Committee on Chamber Music, and a detailed prospectus was developed by Charles Wadsworth, who had been added to the Lincoln Center staff in anticipation of his eventual transfer to a chamber music constituent. An ambitious program called for the creation of an ensemble of chamber music players and a schedule of 120 concerts in the first year of operation. The financial plan would require $290,000 for pre-opening expenses and an amount between $93,000 and $248,000, depending on level of attendance, to cover the first year's deficit. All of this was to be undertaken by Lincoln Center, Inc. prior to the formation of a constituent. However, Schuman was optimistic that an annonymous donor (later known to be Miss Alice Tully) would make a substantial contribution to help launch a chamber music program.

Rockefeller was concerned over the financial implications of this prospectus, and on February 22, 1967, he wrote Schuman, saying:

I am sympathetic to moving forward with the development of the project, [for chamber music] but I am unsympathetic to Lincoln Center's making any further financial commitments in relation to it . . . Such limited funds as we do have, in my judgment, must be conserved for already existing responsibilities and commitments.

What are the consequences of what I am saying? To me it means that no new program commitments can be made until we have assured funds from outside sources to meet them . . .

It is not a question of merit, not a question of importance, but rather the future of Lincoln Center as a whole. You will remember that Winston Churchill once said that he did not wish to preside over the liquidation of the British Empire. Neither you nor I want to preside over the liquidation of Lincoln Center.

Schuman's reply of March 2 carefully reviewed the evolution of the chamber music proposals and defended the financial plans as coming within previously authorized budget plans. He again voiced optimism that Miss Tully would provide important support. Referring to the capital overruns that were then another source of Rockefeller's concern, Schuman wrote:

> Neither you nor I could control these growing capital overages, relating as they do to the building expenses. However regrettable these overages are, in my view we cannot afford at this moment to be diverted from our course, from the very sound programs that have been accepted and, in truth, the programs that give Lincoln Center its position of leadership. To be frank, your letter gives me the impression that you are questioning the timing of our ongoing program because of the capital overages. If so, that is indeed a major issue, going far beyond the question of chamber music alone.

But the problems with respect to chamber music were more than financial. Although the Board had approved the effort to create a chamber music unit when Schuman had first proposed it, at this time there were doubts and rumblings of discontent coming from several of the original constituents. The Philharmonic was questioning whether there was a need for a new chamber music institution. The Metropolitan and Juilliard were raising other questions, emphasizing the competition for financial help from donors.

Rockefeller convened a dinner meeting of key directors to explore these and broader problems of constituent relations and the difficulties in developing a creative partnership. Ames, Ammidon, Houghton, Josephs, McGinley, Schuman, and Young met with him on March 30, 1967. The group defined the term "Lincoln Center" to mean the entire complex—the physical place, the family of constituents, and the educational and artistic force. In program terms, it includes the total of artistic offerings at the center; conversely, its meaning is not limited to the activities of Lincoln Center, Inc. They advocated constituent consultation and participation in all program developments administered by Lincoln Center, Inc. Among the constituents there were feelings that Lincoln Center was a threat, or at least a competitor. This aura of competition must be removed. Insofar as possible, future educational and artistic functions would be carried out through assistance to the constituents. Underlying all of these points of view was their serious concern over the timing of developing programs and financial commitments made in advance of assurance of funds.

There continued to be indications of constituent feeling that Lincoln Center was a competitor in fund raising. All were facing higher costs of operations in their new homes, and through the long period of Lincoln Center's capital fund raising they had cooperated by postponing appeals for large contributions from their most generous supportors. Now they feared that Lincoln Center's appeals for contributions toward its own programs would reduce what they could raise.

At the conclusion of the June 1967 board meeting, David Keiser had a private talk with Schuman, in which he said he had come to feel that Lincoln Center, Inc. should not be presenting artistic programs itself. He was, in effect, challenging Lincoln Center's role as an impressario. Keiser was chairman of the Program Committee; therefore his viewpoint was especially disturbing to Schuman. Both men met with

William Schuman addresses the opening of Festival '67. Seated on platform (left to right): August Hecksher, New York's Administrator of Recreation and Cultural Affairs; Gov. Nelson A. Rockefeller; Archibald MacLeish; and Lawrence A. Wein, member of Board of Directors, Lincoln Center.

Photo by Bob Serating

Rockefeller, McGinley, Drye, and Chapin on June 23. In Keiser's view, program activities were counter to the original objectives for Lincoln Center. They were costly and placed Lincoln Center in fund-raising competition with constituents. Rockefeller felt that program presentations were consistent with original objectives, but agreed that there was a basis for concern over how Lincoln Center was approaching its programming. Although the conference did not lead to a policy change, as Keiser had felt would be wise, it did sound notes of caution on financial and procedural grounds.

Meanwhile, the five-week Festival '67 opened on June 12, and the program offerings of both the constituents and Lincoln Center were successful, as measured by critical and public response. Miles Kastendieck said in his review of the Festival opening

Lincoln Center thrust itself forward dramatically as a cultural force last week. Its Festival '67, the first to blend the offerings of its functioning constituents into a single "presentation," embraces the cause of all the performing arts and qualifies as the largest international project of its kind ever undertaken in this country.

Referring to the colorful decorations of the plaza, made possible by a special contribution from Lincoln Center Director Lawrence Wien, he wrote:

. . . the plaza vibrated with fresh coloring and gaiety. . . . Indeed, the magnificence of Lincoln Center at night attests in itself the creative ideas still growing within it as an institution.[2]

At the end of the festival, the overall attendance had been 85 percent of capacity, and the deficit had been kept within the authorized $775,000. The Times headlined its roundup story "Deficit Can't Hide Festival Success."

This success reduced, for a time, the constituent unrest over Lincoln Center's programming activities, but it did not allay their fears about competitive fund raising. Nor did it reduce Lincoln Center's own deepening financial problems. Nevertheless, plans for Festival '68 were completed and in March of that year, Schuman went to Europe to promote this festival and to make arrangements for a third one in 1969.

Rockefeller continued his talks with other directors and with constituent leaders about the state of constituent relationships. On Schuman's return, Rockefeller wrote to him in April:

. . . Those whom I have talked with individually or in small groups include Messrs. Ames, Hoguet, Keiser, Ammidon, Josephs and Spofford. . . .

The discussions have been worthwhile and meaningful and there is no question that there is a consensus of opinion not only that we must immediately take steps to substantially curtail our current expenditures, but also that we must forthrightly and effectively revamp our inter-family relationships. . . .

My own feeling is that the best approach would be to take a fresh look at the whole interfamily relationship situation with of course particular emphasis on the programming side . . . I am convinced that a major change is in order if we are to end up with a sound working arrangement and one which will be manageable financially.

I appreciate all this is not going to be easy for any of us. As a result of my several conversations I have realized more fully than at any time before the feelings towards Lincoln Center, Inc. on the part of the constituents—feelings of mistrust, fear, competition and even bitterness. We have a long way to go and it is going to be tough, but now is the time in my judgment when the job must be done. Real leadership is going to be required. . . .

In response, Schuman said, in a memorandum to members of the Executive Committee:

It is obvious to all of us that despite the great success that has been achieved in so many aspects of Lincoln Center, the primary one, the "family relationship," remains unsatisfactory. We are all in agreement that the Center will never be the success for which we all hope unless each organization feels a sense of pride and satisfaction in being a part of it, and is wholly free of any feelings toward the Center itself of competition, fear, resentment or any other reservations, however expressed. Whether or not these expressed reservations have reality in fact is quite beside the point. They exist, and some new means, not yet apparent to this writer, must be found to make progress toward their alleviation.

During the remainder of 1968, Lincoln Center's own financial crisis so dominated the attention of all the officers that the related problems of constituent attitudes and relationships were temporarily over-shadowed. A three-year financial plan for the center's programs had been worked out, at the end of 1965, by Ammidon, the new campaign chairman, with Schuman and his staff. They had adopted the term "Lincoln Center Fund" to identify future fund raising as distinct from the capital campaign.

The assets from the Fund for Education and Artistic Advancement and the New Projects Underwriting Fund were merged into the new Lincoln Center Fund, giving it an initial cash balance of $7.37 million at the start of the three year plan. From this total, provision was made to respect donor designations and to meet prior obligations of the corporation such as the $2.5 million to launch the Juilliard drama training program. To support new projects in the fields of education, artistic programming, and new institutional development, the financial needs were forecast for three years beginning July 1, 1966. The total of prior obligations and estimated new project costs for the three-year period, after accounting for ticket sales and self-support programs, came to a total of $7.4 million. Since the projected deficit was, by coincidence, approximately equal to the initial Fund assets, the proposed budgets would wipe out the Fund if new money failed to come in through annual campaigns. The plan expected one-third of the first year's deficit to be met from new money raised, one-half in the second year, two-thirds in the third, and, by the fifth year, 100 percent of the annual deficit. If this could be achieved, the Fund reserves would be drawn down but not exhausted, and in time, financial stability would be reached.

It took over a year to develop the new Lincoln Center Fund organization of volunteers and to prepare for a full-scale annual campaign. In the strategy for future fund raising, strong emphasis was placed on recurring corporate support; a plan for Lincoln Center Associates was developed as a means for seeking recurring gifts from individuals. During the fiscal year 1966-1967, approximately $.5 million was raised.

Josephs, who headed the Budget Review Committee, was greatly disturbed over the delays in achieving a substantial flow of annual contributions, the growing program commitments, and the diminishing reserves of the Lincoln Center Fund. In the spring of 1967 he was convinced that Lincoln Center had to give specific evidence of fiscal control in order to establish donor confidence in its managements. At the end of May, Spofford hosted a breakfast meeting at his home, attended by Rockefeller, Schuman, Josephs, McGinley, and Young. By this date, reserves in the Fund had dropped below $5 million, and current operations were reducing that balance each month. In addition, new contingent liabilities of the center, related to guarantees of bank loans to the Repertory Theater and the Music Theater had to be accepted as potential claims on the limited reserves. Agreement was reached on new controls on expenditures and on a firm policy that assurance of money must precede program commitments. Specifically with reference to the future of film at Lincoln Center, a decision was reached that, soon after the fall film festival, the Film Department would be terminated unless by that time an independent film constituent was clearly assured.

In order to provide for continuous review and fiscal control, the board, on June 5, 1967 approved Josephs' recommendation that the Budget Review Committee be terminated and its function be transferred to the Executive Committee.

During that summer of 1967, in spite of the artistic and public success of the 1967 summer activities, there was growing anxiety over the operating budget and fund raising. For the fiscal year of 1967 and 1968 a gross expenditure of $7 million was budgeted, offset by estimated income of $4 million, leaving a deficit of $3 million. Of that need, $1.3 million could be met if the goal of the Lincoln Center Fund could be reached; the balance of $1.7 million was to be drawn from the income and the reserves of the Lincoln Center Fund. The key to this plan was the reality of the plan to raise $1.3 million, an increase of 160 percent above the $.5 million raised in the previous fiscal year. There were serious doubts that such a rapid increase in giving could be attained.

The budget projection of the administration for the next two years called for a further increase in programs and contribution needs. Ammidon sounded a warning, on September 11, 1967, in a letter to McGinley:

As I look over fund raising forecasts and feel the pulls of current attitudes, I feel strongly that we should not go beyond the present $3 million (contribution need) total costs for yearly operations. I know the projected costs for 1968-69 are the $3.3 million figure and a rise to $3.6 million is contemplated for the following year. It seems to me that we should at all costs try to keep our deficits at or below the $3 million level. In fact I wonder what economies might be effected in the current year's budgets. If we could bring our expenditures down by 10% this might well have a most salutary effect on cost consciousness in our organization and sound planning.

Early in November 1967, concern over the financial problem led to a special evening meeting of the Executive Committee to review the situation. For that meeting, Schuman and his staff prepared a financial report and forecast reflecting the current status of the Lincoln Center Fund and of their future plans for programs and operations. By this time, the estimate of probable receipts in the current year's Fund campaign was only $500,000 in contrast to the goal of $1.3 million on which all previous planning had been based. In planned expenditures, they had deferred certain programs and found economies in operating budgets for a reduction during the year of $238,000. However, this budgetary reduction did not begin to balance the lower fund-raising prospects, with the inevitable result of a much more rapid depletion of the Fund reserves than had been contemplated. The administration projected a budget for the next two years that called for further increases in program expenditure and for higher campaign goals of $1.9 million and $3.3 million.

By February 1968, Spofford's health had improved to the point that he was able to resume the chairmanship of the Executive Committee. On March 5, Josephs, Rockefeller, Spofford, and Young met to consider the deepening financial crisis. An assessment of recent developments gave a clear prospect that the current and projected budgets would draw down the Fund reserves below $1 million by July 1969. The danger signals were flashing, for a base of $2 million had previously been agreed to be a minimum operating fund.

The next day Schuman met with Rockefeller and Young. Following that conference, he wrote Rockefeller to tell him,

> how encouraging it was to find you truly "aroused" by the financial position we are in vis-à-vis operating funds. We must look to you, as Chairman, to provide the same vigorous leadership, however delegated, in helping us raise operating funds as you did in the raising of construction funds.

Rockefeller's reply said:

> You are right, I am "aroused" and I was pleased indeed to find that you had exactly the same reaction. Time is short relatively speaking and we must face up to the situation forthrightly and promptly.

But referring to Schuman's plea for his leadership in raising operating funds, Rockefeller said:

> . . . When we adopted the plan for Lincoln Center Fund raising

two years ago and Hoyt [Ammidon] accepted the Chairmanship of the Fund, it was with the understanding that the responsibility for ongoing fund raising was being accepted by others. It just is not possible for me to consider any change in my relationship which was so carefully worked out among all of us at that time.

This is not only a personal matter with me, it is also a matter of conviction with regard to the future of Lincoln Center. The activities and financial needs of the Center must be tailored to its capacity to command support from the community and that capacity must not be dependent on my personal role as Chairman. Lincoln Center is not a Rockefeller project, and its future activities must not rest on Rockefeller support or efforts.

Within a few days, Schuman left, as previously scheduled, for Europe to discuss plans for Festivals '68 and '69 with artistic and governmental leaders. During his absence, the staff completed the management budget proposal for the next fiscal year. It called for an increase in expenditure of $600,000 over the level of the current year; the directors had expected a substantial reduction. The budget continued to assume that $1.3 million would be raised during the next year, a figure that seemed unrealistic in view of the results up to this time.

On Schuman's return, Rockefeller suggested that the budget be withdrawn for still more intensive study and revision to a bare minimum basis. The next day Schuman indicated, in a memorandum to the Executive Committee, that the preparation of a retrenchment budget was in process. Ammidon could not attend the next meeting and so wrote Spofford to review some of the fund-raising experience of the year:

> Quite frankly, our corporate appeal has been both frustrating and disappointing. . . . [We] made five test calls on major corporations late last year and early this year to see if we could establish some pace-setting giving standards. Unhappily, none of these bore fruit and, as a result, we have had to re-evaluate our first year's corporate appeal and aim at broad coverage with lower amounts rather than a smaller number of leadership gifts. . . .
>
> In great part this has been brought about by the racial tensions which have, unfortunately, coincided with our first appeal and we have had a clear indication from major corporations . . . that the higher level giving which they first contemplated had to be

diverted to more pressing urban problems. . . . It is perfectly apparent that they do not put Lincoln Center in a special category at the moment; it is simply another appeal which calls for a modest contribution.

Stimulated by Ammidon's comments on the situation, Rockefeller wrote Schuman that he felt the budget for 1968-1969 must be reduced by a minimum of $1 million.

Schuman's retrenchment budget was sent to members of the Executive Committee on April 22, 1968. The new budget for 1968-1969 proposed reductions in expenditures of only $548,362, chiefly in educational programs and in supporting services, for a new total of $2,551,224. It continued to assume that $1.3 million could be raised. When the committee met three days later, Schuman did not attend, for he had become ill just as this budgeting process was being completed. He was advised by his doctor to remain at home for some time for rest and recuperation. He was able to see Mazzola and other key staff members to keep in touch with developments at Lincoln Center, and he asked Ames to present the budget proposals to the Executive Committee. Action on the budget was deferred.

During the next month, the staff made further minor reductions of $175,000 in the expenditure budget and accepted a more realistic assumption of $850,000 for contribution income. But these changes only deepened the projection of diminishing reserves. In a breakfast conference involving Rockefeller, Ames, Josephs, Spofford, and Young, all sides of the crisis were carefully reviewed, leading to the inescapable conclusion that major cuts must be made. When the Executive Committee met on May 21, Ames presented both the management's revised budget and the more drastic conclusions reached by the five directors. The committee approved the management proposal, but only on an interim basis, necessary to continue operations, and subject to whatever modification might be made by a new special subcommittee composed of Ammidon, Josephs, Schuman and Mazzola with Ames as chairman.

At this same special meeting, a new crisis in the Repertory Theater had to be dealt with. Hoguet and his board had struggled with continuing deficits and slow returns on their fund-raising efforts. In their discouragement, they had seriously considered liquidation of the Repertory Theater but had been persuaded to try to keep it going for another year. Hoguet felt that the only basis on which that was possible was through cancellation, by Lincoln Center, of the Repertory's indebtedness of $100,000 and continued guarantee by Lincoln Center of a line of bank credit for $200,000. Considering the continuation of the Repertory Theater to be of major importance, once again the Executive Committee approved Hoguet's requests, in spite of their concern over Lincoln Center's own precarious financial future.

The special budget subcommittee met twice weekly during the next month with the advisory help of William Hadley, a businessman who was financial director of the Metropolitan Opera. They outlined a major reorganization and retrenchment of Lincoln Center, Inc. Their policy for the future was to limit administrative costs to realistic estimates of recurring income and project expense to designated contributions. A major objective was a reduction in the costs of the central administration from $1.4 million to $600,000, a target to be reached within one year. The Executive Committee approved the recommendations of Ames' subcommittee on June 26, 1968, and directed implementation to begin at once. It had become clear that Schuman's convalescence would keep him away from the office for the remainder of the summer. A strong day-by-day executive control was needed during this important period and Mazzola was designated chief executive officer of Lincoln Center, with direct responsibility to the Executive Committee and with authority to carry out its mandates. In another move to support the retrenchment proposals of the Budget Subcommittee during this critical period, Ames became chairman of the Executive Committee on October 7, upon Spofford's resignation. Spofford agreed to continue as an Executive Committee member.

During the summer of 1968, Festival '68 was conducted as previously planned. Again it was an artistic and public success, but with greater deficits than had been budgeted and further depletion of the Lincoln Center Fund. Additional deficits occurred later in the summer from the August Serenades and the Film Festival. By mid-October, the undesignated fund reserve had dropped to nearly $500,000. Weekly expenditures were running at a rate of $125,000 per week, and technical bankruptcy of Lincoln Center operations could occur before the end of the year. A report, prepared by Mazzola, was titled: "Analysis of the Disappearing Net Worth of Lincoln Center Fund." He summarized the immediate situation:

It now appears that the shaved but balanced budget projected last June for the year July 1, 1969-70 cannot be achieved nor can the projected deficit be accepted. . . . We can no longer accept any deficits as our funds, for all practical purposes, are exhausted. Therefore, we must adopt an emergency program.

Mazzola and Ames recommended $400,000 in cuts through further reductions in operating expenses and in building operations and "elimination of *all* programs except the Student Program, which is funded." Reference to the continuation of the Student Program and to its separate funding was significant. This program had won not only contribution support but was the one activity of Lincoln Center about which the constituents were enthusiastic and in which they were actively participating. It made no claims on general funds. With its performances, the Student Program was reaching an audience of more than one million young people in the course of a year. With the active cooperation of state and city school administrations, the share of public funding was twice that of Lincoln Center's costs. Hence there was no financial need to curtail its program.

The reduction in operating expenditure was approved; also, Lincoln Center was authorized to establish a line of bank credit to borrow as much as $1 million to tide over inevitable cash-flow fluctuations. In addition, immediate action was taken to reduce future commitments. The earlier authorization for Festival '69 was rescinded. Lincoln Center was not merely in a period of retrenchment, it was in a battle for survival.

The retrenchment program remained in the hands of Ames and Mazzola. Gradually during the late summer and autumn, there was a departure of staff officers from the programming, public relations, accounting, and fund-raising activities as they realized the depth of Lincoln Center's financial crisis. The staff that remained, with a few newcomers, became the nucleus for the continuing staff organization of Lincoln Center.

By mid-September Schuman had recovered from his illness and reentered Lincoln Center's budget balancing effort. He focused his attention on trying to salvage the film and chamber music programs. William F. May, chairman of the Film Committee, reported to the board on October 7, 1968, that "it is uncertain whether there will be enough funds to support an independent film organization." But as the implication of Lincoln Center's critical situation became clear, May and his committee realized that the only alternative to termination of the film program was to find a way to make it an independent organization.

With the encouragement of a grant of $50,000 from the National Endowment for the Arts and a patron pledge of $100,000, payable over five years, a minimum financial underpinning was provided. May and his committee decided to proceed with their plan for a new organization. They streamlined the Film Department and its program and reduced the budget for the next year. Amos Vogel, who had been its director disagreed with the future plans and resigned. In his place the committee appointed Richard Roud, who had previously been involved in the programming of films for the festivals.

In December the Film Committee presented its official proposal to assume independent responsibility for film activities at Lincoln Center during 1969 and for all their financial needs, including a payment to Lincoln Center of $45,000 for administrative and accounting services to be rendered to the new organization. With these assurances, Lincoln Center approved the Film Committee's proposal, terminated its own film department, and credited the Film Committee with previous pledges designated for the film program.

By May 1969, the Film Committee had become incorporated as the Film Society of Lincoln Center, with May as its chairman and Segal its president. Its stated purpose was "to further appreciation of film as a leading communicative art form." It was recognized officially as a constituent institution in Lincoln Center. In subsequent years, the Film Society continued to progress. It eliminated its deficit, broadened its membership base and financial support, and serves a steadily growing audience.

Schuman was eager to organize a resident ensemble group for chamber music, and in October 1968 was proceeding with firm plans for 72 concerts in Alice Tully Hall during the 1969-1970 season of 24 weeks. He felt he had enough assured financing for such a program in the designated pledge from Miss Alice Tully. But within the Chamber Music Committee, voices of caution were raised, advocating a more gradual course of development. Miss Tully herself questioned the wisdom of starting on an ambitious scale that might later have to be curtailed or discontinued. She supported a plan to try to raise an endowment fund for chamber music, but the first such appeals were met by a cool response. Word of such appeals aroused new fears among the other constituents of competition and new doubts about the wisdom of the creation of a new chamber music organization. A policy of "Limitations on Forming New Constituents," adopted by the board earlier in 1968, required approval by existing constituents. A series of meetings between the Chamber Music Committee and the officers of each of the other constituents resulted in a growing consensus among most of the members of the committee to slow down their plans. But Schuman remained unconvinced and maintained his pressure for commitments and public announcement of the program as he had developed it. When the issue was finally drawn late in December, Ames and Rockefeller interceded and stopped the announcement. The removal of pressure enabled the committee to formulate more modest initial plans and to win approval from the other constituents.

In February 1969, the Chamber Music Committee was incorporated as "The Chamber Music Society of Lincoln Center" and became an official constituent, with Charles Wadsworth serving as musical director. Their first program formally opened Alice Tully Hall on September 11, 1969, and in their first season in their new home they presented 16 concerts. Expansion was gradual and was successful both artistically and financially. The Society won a permanent place in the Lincoln Center family and in the musical life of the city.

During November Rockefeller and Schuman continued to confer on the financial crisis, the curtailment of programs, and the difficulties encountered in the relations with constituents. These conversations gradually led to a consideration by Schuman of his own career and of his personal relationship to the future of Lincoln Center. As a result, he decided he should resign from his position as president.

On December 5, 1968, Schuman released to the press a public statement on his resignation:

For some time I have been giving serious consideration to relinquishing the Presidency of Lincoln Center. I have felt that such a move should not only meet my personal wishes but be timed to effect the most orderly transfer of my responsibilities at Lincoln Center. That time is now at hand.

The artistic and educational goals of Lincoln Center, which were my primary reasons for becoming its head, have been clearly defined, and the Center is well on its course towards their achievement. At the same time, I have of necessity, become less involved with the artistic and cultural phases, and more and more with the administrative activities, particularly those dealing with the financial problems of the Center. Consequently, in terms of my commitment as an artist and educator, there is at this time no compelling reason for me to remain.

There is, however, a compelling and overriding personal reason for me to free more time—for composing. After more than three decades of heavy institutional responsibility, I want to engage in activities which directly involve me as an artist and educator, activities which can be flexibly organized and which will not unduly invade the time I require for my own creative work.

I will continue to be available to Lincoln Center for whatever service that is deemed helpful. In this connection, I have agreed to accept the Chairmanship of the Carnegie Study of the Lincoln Center educational program, to begin next year.

It has been a great privilege to have led this important enterprise during its formative years. Triumphs and tribulations have existed in profusion, and there has never been a dull moment. I shall always look back with deep satisfaction on the projects initiated and carried foward during my tenure, and on my very pleasant associations with my colleagues and members of the Lincoln Center Board.

Schuman's resignation, to be effective at the end of the year, was accepted by the board at a special meeting held on December 16, 1968. At the same time, the board designated him "President Emeritus."

The office of president was, by design, left vacant for an indefinite time. Executive leadership was now placed in the hands of Ames, as chairman of the Executive Committee, and of Mazzola, who had been functioning as chief executive officer since the preceding June. In recognition of his continuing executive responsibilities, he was appointed executive vice president and general manager of Lincoln Center. This management team was working well; the directors had confidence in their ability to carry through the reorganization and retrenchment that was underway.

At the board level, other changes marked this period of transition. The size of the board was increased from 28 to 36 members in order to provide a wider representation of community leaders. Under a plan to assure institutional self-renewal, five of the directors retired from the board at age 72 and were made directors emeriti. Two new vice chairmen, in addition to Spofford, were elected: Ames and Wein. Ames remained as chairman of the Executive Committee, but with several new directors replacing others who had provided leadership throughout the formative years of the center.

From an organization to establish and build the center, Lincoln Center became one to administer and develop the institution. The targets of budget reduction were achieved, and by July 1, 1969, the annual cost of administration was $558,000, down 60 percent from the earlier level. Programs were conducted successfully under the policy that funds must precede commitments. The most encouraging sector of the Lincoln Center Fund was the response from corporations. Within a year, the constituents and Lincoln Center had agreed to participate in a joint corporate campaign. This fund-raising approach has resulted in increased corporate support for all the Lincoln Center institutions.

━━━━━━━━━━━━━━━━━━━━━━━━━━━━━━━━━━━━

At the end of 1969, Rockefeller felt that the new institution he had been asked to head in 1956 had been created and was fully established to continue as a vital, operating organization in the cultural life of the city and the nation. He had just been appointed chairman of the President's Commission on Population Growth and the American Future, and he foresaw heavy future demands on his time for that work.

On December 29, Rockefeller wrote Ames:

. . . I have come to the conclusion that I should not stand for reelection as Chairman of the Board at the Annual Meeting which comes in May. Fourteen years of service is a long span of time in our world today. I sincerely believe Lincoln Center would profit by new leadership at the top.

The Executive Committee accepted Rockefeller's decision with understanding and deep regret; they turned to Amyas Ames as the logical successor to fill the position of Board Chairman. On April 8, 1970, the plan was publicly announced. Concerning the choice of Ames, Rockefeller stated:

Two years ago when Lincoln Center was facing very difficult financial and leadership problems, Mr. Ames took on, as Chairman of the Executive Committee, the crucial responsibilities of reorganization and financial retrenchment. He has shown such effective leadership in dealing with these problems that he is the natural nominee to become Chairman of the Board. I support the Committee's choice and I have every confidence in the future of Lincoln Center with Mr. Ames at the helm.

When the board met for its annual meeting on May 11, 1970, Rockefeller was elected Honorary Chairman. On June 23rd, a ceremony was held on the North Plaza to dedicate the bronze plaque which expressed publicly the recognition and appreciation of the leaders of all the Lincoln Center institutions. This plaque inscription quotes Rockefeller's own words:

The Arts are not for the privileged few, but for the many. Their place is not on the periphery of daily life, but at its center. They should function not merely as another form of entertainment but,

THE ARTS ARE NOT FOR THE PRIVILEGED FEW, BUT FOR THE MANY · THEIR PLACE IS NOT ON THE PERIPHERY OF DAILY LIFE, BUT AT ITS CENTER · THEY SHOULD FUNCTION NOT MERELY AS ANOTHER FORM OF ENTERTAINMENT BUT, RATHER, SHOULD CONTRIBUTE SIGNIFICANTLY TO OUR WELL BEING AND HAPPINESS · JOHN D. ROCKEFELLER 3RD, JUNE 22, 1963

*The directors and officers
of Lincoln Center and its constituent institutions honor
John D. Rockefeller 3rd
for his inspiration and leadership in the conception and building
of Lincoln Center for the Performing Arts.*

Metropolitan Opera · New York Philharmonic · The Juilliard School · The New York Public Library · The Repertory Theater of Lincoln Center · The Music Theater of Lincoln Center City Center of Music and Drama · Lincoln Center for the Performing Arts

Photo by Bob Serating

rather, should contribute significantly to our well being and happiness.

In the words spoken at the ceremony, Ames said:

Without John Rockefeller, Lincoln Center could not have been built. It was his leadership and inspiration that carried us through to its completion. Sometimes he pulled us, sometimes he pushed us, but he always carried us onward toward the true goal of completing the Center.

Following the ceremony, over 200 persons who had been involved in the development of Lincoln Center through the years gathered at luncheon. There Rockefeller referred to the

John D. Rockefeller 3rd

. . . generous support from many sources—private and governmental; local, national, and international. To all of these I would express the abiding gratitude of all of us associated with the Center as well as those who use and enjoy it.

He concluded with a look ahead:

And now we are at the point when the physical side of the Center has been completed, and what counts is how the Center will be used for the advancement of the arts and for the benefit of the people who come to attend its performances . . .

Lincoln Center was built not just for today or tomorrow, but for generations to come. We must not be impatient if we do not seem to be solving all our problems as quickly as we would wish. . . . The challenge is great and the stakes are high. The quality of life for all of us is the central issue.

John Rockefeller continued to serve as an active member of the board until his death, on July 10, 1978, in a tragic automobile accident. His leadership in the creation of Lincoln Center had been one of his major activities in a life spent in voluntary service to others.

Epilogue
1970–1980

The creation of Lincoln Center for the Performing Arts was substantially accomplished by 1970. The buildings had been designed, built, paid for, and occupied by artistic and educational institutions. Nine autonomous organizations were constituents. Lincoln Center, Inc. had gradually clarified its role, survived a crisis, undergone reorganization, and was ready to proceed on an established, continuing basis. Active management was under the leadership of Amyas Ames as board chairman and John Mazzola as managing director. The story of how Lincoln Center came into being appropriately ends at this point.

However, in the decade of the 1970s, several developments had such a lasting impact on Lincoln Center that the history of its establishment would be incomplete without their inclusion. Three major gifts gave a fiscal underpinning to the future functioning of the organization. One was made by Mrs. Martha Baird Rockefeller, who died on January 24, 1971 and left a bequest of $10 million to Lincoln Center. Although not required by the terms of the bequest, the board of Lincoln Center decided to use this sum as an endowment, with income available for current expenditure.[1]

In October 1971, the Edna McConnell Clark Foundation made a

grant of just under $4.4 million to Lincoln Center, designated as an endowment for the support of its educational programs.

The third significant contribution came in 1973 from Avery Fisher, who had founded Fisher Radio and achieved his business success in the manufacture of high-fidelity components. He wished to make a major contribution in support of an institution fostering great music. "I owed something to music; it all came out of the world of music, and some of it should go back as a repayment of a personal debt, you might say, but also as a civic responsibility." Fisher chose Lincoln Center and gave approximately $10 million. A portion of his gift was designated to establish the Avery Fisher Fellowship Awards to give further impetus to the careers of outstanding American professional musicians, with selection to be made by Lincoln Center and the New York Philharmonic. Four-fifths of his gift was designated for the maintenance, operation, and improvement of the concert hall. In recognition of his generosity, Philharmonic Hall was renamed "Avery Fisher Hall."

The acoustical properties of Avery Fisher Hall remained the most serious unsolved building problem. The judgment of conductors, musicians, and critics was still negative after the several earlier and costly efforts to improve the hall. Dramatic evidence that a major change must be made came in 1974 with the decisions of both the Boston and Philadelphia Orchestras to leave Avery Fisher Hall and return to Carnegie Hall for their New York concerts.

Amyas Ames, board chairman of both Lincoln Center and the Philharmonic-Symphony Society, in close consultation with Avery Fisher, led the analysis of the problem and the approach to its solution. With further study the conclusion was reached that only a complete redesign and rebuilding of the interior of the hall would suffice. With the use of nearly half of Fisher's gift to Lincoln Center, this was undertaken.

The designers of the new hall were Cyril Harris, who had been an acoustical consultant for the Metropolitan Opera House, Philip Johnson, architect of the New York State Theater, and his partner, John Burgee. In the summer of 1976, during a five-month interval between concert seasons, the hall was completely gutted, leaving only the shell, and a completely new hall was built within the same space. As a part of the reconstruction, the ventilation system was rebuilt, and changes were made in back-stage, office, and box-office lobby facilities. This large and complicated construction task was accomplished in record time under the personal supervision of Carl Morse, who had served as the center's Owner's Representative through the years of its

"Well, here we go again!"

original period of building.[2] The new Avery Fisher Hall was opened on October 19, 1976 to the acclaim of musicians and critics as an acoustical triumph. It has taken its place among the world's great concert halls.

━━━

Lincoln Center's institutional federation continued after 1970 with two constituent changes. The Music Theater brought revivals of American musical shows to the New York State Theater each summer through 1970. The productions met a strong public interest, but operated at a deficit. Its sponsoring group was unable to generate sufficient recurring financial support, and its board with the concurrence of Richard Rodgers terminated the Music Theater operation and liquidated the corporation.

The most persistently troublesome constituent problem has been related to the art of drama. The Repertory Theater developed with

Photo: Susanne Faulkner Stevens

Philip Johnson (left) and Cyril Harris (right) describe their plan for the new Avery Fisher Hall to Avery Fisher, John Mazzola and Amyas Ames.

over 36,000 loyal subscribers. However, it was plagued with constant financial problems, and a succession of changes in leadership of its board brought no lasting solutions. In the fall of 1972, after another crisis and a rescue operation involving $150,000 from Lincoln Center, Jules Irving, their professional director, submitted his resignation to be effective at the end of the 1972–1973 season. Faced with their intractable financial problems and the questions of professional leadership, the board of the Repertory Theater decided that they would cease operations at the end of the season.

Lincoln Center was back at the starting point in its search for a drama constituent. A new committee on Theater at Lincoln Center was formed, and it began a succession of consultations with theater leaders.

At this point, Joseph Papp expressed interest in operating the Vivian Beaumont Theater and in associating his organization, the

Avery Fisher Hall.

New York Shakespeare Festival, with the center. Lincoln Center welcomed Papp's interest, and the New York Shakespeare Festival became a constituent, subject to its condition that the funds necessary for effective operation of the Beaumont would be forthcoming from the community.

Papp opened in the Beaumont in the fall of 1973 and continued for six years. For the first three years, he attempted to develop a new audience, especially from among minority groups in New York, with new works by contemporary American playwrights, but his subscription audience dwindled each season. At the end of his third year, Papp changed his policy to revivals of the classics. After another three seasons of operation at the Beaumont, Papp decided, in 1977, to end the participation of the New York Shakespeare Festival as a constituent in Lincoln Center.

Once again Lincoln Center was left without a drama constituent and with an empty Beaumont Theater. A committee of the board, this time headed by John S. Samuels, 3rd, who was also chairman of City

Center, explored possibilities and decided to create a new theater organization. Richmond Crinkley was chosen executive director and chairman of a directorate, composed of Woody Allen, Sarah Caldwell, Liviu Ciulei, Robbin Phillips, and Ellis Rabb. Samuel's committee was enlarged and established as The Vivian Beaumont Theater, Inc. This group plans to open in the Beaumont in the fall of 1980 as the drama constituent of Lincoln Center.

To enlarge the center's community relations, performance programs were developed by Leonard de Paur to reach beyond the customary audiences of the constituents. An annual Community Holiday Festival was inaugurated in 1970 in Alice Tully Hall during the Christmas season. In cooperation with the five Borough Arts Councils of the city, this festival presents neighborhood dancers, singers, and actors. Free tickets to these performances are distributed through the Borough Arts Councils.[3] An outdoor Street Theater Festival was organized and presented in Lincoln Center Plaza during a two-week period in the summer of 1971. The performing groups came largely from black and Hispanic communities, and all performances were free. By 1974, the Festival was expanded into Lincoln Center Out Of Doors, a series of free performances of musical comedy, dance, cabaret, recitals, and chamber music, as well as street theater. This series has become an annual summer event.[4]

The Lincoln Center Institute was formed in 1974 to conduct a new, major project in aesthetic education in the public schools. In the words of its chairman, Francis Keppel, former United States Commissioner of Education,

> The goal of the Institute is to develop ways of using aesthetic experience as a basic component of education. This represents a shift in emphasis from the traditional teaching of music, dance, drama, opera and film as special subjects, to employing a variety of arts to help young people really to listen when hearing and really to see when looking.

> The Institute evolved out of the experience of the earlier Lincoln Center Student Program. The new Institute absorbed and continued the former program. It has developed new teaching methods and curriculum materials and offers intensive periods of training for teachers in participating schools.[5]

A new era in the dissemination of the arts of live performance began on January 30, 1976 with the first telecast nationally of "Live

Leonard de Pour, Festival Director, with Mayor John Lindsay and Amyas Ames.

"Lincoln Center Out of Doors."

from Lincoln Center." A regular evening concert in Avery Fisher Hall by the New York Philharmonic, with Andre Previn conducting and Van Cliburn as soloist, was seen and heard by an estimated 5 million people. Earlier there had been occasional telecasts of special events at Lincoln Center, but these had required intensive lighting and equipment that was bulky and distracting to the audience in the hall. Technological advancement in the sensitivity of camera eyes, and in small housings and mounts made it possible to telecast with normal stage lighting and without serious disturbance to the audience. For two years preceding that first night of "Live from Lincoln Center," the Media Development Department, under the direction of John Goberman, conducted experiments with the new technology and with new approaches to the technique of transferring a regular stage performance to the home screen. They also perfected the use of simulcasts on FM radio to provide high fidelity sound and developed a nationwide network of FM stations in cooperation with Public Television stations.[6]

This first telecast of a Philharmonic concert was followed by broadcasts of performances by other constituents and by solo artists. In 1977, the Metropolitan Opera started its own series of "Live from the Met" telecasts. These "live" telecasts have proved that there is a large, appreciative audience for quality performances. It has given new meaning to Lincoln Center as a national institution and, through satellite transmission, an international cultural center.

In May 1979 Lincoln Center celebrated the twentieth anniversary of its ground breaking. As such anniversaries can be, it was an occasion for nostalgia. But more significantly, it was an occasion for reflective appraisal. In a message to the performers, builders, artists, patrons, and friends of Lincoln Center, President Jimmy Carter said:

It is a magnet for artists and lovers of the arts everywhere. . . . If an artistic institution can bring us the highest expression and deepest experience of the human spirit, in fleeting but vital moments of our lives, there is little more that we can ask of it. That Lincoln Center has done this so often for so many makes it truly deserving of our respect, our gratitude, our hopes, and our congratulations.

On May 20, 1979, writing in the New York Times, reporter Richard F. Shepard reviewed "Lincoln Center—The First Twenty Years."

It was an innovative cultural togetherness that had never before been tried and it would lead to such a plethora of imitators across

"Live from Lincoln Center"

the nation that esthetes would worry about the emphasis on buildings rather than on what went into them and would prate about a national "edifice complex." Yet, for all that, no other center, from those that linked basketball courts with concert stages, to the impressive Kennedy Center in Washington, D.C. has been able to match the overriding splendor of the artistic concentration at Lincoln Center.[7]

Referring to the group who founded Lincoln Center, the *New York Times* reported:

It was a patrician undertaking. . . . They and the others involved were as dedicated and disinterested a group as one might hope to assemble in modern New York. Not visionaries but, as President Eisenhower observed, men of vision.[8]

These citizens devoted their time and talents to the building of the institution of Lincoln Center. The goals of the founders remain the objectives of the center today: to foster the arts of live performance and to enlarge the opportunities for public enjoyment of those arts.

LINCOLN CENTER FOR THE PERFORMING ARTS, INC.

1980

Officers

Amyas Ames, Chairman of the Board
Lawrence A. Wien, Vice Chairman
Martin E. Segal, Vice Chairman
Leonard N. Block, Treasurer
John W. Mazzola, President
Frank S. Gilligan, Vice-President-Director, Development
John O'Keefe, Vice-President-Director, Public Information
Andre R. Mirabelli, Secretary-Director, Business Affairs

Board of Directors (year indicates date of election)

1963	Amyas Ames	1980	Katharine T. O'Neil
1977	Leonard N. Block	1976	Peter S. Paine
1977	R. Donald Daniel	1977	Richard Salomon
1977	Wilbur Daniels	1975	John S. Samuels 3d
1975	Avery Fisher	1979	Richard Schwartz
1969	Richard L. Gelb	1973	Martin E. Segal
1980	Jerome L. Greene	1978	Peter Jay Sharp
1968	Harry B. Helmsley	1979	Richard R. Shinn
1972	Mrs. Leon Hess	1972	Frank E. Taplin
1972	Mrs. Robert L. Hoguet	1969	Miss Alice Tully
1973	Francis Keppel	1973	Edward R. Wardwell
1976	John D. Macomber	1972	George Weissman
1979	Peter L. Malkin	1979	Taggart Whipple
1967	William F. May	1966	Lawrence A. Wien
1956	Laurence J. McGinley, S.J.	1961	Edgar B. Young
1976	Roger H. Morley	1976	Mrs. Whitney M. Young, Jr.

315

1974 - 1975	Hon. Edwin L. Weisl
1975 - 1977	Richard W. Couper
1975 - 1977	Michael V. Forrestal
1975 - 1977	Hon. Laurence D. Lovett
1976 - 1977	Hon. Martin Lang
1976 - 1977	Hon. H. Claude Shostal
1977	Hon. Joseph P. Davidson

Lincoln Center Council

Anthony A. Bliss, Metropolitan Opera
Richard W. Couper, The New York Public Library
Richmond Crinkley, The Vivian Beaumont Theater
Lincoln Kirstein, New York City Ballet
Joanne Koch, The Film Society of Lincoln Center
John W. Mazzola, Lincoln Center
Peter Mennin, The Juilliard School
Albert K. Webster, New York Philharmonic
John S. Samuels 3d, City Center of Music and Drama, Inc.
Beverly Sills, New York City Opera
Mark Schubart, Lincoln Center Institute
Charles Wadsworth, The Chamber Music Society of Lincoln Center

Administrative Staff

Leonard de Paur, Director, Community Relations
John Goberman, Director, Media Development
Herbert M. Groce, Jr., Director, Operations and Central Facility Services
Delmar D. Hendricks, Booking Director, Concert Halls
William W. Lockwood, Jr., Director, Programming
Robert Ronan, Director, Personnel
Alexander J. Rygiel, Controller
Mark Schubart, Director, Lincoln Center Institute
Robert Turner, General Manager, Concert Halls

Chapter Notes

CHAPTER 1

1. Lincoln Square was named by the city in the nineteenth century when other public squares were named "Washington" and "Madison."
2. Rudolf Bing, *5000 Nights at the Opera* (New York, Doubleday, 1972), pp. 138–140.
3. Houghton knew Harrison well and had confidence in him and his partner, Max Abramovitz, as a result of their architectural work for the Corning and Steuben Glass Companies, of which Houghton was an officer and director.
4. Moses—Col. James M. Hartfield, April 29, 1955.
5. Hartfield—Robert M. Moses, May 3, 1955.
6. Jackson—John D. Rockefeller, Jr., June 2, 1955.

7. John D. Rockefeller, 3rd, "The Evolution: Birth of a Great Center," *The York Times Magazine*, September 23, 1962.

CHAPTER 2

1. Ralph G. Martin, *Lincoln Center for the Performing Arts* (Englewood Cliffs, N. J., Prentice Hall, 1971), p. 15.
2. John D. Rockefeller, 3rd, "The Evolution: Birth of a Great Center," *The New York Times Magazine*, September 23, 1962.
3. Conference participants were Piertro Belluschi, Anthony A. Bliss, Aaron Copland, Charles Dollard, Charles R. P. Farnsley, James Felt, A. L. Fowler, Wallace K. Harrison, Arthur A. Houghton, Henry D. Johnson, Jr., Lewis W. Jones, Lincoln Kirstein,

Goddard Lieberson, Alfred Manuti, Joseph Verner Reed, Samuel R. Rosenbaum, Roger L. Stevens, George D. Stoddard, Helen M. Thompson, Richard F. Walsh, Edgar B. Young, and James D. Zellerbach.

4. Exploratory Committee Press Release, Feb. 18, 1956.

5. William J. Baumol and William G. Bowen, *The Performing Arts, The Economic Dilemma* (New York, The Twentieth Century Fund, 1966), pp. 161-164 and 171.

6. Lincoln Center's legal counsel is now known as Milbank, Tweed, Hadley, and McCloy. Other Milbank partners played important roles in Lincoln Center as it evolved. Paul Folwell, the firm's real estate expert, was the chief draftsman and negotiator of legal contracts with the city. William Jackson represented Lincoln Center in litigation. William D. Gaillard, Jr. and John C. Nelson worked on the formation of the corporation and on contractual relationships between the constituent institutions and Lincoln Center.

3. The concern of the Juilliard directors over discontinuance of their preparatory school was eventually resolved by its transfer to the Manhattan School of Music, which purchased the old Juilliard School building on Morningside Heights.

4. The members of the Advisory Council on Drama were Mrs. V. Beaumont Allen, Mrs. Vincent Astor, Cheryl Crawford, Mrs. Howard S. Cullman, Robert Dowling, Elia Kazan, Walter F. Kerr, Eva Le Gallienne, Sanford Meisner, Joseph Verner Reed, Mrs. George Hamlin Shaw, Roger L. Stevens, William Schuman, George D. Stoddard, Robert Whitehead, and Mrs. William Woodward, Sr.; ex-officio: Reginald Allen and Edgar B. Young.

5. Cf. Ch. 2, p. 25.

6. Rockefeller—the Governor, Mayor, Moses and others, January 12, 1959.

7. Moses—Mayor Robert F. Wagner, January 16, 1959, with copies to Rockefeller and others.

CHAPTER 3

1. *New York Herald Tribune*, May 3, 1957.

2. George E. Spargo—John D. Rockefeller 3rd, May 14, 1957.

3. *The New York Times*, September 12, 1957.

4. *The New York Times*, October 3, 1957.

5. *The New York Times*, November 28, 1957.

CHAPTER 4

1. Rockefeller—Rockefeller Foundation, Nov. 20, 1956.

2. Rockefeller Foundation—John D. Rockefeller, 3rd, Dec. 7. 1956.

CHAPTER 5

1. The concert hall had been officially named Philharmonic Hall by action of the board on March 2, 1959 upon the recommendation of Houghton and Keiser.

2. In addition to the corporate donors listed in the text, there were many others who made gifts or pledges in amounts less than $100,000. Subsequently in the campaign, most corporate donors made additional pledges for approximately half the amount of their original gifts.

CHAPTER 6

1. This study was eventually published in book form. Leo L. Beranek, *Music, Acoustics and Architecture*

(New York, John Wiley & Sons, 1962).
2. Cf. Chapter 3, p. 45.
3. *The New York Times Magazine*, Feb. 9, 1959
4. Cyril Harris was chosen to be the acoustical designer for the rebuilding of Avery Fisher Hall (formerly Philharmonic Hall) in 1976.

CHAPTER 7

1. *New York Herald Tribune*, May 15, 1959.
2. *The New York Times*, May 14, 1959.
3. Ibid.

CHAPTER 8

1. Minutes of the Lincoln Center Board, April 12, 1960.
2. The Boston and Philadelphia Symphony Orchestras continued their New York series in Philharmonic Hall until 1974, when their dissatisfaction with the acoustical properties of the hall caused them to return to Carnegie Hall.
3. Cf. Chapter 10, p. 132ff.

CHAPTER 9

1. Rudolf Bing, *5000 Nights at the Opera* (New York, Doubleday, 1972), p. 297 ff.
2. *The New York Times*, November 14, 1961.
3. Cf. Chapter 4, p. 000.

CHAPTER 10

1. *The New York Times*, May 12, 1965.
2. Cf. Chapter 9, p. 120-121.
3. Laws of New York 1961, Chapter 897.
4. Laws of New York 1962, Chapter 784.

5. *The Performing Arts*, June 30, 1961.
6. *Lincoln Center Summary Report, 1956-1969*, p. 11.

CHAPTER 11

1. The plaza design was later adapted by Robert Indiana in his art poster commemorating the opening of the New York State Theater.
2. Cf. Chapter 10, p. 120-121.
3. Cf. Chapter 10, p. 135.
4. Cf. Chapter 10, p. 130.

CHAPTER 12

1. *New York Herald Tribune*, August 14, 1962.
2. *New York Journal American*, September 23, 1962.
3. *The Performing Arts*, October 31, 1962.
4. *The New York Times*, September 24, 1962.
5. *New York Daily News*, September 24, 1962.
6. *The New York Times*, September 24, 1962.
7. *New York World-Telegram*, September 24, 1962.
8. *New York Daily News*, September 24, 1962.

CHAPTER 13

1. The acoustical consultants were Keinrich Keilholz, Vern O. Knudsen, Paul S. Veneklasen, and Manfried R. Schroeder.
2. *New York Herald Tribune*, April 14, 1963.
3. *New York Journal-American*, October 6, 1963.
4. *The New York Times*, December 27, 1963.
5. *New York Herald Tribune*, September 30, 1964.
6. *The New York Times*, September 30, 1964.

7.` *The New York Times*, September 29, 1965.
8. *New York World Telegram*, April 24, 1964.
9. *The New York Times*, April 24, 1964.
10. *New York Journal American*, April 24, 1964.
11. *Saturday Review*, May 9, 1964.
12. *Musical America*, May, 1964.
13. *New York Herald Tribune*, April 24, 1964.
14. *The New York Times*, July, 1964.
15. *The New York Times*, February 23, 1966.
16. *New York Herald Tribune*, February 23, 1966.
17. *World Telegram and Sun*, October 22, 1965.
18. *New York Daily News*, October 22, 1965.
19. This building was still in use as a high school in 1980.
20. Cf. Chapter 15, p. 225.

CHAPTER 14

1. *The New York Times*, December 20, 1962.
2. *The New York Times*, February 19, 1964.
3. *The New Yorker*, May 9, 1964.
4. *The New York Times*, March 23, 1964.
5. *The New York Times*, November 16, 1964.
6. Herman E. Krawitz, *An Introduction to the Metropolitan Opera House* (New York, Metropolitan Opera Association, 1967), p. 24.

CHAPTER 18

1. *The New York Times*, September 17, 1966.
2. Ibid.
3. *New York World Journal Tribune*, September 17, 1966.
4. *The New York Times*, September 17, 1966.
5. *New York World Journal Tribune*, September 17, 1966.

6. *The New York Times*, September 17, 1966.
7. *The New York Times*, September 25, 1966.
8. *New York World Journal Tribune*, September 17, 1966.
9. *Architectural Record*, September, 1966.
10. *The New York Sunday Times*, September 25, 1966.

CHAPTER 19

1. *The New York Times*, October 12, 1969.
2. *The New York Times*, October 3, 1969.
3. *The New York Times*, October 8, 1969.
4. *Architectural Record*, January 1970.

CHAPTER 20

1. *Lincoln Center for the Performing Arts, Summary Report, 1956-1969* (New York, 1970).
2. From 1960 to 1968, the Engineering News Record Index of major construction cost in New York City increased from 645 to 893—a rise of 38 percent.

CHAPTER 21

1. William Schuman, *The New Establishment*. An address at the Princeton University Conference on The Performing Arts: Their Economic Problems, December 8 and 9, 1966. Published 1966 and distributed by Princeton University.
2. *New York World Journal Tribune*, June 13, 1967.

Epilogue

1. *The New York Times*, February 4, 1971.

2. A detailed account of the redesign and rebuilding of Avery Fisher Hall has been accurately told by Bruce Bliven, Jr. in his article "Annals of Architecture (Avery Fisher Hall)," published in *The New Yorker*, November 8, 1976.
3. Community Holiday Festivals are sponsored by Consolidated Edison Company.
4. Lincoln Center Out of Doors is sponsored by Exxon Corporation, with additional support from the New York State Council on the Arts and the National Endowment on the arts.
5. The Carnegie Corporation financed the preparatory study that led to formation of the Lincoln Center Institute. Initial funding for the Institute came from the National Endowment for the Humanities.
6. The experimental and developmental period of "Live from Lincoln Center" was supported by major grants from the Alfred P. Sloan Foundation, the Ford Foundation, the John and Mary R. Markle Foundation, the New York State Council on the Arts, and the National Endowment for the Arts. The telecasts of "Live from Lincoln Center" are supported by Exxon Corporation, the Corporation for Public Broadcasting, and the Charles A. Dana Foundation. "Live from the Met" is sponsored by Texaco.
7. *The New York Times*, May 20, 1979.
8. Ibid.

Index